"OH, YES IT IS!"

A · HISTORY · OF · PANTOMIME

BY · GERALD · FROW

BRITISH BROADCASTING CORPORATION

Published by the British Broadcasting Corporation
35 Marylebone High Street
London W1M 4AA

ISBN 0 563 20366 8

First published 1985

Set in 11 on 13 pt Bembo Monophoto and printed in England
by Butler & Tanner Ltd, Frome and London

CONTENTS

PICTURE ACKNOWLEDGEMENTS

Catherine Ashmore/Dominic Photography page xix; BBC Hulton Picture Library
page viii; Birmingham Hippodrome/Mel Figures page xx (bottom); Fitzwilliam
Museum, University of Cambridge page xi (top); Harvard Theatre Collection page
i (top); Raymond Mander and Joe Mitchenson Theatre Collection pages ii, iii (top),
v (top), ix, x (bottom), xi (bottom), xii, xiii (bottom), xiv, xv; David Montgomery/
The Sunday Times page xx (top); Courtesy of The Trustees of The Theatre Museum,
Victoria and Albert Museum pages i (bottom), iii (bottom), iv (bottom), v (bottom),
vi, vii, x (top), xiii (top), xvi, xvii; Theatre Royal Drury Lane Archive page xviii.

Front cover: E.T. Archive/Theatre Museum, Victoria and Albert Museum.

A·PROPER·PANTOMIME

No fustian now – no mighty paradoxes
Shall puzzle pit, or gallery, or boxes;
But good old, joyous English pantomime,
And let us hope that it will last our time,
Bringing together in a circle here
All that was scatter'd by the bygone year.
Not wiser than our fathers, let us fairly laugh;
'Care', says the song, 'is but a silly calf!'
I wave my wand – let it not be in vain;
Beneath my spell be children all again!

The sound is recognisably that of pantomime. But the words were not spoken by the Good Fairy as the reference to the 'wand' might lead a modern theatre-goer to suppose. They were spoken by a character representing 'The Spirit of Pantomime' in a Victorian Christmas show of almost a century and a half ago. And if the show's title were exhibited on a bill-board today few people would even realise that it *was* a pantomime. It was called *Moon Queen and King Night; or, Harlequin Twilight* (a comparatively short title for its time!). What's more, the song quoted was one that had been introduced into pantomime some forty years before, in the reign of King George III, by Joey Grimaldi, the greatest Clown of them all. 'Clown' himself has long since vanished from the pantomime (we know him only as a circus figure) yet, for the best part of a hundred years, he was its principal and best-loved character. There was no pantomime without him. His red-hot poker, his string of sausages, and his butter-slide – a grease trap for the unwary – were the pantomime's *raison d'être*; and his songs, such as 'Hot Codlins' and 'Tippity Witchet' were an indispensable part of the entertainment, which a manager omitted at his peril.

I'm not in mood for crying
Care's a silly calf.
If to get fat you're trying
The only way's to laugh.

Audiences continued to demand these songs year after year throughout much of the nineteenth century, and joined in their simple 'fol, lol, de rol' choruses with the same gusto that can be generated to this day by a good comic and a pantomime song-sheet.

Yet Clown himself was a usurper, who had stepped out from among the minor roles to snatch the lead in the Harlequinade that had formed the comic core of the earliest pantomimes. And here, in essence, is one of the most curious things about the pantomime. In almost three hundred years, since it was born on the stages of Georgian London, it has changed out of all recognition, yet it has somehow contrived to remain at heart the same thing. It was not at the beginning specifically a Christmas entertainment. Nor was it directed principally at children. Its form was different; its content was different. Its characters and its stories were not always the characters and stories that are familiar to us. Cinderella and Aladdin and Jack of Beanstalk fame, together with the rest of that select little band of characters we tend to think of as 'traditional', were taken into pantomime at various times over the years, and only very gradually succeeded in seeing off all competition and grabbing the Christmas stages exclusively to themselves. In earlier days they'd had to compete with such as Mother Bunch, the Yellow Dwarf, Riquet with the Tuft, Number Nip, and a host of others, all familiar figures of the old pantomimes. And before them it had been the likes of Valentine and Orson, Perseus and Andromeda, and even Doctor Faustus, medieval romance and classic legend having preceded the nursery tale as a hunting ground for the pantomime deviser in search of a story. In a 'partly new and partly compiled' pantomime of 1790 called *The Fairy Favour; or Harlequin Animated*, the compiled part was taken from 'favourite pantomimes' which included Queen Mab, Fortunatus, The Genii, the Witches, and Lun's Ghost. As the piece was partly compiled from old favourites, only half-price was charged. Right through the eighteenth and for most of the nineteenth century there was a pressing demand for *new* stories, or at the very least for new ways of re-telling or even combining the old ones. Novelty was all important. It wasn't until the 1870s that a small repertory of tried and trusted tales began to be established as the basis for all pantomimes.

Some of the favourite characters of the modern pantomime were very late arrivals. Cinderella had been on the stage for more than a hundred years before Buttons, as we know him, secured a permanent place among the domestic servants employed by her father, the Baron Hardup, or Stonybroke (or Boosey de Blackfriars, as he was once called in the 1890s), and Aladdin's widowed mother had been in pantomime for seventy-three years before she acquired the name of 'Twankey'. Both Buttons, as a character, and Twankey, as a name, originated in the adult and literary world of Victorian burlesque. It was by way of this same world of 'legs and limelight' that the Principal Boy (she has been described as 'the brave, busty, champion of faith, hope and chastity'), born of the 'breeches' parts of seventeenth- and eighteenth-century drama (providing, as the name suggests, the chance for a woman, dressed in man's clothes, to show off a shapely pair of legs), finally came to pantomime, high-stepping it over as if butter wouldn't melt in her mouth. Pantomime was already nearly a hundred and fifty years old when she arrived.

Throughout its history the pantomime has greedily appropriated elements from every other form of theatrical entertainment. It has, after all, been cobbled together over almost three centuries by successive generations of theatre managers in search of an audience, and has thus tended to purloin whatever has proved popular elsewhere. Much of what it borrowed was subsequently discarded or replaced; a good deal was retained and absorbed. The modern pantomime is thus a repository of theatrical forms, styles, traditions and conventions, many of which have long been extinct elsewhere. In pantomime 'breeches' parts survive, and rhyming couplets can still be heard. Here, too (with, alas, some lapses), the ancient theatrical tradition that 'good' shall always enter from the right and 'evil' from the left is still observed. And also preserved are comedic elements, and even whole scenes, that can be traced back to the *commedia dell'arte* of sixteenth-century Italy; or to the inventive clowning of Grimaldi; or to the 'gagging' of stars hauled in from the Victorian music-hall and much abused at the time as vulgar and unwelcome 'invaders' of the genre.

Throughout the long and strange history of pantomime, one thing has remained constant. And that is the firm belief of an older generation (and a sorry number of journalists) that pantomime 'isn't what it used to be', or, with equal certainty, that 'pantomime is dying'. IT LOOKS LIKE CURTAINS FOR THE PANTO proclaim the newspapers from time to time in our own day, above a Christmas-time article regretting pantomime's imminent demise. Similar pieces seem always to have been written.

'Though pantomime seems at present to hold its own, I do not see how it can continue to do so.' That was *The Theatre* in 1882. 'In truth, pantomimes are not what they once were.' That was the *Illustrated London News* in 1876. 'Every season convinces us more, and more, that they have had their day.' That was the *Illustrated London*

9

News again, in 1847. 'Pantomime is no longer what it used to be.' That was *The Times* in 1846. 'The Christmas pantomimes have been getting worse and worse for some years. Ask any respectable playgoer and he will tell you with a sigh that pantomimes are not what they used to be.' That was *The Illustrated London News* once more, in 1846.

'It is agreed on all hands that Pantomimes are not what they were.' That was Leigh Hunt in the *Tatler* in 1831.

And so on, and so on, gloomily back down the years. As early as 1782, Horace Walpole, in a letter written from his 'little Gothic castle' at Strawberry Hill, to the Countess of Ossory, was to complain of Sheridan's pantomime version of *Robinson Crusoe*: 'How unlike the pantomimes of Rich, which were full of wit, and coherent, and carried on a story....' Which takes us back to the very beginning, because John Rich was pantomime's founding father!

Pantomime has *never* been what it was. It has changed constantly down the years. And here, in its amazing ability to meet the demands and reflect the manners and mores of succeeding generations, lies the secret of its continuing survival, and almost continuous success. From the beginning, pantomime was a money-spinner. It was devised to revive the fortunes of an ailing theatre, and down the years has saved a good many from the rocks. More than once it has saved the Theatre Royal, Drury Lane, itself; and but for it Covent Garden might never have been built. 'Theatrical people know that the success or failure of such an entertainment at Christmas has a very serious, and almost incalculable influence, on the proceeds of the remainder of the season.' So wrote that prolific writer of pantomimes and consummate man of the theatre, Tom Dibdin, in 1837. Twenty years earlier Leigh Hunt, the poet and critic, had opined that pantomime 'makes all parties comfortable', and it is recorded that at Drury Lane in the 1720s the employment of four of the greatest dramatic actors of the day (Barton Booth, Robert Wilks, Colley Cibber, and Mrs Oldfield) 'could draw but £500 a week to the Treasury', but that pantomime 'would swell the receipts to £1000'.

Small wonder that managers viewed the possibility of a pantomime failure with something approaching panic. From his diaries we discover the august and eminently sombre tragedian, William Charles Macready, spending some nine and a half hours of a Christmas Eve in the 1830s attending the pantomime rehearsal at Covent Garden, of which he was then Manager. The pantomime, *Harlequin and Fair Rosamond; or, Old Dame Nature and the Fairy Art*, was in a desperate state of unreadiness, principally, it seems, due to the shortcomings of the carpenters and the 'shameful inefficiency' of one Mr Marshall. Macready contemplated cancelling the pantomime, but couldn't bring himself to do so because of the lavish expenditure already incurred. Instead, he contented himself with geeing-up the crew and hoping for the best. 'I have very, very little hope, and great fear,' he wrote. 'God befriend me in all my doings! Amen!' Come Boxing Day and things were still not right. Macready confesses to having given an indifferent performance of Lord Hastings in the forepiece, Nicholas Rowe's historical tragedy *Jane Shore*, because his mind was on the pantomime that was to follow. His forebodings were, in the event, justified. On the first performance the pantomime failed. At home that night he confided to his diary: 'What will be the result I cannot guess – it will go near to ruin me.' However, on the second night all went 'very smoothly' – for which Macready was pleased to thank God rather than the carpenters and Mr Marshall!

In those days, the pantomime formed only part of the long evening's entertainment. It might be preceded by a comedy, a drama, or, if it were at one of the 'minor' theatres, a mixed bag of entertainment. But there was a tradition, instituted in 1759 at Drury Lane by David Garrick, of opening the evening with something 'worthy', principally for the benefit of the London apprentices who tended to pack the upper galleries, and who were generally considered to be in need of moral uplift, especially when they were out to enjoy themselves.

Two plays in particular came to fill this bill. One was *Jane Shore*, as Macready's diary records, and the other a piece called *The London Merchant; or, The History of George Barnwell*, which told the salutary tale of an apprentice who murdered his uncle and ended up swinging for it. Just the thing to make them sit through whilst waiting for the pantomime to start! Though most of them happily passed this part of the evening chatting, eating, drinking, and fighting, so that very little of the piece was ever heard. Finally, both these forepieces got their come-uppance when imaginative writers turned them into pantomimes! Nothing was sacred.

The earliest pantomimes were something under an hour long. But, with increasing popularity they grew gradually longer, until, in 1855, *The Times* critic was complaining that he'd had to rush his notice of the one at Covent Garden because the curtain hadn't fallen until one o'clock in the morning. Fourteen years before this the same newspaper had suggested that, as the pantomime was directed principally at children, it should really be placed first on the bill, rather than be delayed 'to so late an hour that their spirits are flagged and their energies exhausted just as the treat is about to be prepared for them'. But no matter where it was placed on the bill, the truth was that the pantomime had simply become far too long. Charles Dickens, in *The Uncommercial Traveller* (1860), recalled one 'so long, that before it was over I felt as if I had been travelling for six weeks – going to India, say, by the Overland Mail'.

Even when the fore- and after-pieces were dropped, and the pantomime left to stand alone, it made no difference; the pantomime merely 'spread' to fill the available time. When, in the late 1890s and early 1900s, Arthur Collins was manager and pantomime supremo at the Theatre Royal, Drury Lane, he always took his customary call at the end of the first half, because it would have been too late at the end. And there is a famous story of kindly, plump little Herman Finck (composer and conductor of theatre orchestras), leaving the Lane one Boxing Night after a Collins' pantomime, to be asked by his wife, 'I wonder what time it is?' Finck is said to have replied: 'You mean you wonder what day it is!'

The problem remains. To this day critics regularly complain about the excessive length of the pantomime. As one of them has put it, they are 'hours beyond the attention span and bladder control of the young spectators for whom they are intended'. This same writer, incidentally, despatched by his paper a year or two back to cover some dozen pantomimes nationwide, concluded that, as entertainment, the pantomime was generally speaking 'abysmal', even by the standards of television! 'The plots', he wrote, 'are ludicrous. Even the most incompetent performers are in ruthless competition with each other. None of the dancers match, and few of them can dance anyway. The pit orchestra is ham-fisted, blubber-mouthed, and almost as stoned as the stage hands who have to shift mountains of battered scenery that has seen better days, and better pantos. Yet,' he had to admit, 'more people visit more theatres than at any other time of the year.'

Again, it is a sentiment that has often been expressed down the years. In December 1823, for example, *The Times* wrote: 'Everybody pooh-poohs the pantomime, but everybody goes to see it. It is voted "sad nonsense", and played every night for two months!' Its very popularity has regularly pulled down upon its head the castigation and earnest disapproval of the literati, from Alexander Pope to Bernard Shaw, and even those who did not despise and reject it outright as a valid theatrical form have sought to turn it into something altogether more 'artistic'. Somebody in the 1920s suggested that it really needed an 'Elizabethan' dramatist to re-work the old fairy-tales in order to get shot of 'the pinchbeck couplets' of the modern librettists, and there were those before him who seem to have seen the ideal pantomime as having a book by Ibsen and music by Wagner. W. Davenport Adams, in 'A Plea for Pantomime', printed in *The Theatre* magazine of 1st February 1879, while granting pantomime certain rude virtues, set out to suggest that 'something more should be made of it', in order, as he put it, 'to bring it to a higher level'. It transpired that he wanted to get rid of all political and local allusions that were 'of a character quite foreign to the circumstances'; to get rid of all music-hall and other recent popular songs; and to banish all speciality acts, whether they be acrobats or performing dogs. He saw these elements as vulgar and unnecessary.

These are invariably the nits picked on by the more serious-minded. Yet they have been an essential part of pantomime almost from the very beginning. Remove them, and you may be left with a fairy extravaganza, or even a musical comedy, but you will not have a pantomime. Its the incongruities and unexplained intrusions that give pantomime its essential flavour. It has, after all, always been a 'holiday' entertainment, whether staged at Christmas, Easter, or in the Summer, and it is therefore entirely appropriate that it should offer what the pantomime historian A. E. Wilson has called 'a truce to reason, a holiday to common sense'.

There was, for example, a pantomime based on the story of King Alfred the Great in which the King at one point, and in the cause of topicality, imitated Blondin's famous performance (the French acrobat had crossed Niagara Falls on a tight-rope in 1859). And what better way to get into a couple of dance numbers than that employed by the King in the Palace Gardens during the Ball Scene of an 1883 *Cinderella*? Marching down to the footlights, he declared:

> Well, things so far, are going very pleasantly!
> I think I'll dance a little hornpipe presently.
> But as the children soon to bed must go,
> I think they first should have a dance you know.

Whereupon enter the children.

Leopold Wagner, one of pantomime's first historians, recalled a pantomime version of *The Yellow Dwarf*, staged in the provinces during the 1880s, in the course of which 'were discovered Tyler's Silver Band in oriental costume, playing "Come Back to Erin" on the terrace of King Rombo's Palace on the banks of the Ganges' – a 'holiday to common sense' indeed!

In the following chapters we take a look at 'the delights – the ten thousand million delights of a pantomime', as Charles Dickens has put it. We survey its history; examine the curious rag-bag of literary and theatrical ideas and conventions from which it has evolved; see where the familiar characters and stories came from; and discover why the original characters and stories died out. We take a look at the way in which the pantomime came to reflect the world about it, and is thus today a valuable source of social history. We follow the pantomime from its early 'silent' days to the coming of the famous pantomime writers who packed it with outrageous puns and rhyming couplets and gags which are still in use today. ('I will now get my foot in the crystal slipper.' 'You couldn't get your foot in the Crystal Palace!') We shall see how pantomime was infiltrated by extravaganza and burlesque; how it came gradually to be identified with Christmas and childhood; how the Victorians larded it with moral significance:

> From what you have seen henceforth, fair maiden, learn
> That all must work, a recompense to earn;
> Without the labourer's hands were thus employed,
> England would perish, Commerce be destroyed.
> There's not a sail that studs some distant sea
> But bears the product of man's industry;
> And even monarchs find their wealth arise
> From those same workmen they despise.

A neat lesson given to Princess Margery Daw by a character chillingly called 'Necessity' in a Drury Lane pantomime of the 1850s!

We glimpse again the high Victorian days of unparalleled scenic splendour; trace the invasion of music-hall stars that began in the 1870s, brought new life and lasting glory with names like Dan Leno, Vesta Tilley and Marie Lloyd, and caused apoplexy among the old-guard, and outrage in the press:

> I object to the intrusion of such artists into the domain of pantomime. They bring with them not only their songs which, when offensive in their wording, are sometimes made doubly dangerous by their tunefulness; not only their dances, which are usually vulgar when they are not inane; but their style and manner and 'gags', which are generally the most deplorable of all....

We take a look at the development and practical operation of some of the mechanical tricks and transformations that have long given the pantomime its element of 'magic'; glimpse the workings of the 'skin' parts (the cow, the goose, the cat, and others); and see how the pantomime roles have changed across the years.

In sum, we pose (and attempt to answer) the two questions that have intrigued and exasperated people (especially foreigners) since it all began, namely, what exactly *is* pantomime, and W H Y?

ORIGINS

On 2nd March 1717 the London *Daily Courant* carried an advertisement announcing that at the Theatre Royal, Drury Lane, that evening there would be presented 'a play call'd The Maid's Tragedy', together with 'a New Dramatick Entertainment of Dancing, after the Manner of the Ancient Pantomimes, call'd The Loves of Mars and Venus'. It was the first time the word 'pantomime' had been used in the billing of an English entertainment.

The advertisement went on to list the cast of this 'afterpiece'. A Monsieur Dupré appeared as Mars and a Mrs Santlow as Venus. There were 'three Graces' in the varied shapes of Mrs Bicknell, Miss Younger, and Miss Willis; and 'four followers of Mars' played by Mr Prince, Monsieur Boval, Mr Wade and Mr Birkhead. (A subsequent advertisement for the same piece added: 'The 4 Cyclops by the Comedians'.) Of most interest to us, however, is the fact that the part of Vulcan was taken by a 'Mr Weaver'. This was John Weaver, the Lane's Dancing Master, who had also devised the piece. He was a 'little, dapper, cheerful man', then aged forty-three, a native of Shrewsbury in which ancient town he continued to reside when not engaged in theatrical enterprise in London, and where he is said to have taught dancing to three generations.

As both a teacher and a performer of dancing, Weaver had long been concerned that the dance was treated in England with insufficient seriousness. In a letter written to Addison and Steele's *Spectator* in March 1712, he posed the question: 'Why should Dancing, an Art celebrated by the Ancients in so extraordinary a manner, be totally neglected by the Moderns?' He went on to complain that dancing was, in England, 'esteem'd only as an amusing trifle' and that 'capering and tumbling is now preferred to, and supplies the Place of just and regular Dancing in our Theatres'.

Weaver attributed what he called 'the low Ebb to which Dancing is now fallen' to the fact that there was no serious written work on the subject, relating its history, extolling its virtues, and expounding its possibilities. And he announced his own intention of taking a first step towards supplying that deficiency by the publication of 'a small Treatise as an Essay towards an History of Dancing', concluding what was virtually a 1000-word puff for his treatise by asking 'Mr Spectator' to give it his blessing prior to publication. It was one of several such pieces on the history and technique of dancing that Weaver published between 1706 and 1728. In it he included an account of the dances of the Greeks and Romans 'whether religious, warlike, or civil', in which he paid particular attention to 'that Part of Dancing relating to the ancient stage, and in which the Pantomimes had so great a share'.

Here, as in his description of his Drury Lane entertainment, Weaver was using the word 'pantomime' in its classic sense, to signify the performer, rather than the work performed. 'The pantomime is above all things an actor,' wrote Lucian of Samosata in the second century AD. He went on to tell the tale of the uninitiated foreign spectator who noticed that although five masks were laid out ready, there appeared to be only one actor preparing to perform. 'Where are the other four?' he is said to have asked, to be told that all five parts in the entertainment were to be played by the one man. This was the *pantomimus* – the 'imitator of all'. The foreigner was much impressed. 'Your humble servant, sir!' (or words to that effect) he is reputed to have said to the actor. 'I observe that you have but one body; it had escaped me, that you possessed several souls.'

These *pantomimi* had originated in Greece and come to fashion in the theatres of Imperial Rome during the reign of the Emperor Augustus where they achieved huge popular success, and were to continue to do so for many years, so much so that one of them, Paris, was put to death by Nero in a fit of professional jealousy! They told their stories in dumb-show and dance, accompanied by music (usually flutes, pipes, cymbals, and trumpets), and were backed by a chorus who sang the story that was being enacted.

Lucian, a great admirer of the pantomimes, details the considerable mental and physical prowess that a good one needed to possess – above all extreme grace and agility and quite extraordinary powers of expressiveness in gesture and movement. 'His performance is as much an intellectual as a physical exercise; there is meaning in his movements; every gesture has its significance.' He writes of one who 'by himself danc'd the Adultery of Mars and Venus, the Sun betraying them, and Vulcan plotting, and catching them in a Wire Net; then every God, who was severally spectator; then Venus blushing; and Mars beseeching'.

Weaver, in his *History of the Mimes and Pantomimes* (1728), expresses similar admiration for these performers whose 'chief art lay in acting, and silently demonstrating all sorts of manners and passions', and who might 'on the same day, at one time' be called upon to represent 'Athamas mad, Ino trembling; now Atreus, then Thyestes'. He concludes in wonder: 'And all this done by one man.' Here lay his inspiration for the staging of entertainments in which the story was 'carried on by Dancing, Action and Motion only', in what he liked to call 'Scenic Dancing'. His own version of the Mars and Venus story was later described by Colley Cibber (at the time of its performance one of a triumvirate of actors running the Drury Lane Theatre) as 'a connected presentation of dances in character, wherein the passions were so happily expressed, and the whole story so intelligibly told, by a mute narration of gesture only, that even thinking spectators allowed it both a pleasing and a rational entertainment'. The description of Weaver's piece given in the printed 'book' (sold in the theatre at a price of 6d, or 2½p) is: 'The Loves of Mars and Venus: a Dramatick Entertainment of Dancing, Attempted in Imitation of the Pantomimes of the Ancient Greeks and Romans.' In his Preface Weaver writes: 'I call it an Attempt ... because this is the first Trial of this Nature that has been made since the Reign of Trajan,' and goes on to explain that he'd not been able to get all his dancers 'equal to the Design' because it was so 'entirely novel and foreign to the present manner of Dancing'. He then advises any of his audience who want to know more about the ancient pantomimes to look at the essay on the history of dancing that he'd so energetically 'plugged' in his letter to *The Spectator* five years previously.

Finally, Weaver explains in brief the 'language' of the Dance: how, for example, Admiration is expressed 'by the raising up of the right Hand, the Palm turn'd upwards, the Fingers clos'd; and in one Motion the Wrist turn'd round and Fingers spread; the Body reclining, and Eyes fix'd on the Object'; how a threat is expressed by 'raising the Hand, and Shaking the bended Fist, Knitting the Brow, biting the Nails, and catching back the breath'; and impatience by 'Smiting of the Thigh or Breast with the Hand'.

In this way Weaver sought to emulate in some degree the ancients. His efforts were to ensure him a place in the theatrical history books. But, paradoxically, he was to be remembered, not as the initiator of a renaissance in the art of the dance, but as the man who, albeit unintentionally, provided the name for a theatrical form in which 'capering' and 'tumbling' were to be forever enshrined – the English pantomime.

2.

The man who was to be mainly responsible for determining the early shape and form of that pantomime and for establishing it as a popular success was a genial, eccentric, but immensely gifted actor-manager called John Rich. Rich, who was some twenty years younger than Weaver, was in that second decade of the eighteenth century manager of what was then still known to Londoners as the 'New' Theatre in Lincoln's Inn Fields. It stood on the southern fringe of the Fields in Portugal Street, some quarter of a mile to the east of Drury Lane, in what was then a fashionable residential area of London, and was the third theatre to have stood on the site since 1661. The site, incidentally, is now occupied by the Royal College of Surgeons.

The 'New' Theatre in Lincoln's Inn Fields had been built by John Rich's father, Christopher Rich, 'as sly a Tyrant as ever was set at the Head of a Theatre'. Old Rich has been described more specifically as 'infamous, thieving and penny-snatching', and more graphically as 'an old snarling lawyer, a waspish, ignorant pettifogger, who disregards the rights of all others'. That he was all of these things there seems to be little doubt. No one had a good word to say for Christopher Rich. He started his professional life as a lawyer, but in 1690, for £80, bought his way into the management of the Drury Lane Theatre.

At that time (and for well over a century to come) the London theatre operated under the restrictions of two Royal Patents that had been granted at the Restoration by King Charles II. These had established what was virtually a theatrical monopoly in London and prevented anyone else from entering the field of 'spoken drama'. It was a monopoly which was to be confirmed by the Licensing Act of 1737, and it was to prove of singular importance in the development of pantomime.

Both of these Patents had been granted in the first place to dramatists. One had gone to Thomas Killigrew, who was, according to Pepys, 'a merry droll, but a gentleman of great esteem with the King' and one who, as Pepys heard it, received an allowance from the Royal Wardrobe 'for cap and bells' as King's Fool or Jester – a post, incidentally, which entitled him to 'revile or jeer anybody', even the greatest person, 'without offence'. He was, in fact, Master of the Revels. Thomas Killigrew was the man who built the first Theatre

Royal in Drury Lane to house his company, the King's Men.

The second Royal Patent had been granted to Sir William Davenant whom gossip (relayed to posterity by John Aubrey) had named as the natural son of William Shakespeare 'by the hostess of the Crown Inn, Cornmarket', in Oxford. Shakespeare was certainly his godfather. Davenant's Company was known as the Duke's Men, their patron being Charles II's brother, James, Duke of York, later King James II. Davenant took his company into the newly-built Duke's House, the first of the three theatres to stand in Portugal Street, Lincoln's Inn Fields, on a site 'within the walls of a Tennis Quaree Court'. Subsequently, the company moved into a new and larger Duke's Theatre, designed for them by Sir Christopher Wren and described as 'a stately edifice, the front supported by lofty columns'. It stood, fronting the river, off Salisbury Court, to the south of Fleet Street, in what was known as 'Dorset Gardens', the site having been formerly the garden of Dorset House, London home of the Duke of Dorset. Davenant himself had died shortly before the completion of the new house. His Patent subsequently passed to his sons.

For some years there was intense rivalry between the two Royal Companies at Drury Lane and Dorset Gardens, but in 1682 they merged to form a united company based on the Theatre Royal at Drury Lane. The theatre in Dorset Gardens, now without a Patent, fell to displays by jugglers, tumblers, strong men and wild animals, and was eventually demolished in 1709. For various reasons, though, the merger proved to be a somewhat unhappy affair, despite a highly gifted acting company. There were deep internal divisions and it all proved rather too much for Davenant's sons. It was at this point that rascally old Christopher Rich entered the scene, offering to buy the Davenant Patent. Within three years of getting it, he had contrived to gain total control of the theatre. He was now Patentee and Manager of the Theatre Royal, Drury Lane, a position of unrivalled theatrical power.

Rich was to control the Lane's destiny for almost twenty years in that 'thieving, penny-snatching' manner for which he was soon to be renowned. As one of the younger members of his company was later to complain, 'He gave the actors more liberty and fewer days' pay than any of his predecessors; he would laugh with them over a bottle, and bite them in their bargains. He kept them poor that they might not rebel, and sometimes merry that they might not think of it.' The actors stood little chance against Christopher Rich for, we are told, 'all their articles of agreement had a clause in them that he could creep out at', and 'whenever they were mutinous he would threaten to sue them'. He obviously made good use of his knowledge of the law and is said to have been ably assisted in his financial chicanery and book-cooking by his Receiver and Treasurer, one Zachary Baggs.

Rich's actors frequently received short wages on a promise that they would be made up 'when the money came into the house'. But, of course, it seldom did – at least as far as they were concerned. Even if settling-up became finally unavoidable, Rich could usually conjure up a deduction or two that would serve to keep the financial balance weighted in his favour, and most monies were, in fact, swept swiftly into his own pocket. One of his favourite little tricks was to inveigle members of the company to enter into 'profit-sharing' agreements which also, in the small print as it were, committed them to sharing any losses with him. Rich and Baggs could always be relied upon to come up with a 'paper' loss. Not that members of the company were ever allowed sight of the books. They had to take Rich's word for the financial state of things and this word, quite freely given, invari-ably proved too complicated for them to understand. Another favourite ruse for reducing overheads was to keep the older, more experienced, and therefore more expensive, players off the stage as much as possible. To this end Rich would regularly scour the country for aspiring young performers to whom, for the honour of appearing on the stage of the great Theatre Royal, he would pay, perhaps, fifteen shillings a week – less ten shillings 'for instruction'.

The upshot was, of course, that the theatre existed in a state of almost constant and seething discontent which, on occasion and de-spite the threats of legal action, flared into open rebellion and mass defections. Finally, a group of actors appealed to the Lord Chamber-lain who ended the rapacious and tyrannical reign of Christopher Rich by serving a 'Silence Order' on him. This temporarily closed the Theatre Royal and, in effect, withdrew Rich's licence to manage it. Not that he went quietly; troops armed with swords and muskets had, in the end, to break their way into the theatre to take possession and chuck Rich out. Even then theatrical London had still not heard the last of him. Shortly afterwards he moved into the deserted theatre in Lincoln's Inn Fields with, he claimed, his Royal Patent and a 'curious wild scheme' of rebuilding it. He was not, however, destined to finish the job. On 4th November 1714, with the new building almost completed, Christopher Rich died. The theatre passed into the hands of his two sons, John and Christopher, who 'perfected and finished' it. It finally opened on 18th December that same year with a production of George Farquhar's *The Recruiting Officer*. The company was announced as playing 'under Letters Patent granted by King Charles II'.

On that opening night John Rich, dressed in mourning, delivered an elegaical prologue which contained the lines:

> But, O my poor father, alas he died
> Ere he beheld this house in finished pride.
> He raised the stately pile by slow degrees,
> But with the hopes a curious town to please.

It was John who quickly assumed managerial control of the new theatre. In the first few years of his management he was to be faced with a great many difficulties. Some of these were later described by his contemporary Thomas Davies, actor, friend and biographer of David Garrick, and, in later years, bookseller (it was in his bookshop at No. 8 Russell Street, Covent Garden that, in 1763, Davies introduced the young James Boswell to Doctor Johnson). As Davies reminds us, Rich was at the time of his father's death very young and inexperienced. He was still only twenty-two. Because of this, some of the older members of the acting company 'considered him as one very unfit to give laws to them, and manage the business of a theatre'. He was further handicapped by the fact that his education had been 'grossly neglected'. His father had been far too mean to squander money in that direction. The result was that his language was 'vulgar and ungrammatical'. He spoke, as another contemporary put it, 'in false English' – he would, for example, speak of 'larning' someone to act, and he had an unfortunate knack of making what, before the end of the century, were to become known as 'malapropisms' (after Sheridan's character in *The Rivals*). He's quoted as having referred to a turban as a 'turbot', and on one occasion as having instructed an actress to lay the stress on 'the adjutant'. Davies, who greatly admired him, declares him 'a perfect male slipslop', a reference to Mrs Slipslop, the chambermaid, in Henry Fielding's *Joseph Andrews* who was 'a mighty affector of hard words' and considered that 'want of shame was not the currycuristic of a clergyman'.

Rich's oddities of speech went hand in hand with a number of wilful eccentricities hardly calculated to endear him to the more self-opinionated members of his company or, indeed, to anybody who took themselves too seriously or tended toward the pompous. He derived, for example, a peculiar and perverse delight in pretending never to remember anyone's name. Even the most important might find themselves referred to simply as 'Mister'. Alternatively, he might choose deliberately to get their names wrong. In the course of a single interview with the actor Tate Wilkinson, Rich called him 'William-shun', 'Williamskin', 'Whittington', and a succession of similarly fanciful variations of his real name.

Certain of his contemporaries were to damn Rich to posterity on account of these peculiarities of speech and manner. Tate Wilkinson was to write of his 'natural stupidity', and that renowned and prolific song-writer Charles Dibdin ('the British sailor's Poet Laureate') to describe him as 'perhaps the most ignorant of all human beings'. Subsequent writers have compounded these descriptions into the picture of a man both uncouth and totally illiterate, and boorish, for which there seems scant justification. Rich was, after all, founder of the famous 'Sublime Society of Beefsteaks' (of which more later), and as such regularly enjoyed the company of some of the greatest illuminaries and wits of the time. We are told that his colloquial oddities were 'much relished' by the members of this Society. We are also told that they found his 'chat' very agreeable, and that 'he had much entertainment in his conversation'.

The fact is that Rich was never very fond of 'dramatic' actors. He had little time for their whims, their petty jealousies, or their irritating readiness to feel 'slighted'. His attitude toward them, which has been described as *'non chalons'*, was no doubt picked up at his father's knee and reinforced by his own early experience with the Lincoln's Inn Theatre company. It is well illustrated by the famous exchange of letters between himself and James Quin, one of his leading players. Quin had been staying in his beloved city of Bath (he would eventually retire there, and is buried in the Abbey), and despite the approach of a new London season, had received no word at all from Rich. Picqued at this lack of attention, he sent Rich a brusque reminder of his whereabouts:

> I am at Bath.
> Quin.

He received an immediate and equally brusque reply:

> You may stay there and be damned.
> Rich.

Parental indoctrination and sombre experience aside, Rich's readiness to take his actors down a peg or two more than likely stemmed in part from an awareness of his own limitations. He was, after all, ill-equipped to be a dramatic actor himself, and this obviously rankled with him. John Jackson, who came to know Rich well towards the end of his life, states categorically in his *History of the Scottish Stage* that Rich, by then hugely successful and much acclaimed as a pan-tomimist, 'would have preferred performing the part of "Cato" with six people in the pit, to exhibiting in his natural cast, to constant crowded and *overflowing* houses'. It was the familiar problem of the Clown and Hamlet. We know that Rich made a number of excur-sions into the drama, such as in November 1715 when he essayed the title role in a play called *The Unhappy Favourite; or, The Earl of Essex*, but he appears to have made little mark in this or any of them. He was by then close to discovering what Jackson was to term his 'natural cast'. But he was still some years away from the sort of success that he and the Lincoln's Inn Theatre so desperately needed.

Drury Lane meanwhile was experiencing a Golden Age. Since the departure of Christopher Rich, it had been run by a triumvirate of first-rate actors, all of them former members of Rich's old company. The three were Colley Cibber, who was also a dramatist and a future Poet Laureate (it has been said that he wrote 'some of the worst odes in the language'); the fiery-tempered and extravagant Robert Wilks; and comedian Thomas Doggett who, in 1716, instituted the annual Thames sculling race in which, to this day, apprentice watermen compete for the much-prized Doggett Coat and Badge. By this time he had been replaced at the Lane by tragedian Barton Booth who, originally intended for the Church, had been bitten by the acting 'bug' at Westminster School and had 'run away' to join 'the players'. Because of the Lane's immense success under the Triumvirate, Lin-coln's Inn was soon feeling the draught. Gabriel Rennel, in a pamphlet describing the state of the two theatres, tells us that Rich's actors were ultimately reduced 'to a more hungry and ragged condition than a company of country strollers'. Their audience every night was 'chiefly made up of Bailiffs and catchpoles, who arrested the poor devils whilst they strutted on the stage'. The picture Rennel paints of the pitiful condition of this unhappy company grows ever more pathetic: 'Their theatre became their prison, and a smart fellow would much sooner have been carried to the Round House, as a place that was less formidable and more polite, than be a spectator of so dismal a scene of misery and want. In short, everybody fled from a set of people who looked like real ghosts, and who appeared in such frightful shapes as scared even parsons and undertakers from their House.' Rennel's picture is particularly highly coloured to suit the political purpose of his pamphlet, but there are, indeed, reports in the press at the time of productions being postponed due to 'the unexpected arrest' of leading actors, and the essayist Richard Steele was of the opinion that the theatre was on the verge of closure. And all this while, we are told, Drury Lane 'hoisted its sails with a strong wind and with a high tide of prosperity and wealth'. But the tables were to be dramatically turned. As one contemporary satirist put it:

> Long labour'd Rich, by Tragick Verse to gain
> The Town's Applause – but labour'd long in vain;
> At length he wisely to his Aid call'd in,
> The active Mime, and checker'd Harlequin.

3.

Harlequin's roots may be traced back to classical times, but he was born 'Arlecchino' into the Italy of the sixteenth century where he was one of the stock characters of the *commedia dell'arte* or, more fully, the *commedia dell'arte all'improviso*, 'professional improvised comedy', which was just one of several names which were given to it. It was a rumbustious, low and earthy form of comedy with no literary or artistic pretensions, and it was originally not scripted. Players were merely provided with the names of the characters they were to play, and a broad storyline in the shape of a scene-by-scene breakdown of the plot. They were also instructed in their entrances and exits and given a rough timing for the piece so that it played neither too short nor too long. The scenario was hung up somewhere behind the scenes where it could readily be referred to during the performance. Apart from that, the players were left to their own devices, the detailed content and business of each scene and the actual dialogue spoken being made up as they went along. As Thelma Niklaus has written in her comprehensive study of Harlequin, *Harlequin Phoenix; or the Rise and Fall of a Bergamask Rogue*: 'Every actor of experience had, tucked away in his prodigious memory, his *repertorio*, a vast collection of phrases and speeches that could be drawn upon to fit any occasion. According to the type of role he normally played, his *repertorio* would consist of reproaches, boasting, obscene jokes, angry tirades, declarations of love, challenges to mortal combat, protestations of despair, delight, or delirium, streams of wild oaths, soliloquies that were rhetorical, impassioned, or gibberish, all ready to spring to mind when required.' It was called 'professional' comedy because it required very special skills and was invariably played by members of the actors' guild, or *arte*, who alone possessed them. It was said that it was easier to train ten actors for ordinary comedy than one for *commedia dell'arte*.

The basic stories were nearly always the same. They told a tale of a pair of young lovers whose love was constantly being frustrated by the intervention of an aged father or guardian and his friend, another old man. These two old men were, in their turn, constantly being thwarted in their efforts by a gaggle of comic and greedy servants (or *zannis*, from which comes our word 'zany'), eager to spite and humiliate their masters by aiding and abetting the young lovers. Such plots invariably involved a chase, and such chases could lead anywhere, even into the realms of the ancient gods of Greece and Rome. Thus Harlequin and his cronies might find themselves suddenly atop Mount Olympus or plunged into the Nether Regions where Pluto ruled.

The older and the comic characters of the *commedia* plays were generally played in leather half-masks, which left the mouth free. (Another name for the form was *commedia a maschera*, 'Comedy of Masks'.) They were stock characters and represented standard Italian regional 'types', as we might have a brash and chirpy Cockney in a flash 'whistle and flute' and jaunty 'titfer', all 'wotcher' and 'me old cock sparrer'; a canny and bewhiskered Scot with a tartan Tam o'Shanter and a stick like Harry Lauder; or a gangling sad-faced Lancastrian replete with cloth-cap, muffler, a whippet and a vocabulary larded with 'ee ba gums'. The *commedia* companies possessed a large repertoire of such 'types' which was constantly being changed and expanded as they strolled the country from one town or province to another and discovered new 'models'. But there was a handful of stalwart characters that were in more or less constant use. Among these were the two old men, Pantalone and Il Dottore. The former, usually the father or guardian of the 'heroine', was an aged Venetian merchant, a crabbed, spindle-shanked and beslippered figure in scarlet trousers with the tall red woollen cap much favoured by Venetian merchants atop his ancient head. He was by turns avaricious, suspicious, amorous and gullible, and was the main butt of the other characters. His friend, Il Dottore, was a pompous Doctor (it might be of law, medicine or philosophy, according to the plot) who hailed from the ancient University town of Bologna, wore an academic gown, spoke Latin with a broad Bolognese accent, pedantically pronounced ill-considered opinions in a mixture of jargon and gibberish, and invariably succeeded in proving that a little learning is, indeed, a very dangerous thing.

The principal servant characters were Arlecchino and Brighella. The former was to become the most important, most popular, and longest-lived character of the entire genre, though he survives today principally on chocolate boxes, biscuit tins, and in porcelain. Arlecchino hailed originally from Lower Bergamo, some 54 kilometres north-east of Milan and not far from Lake Como in Northern Italy. It was an area famous for its fools, and Arlecchino was one of them. He was stupid, gluttonous, cowardly, and he lusted after anything in skirts. He was constantly in trouble, was frequently kicked and cuffed (which neither affected nor improved him), and he was extraordinarily agile, a fact signified by the hare's foot that he always wore in his cap. Traditionally accoutred in a loose-fitting suit of rags and patches, a purse and a wooden sword hanging from his belt, he was carefree and he was incorrigible. He was to change a good deal down the years and in other places.

Brighella, the second servant, was originally from Bergamo too, though he came from Upper Bergamo where they weren't so daft, and he was subsequently to evolve into something more akin to a Neapolitan street-corner boy. He was a clever and unscrupulous rogue, willing to do anything provided he was paid for it. He was liar, thief, braggart and cheat, and, like Arlecchino, adept at acrobatics, dancing and tumbling. The two of them formed what we would call a popular comedy 'double'.

Other popular 'masks' were Scaramuccia and Il Capitano, both braggart soldiers; and the servants Pulcinella and Pagliaccio. Pulcinella was a hump-backed, hook-nosed, dolt of peasant origin, egotistical and brutish, whose best friend was the stout cudgel he always carried and which he put to good and frequent use. He survives to this day, little changed, as the 'Mr Punch' of our Punch and Judy shows. Pagliaccio was likewise a peasant, but almost childlike in his honesty and simplicity. He was mischievous and delighted in playing practical jokes, despite the fact that they invariably landed him up to the neck in hot water.

The 'Lover' character was always played without a mask. He was a young gallant, or man-about-town, elegant, aristocratic, and handsome. He dressed in the height of fashion and always bore a suitably romantic name such as Flavio, Silvio or Orazio. His lady-love was similarly played without a mask. She, too, was always elegantly dressed and was probably a Lavinia, an Isabella, or an Ortensia. But a character more important than either of these two in the future anglicising of the *commedia* characters was my lady's maid. She didn't wear a mask either. None of the female characters did. Furthermore they were actually played by women, rather than by youths, as was at that time normal throughout Europe in every other theatrical form. (It was to be over a century before women appeared on the English stage.) Here, no doubt, was yet another reason for the extraordinary success of the genre in Continental Europe. My lady's maid was a smart and saucy young thing, bright as a button and pretty as a picture, and she invariably took a shine to Arlecchino. She usually took a shine to more than one of the masked characters, but she always returned to Arlecchino, the ups and downs of their relationship usually forming a complicated and comic sub-plot. She might be known as Rosetta, Carmosina, Diamantina or Nespolia (to name but a few), but she was finally to settle down as Columbina.

The *commedia* plays were larded with music and dance, knockabout buffoonery, tumbling and acrobatics. They were lively, satirical and above all funny, both visually and verbally. Their popularity spread throughout virtually the whole of Europe and endured for well over two hundred years. It is said that they even reached as far as Moscow. Italian companies that settled in France were to influence the work of Molière, who for a time shared the stage of the Petit-Bourbon theatre, and later the Palais-Royal, with one; and, in the following century, the work of Marivaux, who began writing for the Comédie-Italienne in 1720 and was to write chiefly for them for the rest of his working life.

But it was in the English pantomime that certain of the *commedia* characters (much changed), and a good deal of the basic business, were to find their longest and their final regular employment on the stage. And this, despite the fact that England was one of the very few corners of Europe in which they didn't at first find popular favour. The famous English dislike of anything 'foreign' was against them for one thing. So, too, was that broad deep seam of Puritanism which had its culmination in Cromwell and the Commonwealth. 'They have now their female players in Italy and other foreign parts,' wrote William Prynne with burning disapproval in his famous diatribe *Histriomastix*, early in the reign of King Charles I. 'And Michaelmas, 1629, they had French women-actors in a play personated at Blackfriars, to which there was great resort.' He went on to describe the women as 'monsters', and to berate their appearance on the stage as 'impudent', 'shameful', and 'unwomanish'. Prynne was, of course, a Puritan fanatic. He was to have both his ears cut off because of it, and later to have his cheeks branded with the letters 'S.L.' – 'Seditious Libeller'. But another writer tells us that the audience which had such 'great resort' to the Blackfriars Theatre to see the French actresses didn't think much of their display either, and let them know it in no uncertain terms. 'Glad am I to say they were hissed, hooted, and pippin-pelted from the stage,' he wrote. And he added: 'I do not think they will soon be ready to try the same again.'

Apart from such disastrous early excursions into the public theatres, foreign companies had appeared at various times in the previous fifty years before the English court where, no doubt, their language (and, indeed, their morality) was better understood. We know, for example, that an Italian *commedia* company was included in the non-stop programme of plays, masques, pageants, feasts, revels, hunts, bear-baitings, and firework displays that was laid on by Robert Dudley, Earl of Leicester, to entertain Queen Elizabeth during her two-and-a-half week sojourn at Kenilworth Castle in the high summer of 1575. It was the Queen's third and final visit to her favourite, and the entertainment is said to have cost him £1000 a day. One spectator was afterwards to write: 'Now ... was there showed before her Highness by an Italian, such feats of agility, in goings, turnings, tumblings, castings, hops, jumps, leaps, skips, springs, gambols, somersaults, caprettiez, and slights; forward, backward, sideways, downward, upward, and with such sundry windings, gyrings and circumflexions; also lightly and with such easiness as by me in a few words it is not expressible by pen or speech, I tell you plain.'

The *al fresco* performance of the *commedia* company before the queen and her court at Kenilworth that July day is recorded on a painting that has been attributed to Marcus Gheeraerts the Elder, a fashionable artist of the time. The visit was the culmination of a summer progress that had taken the queen through the Midland counties, just one of the long, slow processions through different parts of her kingdom that were a feature of her reign. Such a procession, which would include her entire court, might consist of upwards of 400 carts and 2400 horses and pack-mules, and cover no more than ten or twelve miles a day.

Companies of Italian performers were much in evidence during such progresses. The Revels Accounts for 1573, for example, list payments for 'setting forth of sundry kinds of apparel, properties and furniture for the Italian players that followed the progress and made pastime first at Windsor and afterwards at Reading'. Among the items charged were 'a plank of fir and other pieces of sawn wood'; 'gold leather for coronets'; 'arrows for nymphes'; and 'the hire of a scythe for Satan'.

References to the characters and methods of the *commedia* companies are numerous in the writings of the English dramatic authors of the sixteenth and seventeenth centuries. Best known, of course, is Shakespeare's reference to the 'lean and slipper'd Pantaloon' in *As You Like It*, but Thomas Heywood writes of 'Zanyes, Pantaloons, Harlakeans, in which the French, but especially the Italians, have been excellent as known in this country', and in *The Spanish Gipsie* of the 1620s Thomas Middleton and William Rowley indicate their familiarity with the techniques of improvisation when they have a character say:

> ... there is a way
> Which the Italians and the Frenchmen use
> That is, on a word given, or some slight plot
> The actors will extempore fashion out
> Scenes neat and witty.

Some of the actual *commedia* characters also began gradually to find their way into the English drama. At Drury Lane in 1677, for example, Joe Haynes, the famous comic actor and clown of Charles II's day, appeared as Harlequin in Edward Ravenscroft's *Scaramouch a Philosopher, Harlequin a Schoolboy, Bravo, Merchant and Magician*, which was described as 'A comedy after the Italian Manner in 5 Acts and in prose'. The piece is said to have been inspired by the sensational visit to London four years earlier of a *commedia* company headed by Tiberio Fiorelli. Fiorelli, held by many to be the greatest of all exponents of the role of Scaramuccia (or Scaramouch), had actually been a member of the Italian company that had shared the Petit-Bourbon with Molière. Ravenscroft's piece was, in fact, 'taken from' no less than three of Molière's plays, among them *Les Fourberies de Scapin*, and he was justifiably furious when he was pipped at the post by the production of Thomas Otway's *The Cheats of Scapin* at the rival Dorset Gardens theatre. In his play, Ravenscroft includes a *commedia* scene which occurs in pantomime to this day, 'The School-Room Scene'. It is the opening scene of the third act, and Harlequin is discovered 'amongst a company of little children at school, all gabbling together'. In the middle of the room sits the schoolmistress armed with the necessary rods and rules for hand- and bottom-thwacking. After a knockabout introduction between Harlequin and the rest of the pupils, the mistress calls the class to order and instructs Harlequin to 'shut his book and say over his alphabet':

HARLEQUIN (*reciting*): A,B,C,D,E,F,G,H,I,K,L,M,N,P ...
MISTRESS: N-P? What's the next letter to N?
HARLEQUIN: P.
MISTRESS: P, again? Hold out your hand.
HARLEQUIN: My hand?
MISTRESS: Hold it out to receive instruction thus. (*He holds his hand out.*)
So, now look on the top of the house, and see what letter sticks on the ceiling. (*He looks up, and she hits his hand with the cane.*)

HARLEQUIN   (*crying out*): O!
MISTRESS: 'O' then is the next letter! L,M,N,O . . . This I see (*indicating the cane*) will make you a scholar. . . .

There's a bit more 'business' and they move on to something a little more advanced – the stringing together of *two* letters and the sounds that these form:

MISTRESS: Now, open your book and read.
HARLEQUIN: A,B = ab; E,B = eb; I,B = ib; O,B = ob; U,B = ub; B,A = ab. . . . .
MISTRESS: How's that? BA spells 'ab'?
HARLEQUIN: Yes.
MISTRESS: A,B spells ab. B,A spells . . . what? What says the sheep?
HARLEQUIN: What says the sheep? (*and he roars with laughter*) Ha! ha! ha! he!
MISTRESS   (*more sternly*): What says the sheep?
HARLEQUIN: The sheep says . . . (*But he is unable to contain himself.*) Ha! he! he! Nothing can a sheep speak!
MISTRESS: Did you never hear a sheep cry 'Ba'?
HARLEQUIN: Ba? Yes.
MISTRESS: Well, then, B,A spells 'Ba'. A sound whipping will quicken your apprehension.

In order to administer the punishment, she tells Harlequin to bend over a chair, and stick his head through the back of it. This he does. And the scene ends as he lifts it up and 'runs about the Room with it hanging on his neck' while 'all the children take rods, and with the Mistress, run about the stage whipping him' until he finally runs out.

Some ten years after Ravenscroft's comedy Aphra Behn essayed a Harlequin farce called *The Emperor of the Moon*. Mrs Behn (the 'incomparable Astrea'), a one-time spy in the Netherlands and the first Englishwoman to earn a living from writing, was even in her own uninhibited day famous for her robust dialogue and indelicate situations, as Alexander Pope reminds us in the couplet:

> The stage how loosely does Astrea tread
> Who fairly puts all characters to bed.

More brutally, one Victorian lady critic was to write of her: 'It is amply evident her mind was tainted to the core.'

The Emperor of the Moon was taken from a French play called *Arlequin Empereur dans la Lune*, which in turn had been based on a scenario taken from the *commedia dell'arte*. The story is typically simple. There is a father (Doctor Baliardo) who has two female charges, a daughter (Elaria) and a niece (Bellemante). Each of these girls has a young lover (Don Cinthio and Don Charmante, respectively). But the father, who's described as being 'a little Whimsical, Romantick, or Don Quick-sottish' and also as 'Lunatick', is moon-mad, and thinks he perceives an opportunity for his charges to marry the 'Emperor of the Moon' and his lieutenant the 'Prince of Thunderland'.

There are three servant characters, who provide the comedy and the romantic sub-plot. There is Scaramouch, who is the father's servant; Harlequin, servant to Cinthio, the daughter's suitor; and there is Mopsophil, who is 'Governante' to the girls and, in effect, fills the Columbine role. Both Scaramouch and Harlequin are in love with her.

Of special interest in this piece, as well, are the comedy sequences, routines that had been invented by *commedia* players and honed to a nicety by being 'worked' in front of countless audiences down the years. Their comedic possibilities in the hands of skilled performers are again immediately obvious. Perhaps the most famous of them is the 'suicide scene' in Act I. Here, Harlequin, eavesdropping as ever, has heard his rival ask Doctor Baliardo for the hand of Mopsophil. Even worse, he has heard the Doctor reply: 'Set not thy Heart on Transitories, mortal, there are better things in store – besides, I have promis'd her to a Farmer for his Son.' Harlequin is mortified. 'My Mistress Mopsophil to marry a Farmer's Son! What am I then forsaken, abandon'd by the false fair One!' Alone now on the stage, he determines, in mockery of the heroic manner, to end it all.

HARLEQUIN: It is resolv'd, I'll hang myself – No, – When did I ever hear of a Hero that hang'd himself? No – 'tis the Death of Rogues. What if I drown myself? – No, – Useless Dogs and Puppies are drown'd; a Pistol or a Caper on my own Sword wou'd look more nobly, but that I have a natural aversion to Pain. Besides, it is as Vulgar as Rats-bane, or the sliceing of the Weasand.★ No, I'll die a Death uncommon, and leave behind me an eternal Fame. I have somewhere read in an Author, either Ancient or Modern, of a Man that laugh'd to death. – I am very Ticklish, and am resolv'd – to die that Death. – O Mopsophil, my cruel Mopsophil! (*Pulls off his Hat, Sword and Shoes.*) – And now, farewell the World, fond Love, and mortal Cares . . .

And he 'falls to tickle himself, his Head, his Ears, his Arm-Pits, Hands, Sides, and Soals of His Feet; making ridiculous Cries and Noises of Laughing several ways, with Antick leaps and Skips, at last falls down as dead'. At this point Scaramouch enters looking for him, and 'going forward, tumbles over him' – of course! Harlequin now leaps up and suggests that as Mopsophil is apparently lost to *both* of them they should really kill themselves together. He suggests they might 'like

---

★ 'sliceing of the Weasand' – cutting the throat.

loving Brothers, hand in hand, leap from some Precipice into the Sea'. But Scaramouch doesn't like that idea:

SCARAMOUCH: What, and spoil all my Clothes? I thank you for that; no I have a newer way: you know I lodge four pair of Stairs high, let's ascend thither, and after saying our Prayers ...

HARLEQUIN: Prayers! I never heard of a dying hero that ever pray'd.

SCARAMOUCH: Well, I'll not stand with you for a Trifle – Being come up, I'll open the Casement, take you by the Heels, and fling you out into the Street, – after which, you have no more to do, but to come up and throw me down in my turn.

HARLEQUIN: The Achievement's great and new; but now I think on't, I'm resolv'd to hear my Sentence from the mouth of the perfidious Trollop, for yet I cannot credit it. I'll to the Gypsie, tho' I venture banging, To be undeceiv'd, 'tis hardly worth the hanging.

And he exits, and the scene ends with a device that was to become forever associated with the pantomime, a rhyming couplet.

Another famous scene from the piece is that in which Scaramouch and Harlequin, unbeknown to each other, enter Bellemante's bedroom in the dark hoping to have a quiet and persuasive word with Mopsophil. They are both groping about in the pretended darkness of the stage, each still unaware of the other's presence, when Harlequin walks smack into a table. He lets out an exclamation, and Scaramouch, hearing a man's voice, is terrified that it might be his Master, the Doctor. By way of deception he decides to put himself 'into such a posture, that if he feels me, he shall as soon take me for a Church Spout as a Man'. A stage direction then instructs: 'He puts himself into a Posture ridiculous, his Arms akimbo, his Knees wide open, his Backside almost touching the Ground, his Mouth stretched wide, and his Eyes staring.' Whereupon Harlequin, groping, 'thrusts his hand into his mouth'. Scaramouch 'bites him, the other dare not cry out'. So, there stands Harlequin 'making damnable Faces and Signs of Pain', frightened to yell in case he attracts the Doctor, his hand held fast in the darkness by he knows not what, but something that feels to him as if it were 'all Mouth, with twenty Rows of Teeth'.

Finally, in Act III, there comes a scene in which the fun stems entirely from the confusion caused by quick changes of costume and stage property. The scene is a street in Naples, with the Town Gate, at which stands an official 'with a Staff like a London Constable'. Harlequin enters 'through the Gate towards the Stage'; he is 'dress'd like a Gentleman', and is 'riding in a Calash', which was a particular type of light, low-wheeled carriage equipped with a removable hood that folded down at the back like a perambulator hood. The official 'lays hold of his horse', stops him, and points out that everybody entering Naples in a coach, a chariot or a calash has to pay a toll. Harlequin is amazed. What has this to do with him? He is *not* in a coach, a chariot, or a calash, he insists. He's a baker bringing bread to the city and he's in a baker's cart. Is the man drunk? There's a heated argument, a bit of a scuffle, and the poor confused official hurries toward the office to fetch help in the shape of the clerk. The minute his back is turned, Harlequin, by a lightning change of clothes and a deft bit of trickery with the hood of the carriage, transforms himself before our eyes into a baker driving a cart. At this point, of course, the official returns with the clerk, and the confusion is complete – or very nearly. The trick is, in fact, repeated several times, backwards and forwards. The official has only to avert his eyes for a moment and Harlequin is changed from baker back to gentleman or gentleman to baker, his cart to calash and back again to cart. Here, in embryo, is the sort of comedy routine that was to pass into English pantomime and to be wonderfully developed down the years.

Later critics, viewing *The Emperor of the Moon* with hindsight, have frequently attached the word 'pantomime' to it. It has been called 'one of the best pantomime farces ever seen' (though Aphra Behn herself described it simply as 'A Farce'), and it has been hailed as 'the forerunner of the many Harlequinades which later led to English pantomime'. It is true, that with its Harlequin, its simple story, its comedy routines, and its ample provision for song, dance and lavish scenery, it does have something of the spirit of what were to become known as the 'Harlequin pantomimes' of the eighteenth and early nineteenth centuries. But the truth is that Aphra Behn's play appears somewhat similar to the Harlequin pantomime only because they shared the same root-stock, the *commedia dell'arte*. The play is interesting in that it indicates a growing acceptance of Harlequin and his cronies of the *commedia* in the London theatre, and although it was some twenty years after Aphra Behn's farce that the pantomime began to emerge, it is perhaps significant that her piece was revived numerous times at both Patent Houses during its formative years.

However, the Harlequin that finally crossed the Channel to settle in Britain as pantomime's first hero was very different from Aphra Behn's Harlequin. He was different, too, from previous visiting Harlequins. And he came to England via France. The most significant difference between him and his predecessors was that he had lost his tongue – he did not speak.

THREE

ENTER·THE·SPECKLED·WIZARD

By the end of the seventeenth century, the art of *commedia* was in decline in Italy and its main European stronghold was France. Here, Arlecchino had become Arlequin; Scaramuccia, Scaramouch; Pantalone, Pantaloon; Columbina, Columbine (and heroine rather than servant); and from Pagliaccio the French had developed Pierrot.

In France, the great range of 'masks' that had evolved in Italy had, outside the Paris theatres, been gradually reduced to a mere handful of the most popular ones to meet the needs of a host of small groups, some of them perhaps only three or four players strong, that regularly toured the country playing the booth theatres of the numerous fairs that were staged every year. These actors were known as *forains*, actors from the 'Théâtres de la Foire', itinerants, travelling showmen, 'strollers'.

The huge popular success of some of these *forains* at the great Parisian fairs, such as those of Saint-Germain and Saint-Laurent, was eventually to draw down upon the heads of this fraternity the wrath of the mighty Comédie Française, which became increasingly picqued at the competition. In the manner of the London Patent Houses, the Comédie demanded the sole right to use the spoken word. Thus, by Royal Decree, the *forains* were finally forbidden to speak, and the loquacious Arlecchino of Italy became the mute Arlequin of France.

The companies, though, were nothing if not inventive. When first deprived of speech, they resorted to writing essential lines of dialogue or twists of plot onto scrolls which they carried in their pockets and unrolled to exhibit to the audience at the appropriate moments. Later, they changed to placards that were flown in from the stage roof and upon which, and perhaps in verse, they would inscribe their 'captions'. When these were banned, they tried handing out leaflets on which would be printed not only the necessary plot details, but also the words of the songs, so that audiences could join in. Another ruse was to enact only isolated scenes which enabled them to plead that they were not staging 'plays' as such, anyway.

Towards the end of the seventeenth century, companies of *forains* had begun to find their way across the Channel to the numerous English fairs, at which mute, dancing and tumbling Harlequins were becoming increasingly popular. At London's May Fair in 1696, for example, we find a booth theatre near Hyde Park Corner in which was presented *King William's Happy Deliverance and Glorious Triumph over his Enemies*, and, we are told, *The Conceits of Scaramouch and Harlequin*, and at Bartholomew Fair we read of an Italian Scaramouch dancing on the rope with a wheelbarrow before him, with two children and a dog in it, and with a duck on his head – who 'sings to the company and causes much laughter'.

In the theatre, too, at this time the English stage was, to quote one authority, 'pestered' with tumblers and rope dancers from France, Italian squallers, and dancing masters with dancing dogs. In an epilogue to a play written in 1700 one dispirited London playwright complained to his audience:

> Show but a mimic ape, or French buffoon,
> You to the other house in shoals are gone,
> And leave us here to tune our crowds alone.
> Must Shakespeare, Fletcher and laborious Ben
> Be left for Scaramouch and Harlequin?

The house to which the audience 'in shoals' was gone was the Theatre Royal in Drury Lane, and the manager who had invited Scaramouch and Harlequin on to that august stage was none other than wily old Christopher Rich. Among the *forains* who appeared for Rich at Drury Lane in those first years of the eighteenth century were the Sieurs Alard. They performed what were called 'Italian Night Scenes', which the Lane's Dancing Master, none other than John Weaver, was subsequently and publicly to scorn as 'ludicrous representations of Harlequin, Scaramouch, Columbine, Pierrot, etc.'.

Equally scornful was the anonymous *Comparison Between the Two Stages* published in 1702, which described the Sieur Alard and 'the two Monsieurs his Sons' as 'rogues that show at Paris for a Groat a piece'. The anonymous writer went on to describe the sort of entertainment they gave: 'What a rout here was with a Night piece of Harlequin and Scaramouch with the Guitar and the Bladder! What jumping over Tables and Joint-Stools! What ridiculous Postures and Grimaces! and what an exquisite trick 'twas to straddle before the Audience, making a thousand damn'd French Faces, and seeming in labour with a monstrous Birth, at last my counterfeit Male Lady is delivered of her two Puppies Harlequin and Scaramouch.' The writer professed himself 'scandaliz'd' by the fact that 'these Rascals', as he called them, 'brought the greatest Houses that ever were known'. It was a lesson that was not lost on Christopher Rich's son, John.

'Italian Night Scenes' were stories told exclusively through dance, and customarily set in some place of pleasure to which people resorted of an evening, such as an inn, a tavern, a pleasure garden, or a fair. The action was comedic, knockabout, and uninhibited, usually involving misunderstandings and upsets between the characters of the *commedia* and the ordinary townspeople. Such 'Italian Night Scenes' were to become a frequent feature of the bill at the Lincoln's Inn Fields Theatre. They were just the sort of thing John Rich needed. His company was, after all, no match dramatically for the weight and talent of the Drury Lane company under the triumvirate. At that period both theatres included 'Entertainments of Dancing' in their programmes. They invariably followed the play and concluded the long evening's entertainment. It was a policy that was not wholly approved of by the Drury Lane management, but as Colley Cibber was later to explain, 'When one company is too hard for another, the lower in reputation has always been forced to exhibit fine new-fangled foppery to draw the multitude after them. Of these expedients, singing and dancing had formerly been the most effectual; but, at the time I am speaking of, our English music had been so discountenanced, since the taste of Italian operas prevail'd, that it was to no purpose to pretend to it. Dancing therefore was now the only weight in the opposite scale, and as the new theatre sometimes found their account in it, it could not be safe for us wholly to neglect it.'

Advertisements that regularly appeared in The *Daily Courant* show that in 1715 such entertainments were far more frequent at Lincoln's Inn than at Drury Lane, but over the next few years the triumvirate, much against its will, was to be forced to take increasing notice of what young John Rich was up to. At the start of the period, however, Drury Lane was attempting to satisfy the public demand for 'things Italian' with a 'new Musical Masque call'd Venus and Adonis ... compos'd in the Italian Manner, and perform'd all in English' rather than the 'Italian Night Scenes' or 'Italian Mimick Scenes' that John Rich was beginning to stage with increasing regularity.

The Lincoln's Inn bill for Thursday, 31st March 1715, for example, included a revival of the play *Theodosius; or, The Force of Love*, plus 'a piece of Vocal and Instrumental Musick' called *The Beau Demolish'd*; a Dialogue by Mr Leveridge and Mr Pack; a trumpet song by Mr Rawlins; singing by 'the New Boy'; and several entertainments of dancing, 'Particularly an Italian Night Scene (perform'd but once these ten years) between a Harlequin, a Scaramouch and Punch'. Five days later Harlequin was back on the stage of Drury Lane in a revival of Aphra Behn's farce *The Emperor of the Moon*. (It was to be staged several times that year at both houses.) On Easter Monday (18 April) Rich's bill included 'an entertainment between a Harlequin and two Punches' *and* 'A Dance of Two Scaramouches'. The following Saturday he announced 'An Entertainment betwixt a Countryman and a Harlequin'. A week later Drury Lane countered with 'A Tub-Dance between a Cooper and his Wife, and Man, a Scaramouch and Harlequin', to which was added a couple of days later 'the Dance of Four Scaramouches'. And the ding-dong between the two houses continued throughout that year and into the next with the competition gradually becoming more fierce.

On 12th November 1716, Rich at Lincoln's Inn Fields staged 'A Dance between 2 Punchinellos, a Harlequin and Dame Ragonde'. Two days later Drury Lane came up with 'A Mimick Night Scene after the Italian Manner, between a Harlequin, Scaramouch, and Dame Ragonde"! Next, on 26th December, came Rich's 'New Italian Mimick Night Scene (never perform'd before) between a Scaramouch, a Harlequin, a Country Farmer, his wife and others'. By 1st January the following year this appears to have been re-titled *Harlequin Executed; or, The Farmer Disappointed*.

It was in the March of this same year that Drury Lane staged John Weaver's *The Loves of Mars and Venus*, an 'Entertainment of Dancing' that did *not* use Harlequin or any of the *commedia* tribe, but instead harked back to 'the ancient pantomimes'. Weaver, as we have seen, thought very little of 'capering' and 'tumbling'. His next piece, however, staged a month later, was advertised as 'A New Dramatick Entertainment of Dancing in Grotesque Characters call'd "The Shipwreck; or, Perseus and Andromeda", Perseus by Harlequin, Andromeda by Columbine, Monster by Crocodile.' It was performed by Mr Weaver, Mr Wade and Mrs Bicknell with '4 sailors and their wives by the Comedians'. Weaver himself was later to explain that in his use of the words 'Grotesque Characters' he had meant 'unnatural' characters, characters 'where, in lieu of regulated Gesture you meet with distorted and ridiculous Actions, and Grin and Grimace take up entirely that Countenance where the Passions and Affections of the Mind should be expressed'. His Harlequinade version of a classic legend is said to have confused the public. But his use of the word 'pantomime' in the description of his earlier piece had given them a good 'fun' word that came trippingly off the tongue – certainly a good deal more trippingly than 'Italian Night Scene', 'Mimick Night Scene after the Italian Manner', or 'Dramatic Entertainment of Dancing' whether 'in Grotesque Characters' or 'in Imitation of the Ancient Pantomimes'. It thus began to be applied by the public to *any* entertainment along any of these lines.

It would seem also that Weaver was the first to suggest the possibility of linking the English Harlequin with a classical, mythological or legendary story which was to become the central device of Rich's later and most successful pantomimes. Certainly there is no suggestion of the use of such themes in Rich's mimic entertainments up to this point. Furthermore, Colley Cibber was to name *The Loves of Mars and Venus* as the 'original hint' from which sprung 'that succession of monstrous medlies, that have so long infested the stage'. It is easy to accept Cibber's statement as one of accurate historical record. After all, it is hardly likely that he wrote it to claim for his own theatre the credit for having originated a succession of works which he considered 'poetical drams', 'gin-shops of the stage', and mere 'fooleries'. On the play-bills at Lincoln's Inn Fields, meanwhile, there now frequently appeared the words 'Harlequin by Mr Lun'. 'Lun' was the stage name taken by John Rich. In the character of the silent Harlequin he had discovered the perfect role. Peculiarities of speech and the vagaries of an uncertain memory were no longer of any consequence. It was a role he was to make peculiarly his own. Indeed, some few years later a visitor to London was to declare him the best Harlequin in all Europe.

2.

Thus, Harlequin came to dominate the earliest English pantomimes. But Rich's genius was to endow the character with a capability he had never before possessed – the power to perform 'magic'. In Italy, at the beginning, Arlecchino had been a rustic dolt, gluttonous and stupid. In France, as Arlequin, he had become altogether more wordly, an impudent, street-wise rogue, sharp and cynical. In England, Rich was to transform him into a witty, mischievous, and virtually indestructible magician, a direct instrument of those 'immortals' with whom, in the past, he'd been permitted only sporadic, brief and unequal associations.

Black-masked and parti-coloured, Rich's Harlequin was to be dubbed 'the speckled wizard' and 'the wooden-sword magician'. Through him, Rich would be able to realise to the full not only his talent as a mimic dancer, but also his inventiveness as a machinist (in which area, too, he was said to have had no equal), and his natural flair for mounting stage spectacles. Rich devised a form of entertainment which, as Thomas Davies has described it:

> Consisted of two parts, one serious, and the other comic. By the help of gay scenes, fine habits, grand dances, appropriate music, and other decorations, he exhibited a story from Ovid's *Metamorphoses*, or some other fabulous writer. Between the pauses or acts of this serious representation, he interwove a comic fable, consisting chiefly of the courtship of Harlequin and Columbine, with a variety of surprising adventures and tricks, which were produced by the magic wand of Harlequin; such as the sudden transformation of palaces and temples into huts and cottages; of men and women into wheel-barrows and joint-stools; of trees turned to houses; colonnades to beds of tulips; and mechanic shops into serpents and ostriches.

In bringing together all these disparate elements, Rich finally produced the first real English pantomime. It opened at the Lincoln's Inn Fields Theatre on Thursday, 16th March 1721, following a performance of *King Lear*, and it was called *The Magician; or, Harlequin a Director*. It was a suitably topical title. That spring, England was still in the chaotic aftermath of the South Sea Bubble which had finally burst the previous autumn, ending a mania for speculative dealing in the stock of the South Sea and other companies and leaving a host of investors nationwide to face ruin. The South Sea Company's directors (among them a number of MPs) were at that very time being investigated. Public excitement was intense – and the word 'director' was a dirty one.

There's a song in Rich's piece in which a mountebank offers 'a whim-wham new come over' (from France) as an alternative, he assures us, to a 'bubble' company in which to invest. He promises that:

> T'will ease you of all your Troubles ho!
> By a Chymical new Chymerical way;
> But first of all down with the Bubbles ho!
> For this is the fairest play.

Judging by the number and sequence of performances given (eighteen in all during 1721; twenty-seven the following year; and ten in 1723), *The Magician* was neither an immediate nor ever an immense success, though its popularity obviously grew, and it was to remain in the repertory for several more years, and to be revived as late as 1780. But it was innovative. It established the pattern. Rich was on the right track at last and the fortunes of his company were on the turn. His first huge popular success came in December 1723 with a piece called *The Necromancer; or Harlequin Doctor Faustus*. Actually, Drury Lane had pipped him to the Faustus legend as a subject for pantomime with their *Harlequin Doctor Faustus – with the Masque of the Deities* staged in November, but within four weeks of its opening Rich had *his* version on stage at Lincoln's Inn Fields. It took the town by storm, running continuously right through January and February 1724 and clocking up some sixty-odd performances in 1724 alone.

The *Daily Journal* for 9th January that year reports one performance for which 'the concourse of people to see it was so exceeding great, that many hundreds were obliged to go back again, as not being able to obtain admittance'. It concludes: 'The Entertainment was wonderful satisfactory to the audience, as exceeding all the Legerdemain that has been hitherto perform'd on the stage.'

It is not easy to discover exactly what these pieces were really like. Very few of the 'books' survive, and those that do provide only the 'vocal parts', the songs and the recitatives (the gods, goddesses and heroes of the 'serious' scenes always sang their parts). Of the comic interludes we're often told no more than: 'Scene, A Farm-Yard. The Grotesque Part Begins.' And a little later on, perhaps: 'Scene, the Side of a Wood. The actions of Harlequin continued.' Alternatively, as is the case with Drury Lane's *Harlequin Doctor Faustus*, we may find that a complete printed description of the piece exists, but that this omits the songs and recitatives!

We can, however, piece together one complete show of Rich's. It was a 'Dramatick Entertainment' (the word 'pantomime' would then have been applied only to the mute comic interlude) called *Harlequin a Sorcerer; with the Loves of Pluto and Proserpine*. The 'vocal parts' were written by Lewis Theobald, a true 'Man of Kent' (he hailed from Sittingbourne) and, like Rich, the son of an attorney. Together, these two devised many of the most successful pantomime entertainments of their day, Theobald contributing the written scenes; Rich 'inventing' the comic interludes and the trick-work.

Harlequin a Sorcerer, one of their most brilliant successes, opened at the Lincoln's Inn Fields Theatre on 21st January 1725. (There was, as may be seen, still no set time of year for the mounting of such pieces.) The printed 'book' of 'vocal parts' was, as usual, published for sale in the theatre and, as usual, contains no details of the comic portion. However, Rich revived the piece many times and during one such revival ('with alterations') at Covent Garden in 1752, the *Gentleman's Magazine* printed a 'summary' of the piece which, in fact, gives the Harlequin interlude (there was only one in this particular show) in full. So, putting these two together we can see precisely what a John Rich entertainment, at its best, was like.

The principal characters of the 'serious' part were Pluto (Mr
Leveridge); Ascalax, Chief Minister and an Attendant on Pluto (Mr
Legar); and Proserpine (Mrs Barbier). There were also five witches
(four of them played by men), a chorus of witches, and 'Several
Shades, Infernals and others'. The characters of the 'pantomime' interlude were Harlequin (Mr Lun), Columbine, Pantaloon, and Pantaloon's servants. Who played these parts we are not told. So, the
overture is played; the curtain rises . . .

> . . . and discovers dark rock Caverns, by the Side of A Wood, illumin'd by the Moon;
> Birds of Omen promiscuously flying, Flashes of Lightning faintly striking. While the
> Symphony is playing, divers Witches enter severally.

1ST VOICE	Why sisters, why – Why thus d'ye stay;
	Our works admit of no Delay.
	The Noon of Night is hurrying on,
	When all must meet, salute and own,
	Our Master's new contracted Son;
	Meanwhile, on all the Winds that blow,
	Our new wrought Mischief let us throw.
3RD VOICE	This – To the East.
4TH VOICE	This – To the West.
5TH VOICE	This – To the South.
1ST VOICE	This – To the North.
ALL	Let dire Contagion now go forth.

(A Noise in the Air.)

1ST VOICE	Our new Companion's posting here,
	To welcome him, let's all prepare.

*(Symphony, while a Flock of Witches fly cross, Harlequin in a Post Chaise flying Swiftly
after.) Witches and Harlequin Enter.*

3RD VOICE	Welcome.
4TH VOICE	Welcome.
2ND VOICE	Welcome.
1ST VOICE	Welcome.

AIR

Welcome to our Place of Sporting:
Health and Treasure
Ev'ry Pleasure
Now command.
Here each night, at our Resorting,
We redouble
Ev'ry trouble
Through the Land.

1ST VOICE	How have you sported all this Night?
	What Deeds perform'd for his Delight?
3RD VOICE	On the new Justice and the Squire
	We've had our Will – Our full Desire;

41

We've fool'd 'em to the highest Pitch,
And sous'd 'em both into a Ditch.

CHORUS   Ho, ho, ho.
Ho, ho, ho.

3RD VOICE   The Farmer's Hogs too we have drown'd
And laid his Barns flat to the Ground.

CHORUS   Ho, ho, ho.
Ho, ho, ho.

2ND VOICE   The Mayor o' th'Town I lugg'd by th'Ears,
And threw him Head-long down the Stairs.
The Pinder★ in my Way I found,
And whipp'd him nine times round the Pound.

CHORUS   Ho, ho, ho.
Ho, ho, ho.

1ST VOICE   Let us embrace – Thou shalt be wise,
And overcome thy Enemies.

AIR

Let the Thunder crack and roll;
No Pow'r thy Charms shall e'er control.
Nature shall yield to your great Skill:
    Your Art, with Ease,
    Shall, when you Please,
Transform all things to what you will.

3RD VOICE   Now let our Art a Dance Prepare,
To Notes that may regale the Ear,
Whilst merry Sprights obey the Sound,
And, in brisk Measure, beat the Ground.

A DANCE OF WITCHES

1ST VOICE   The hated Morn comes on apace;
'Tis time we shou'd depart this Place,
Till the great Planet of the Sun,
His vig'rous Course of Light has run,
Which still creates more Mischiefs to be done.
Now throw off all Remorse and Fear,
Revenge shall be to thee most dear;
On sweet Revenge still fix thy Mind,
With us 'tis Joy to plague Mankind.

CHORUS OF ALL   With us 'tis Joy to plague Mankind.
(*Exeunt Severally.*)

Here in the 'book' appears the line 'Scene changes, and the Actions of Harlequin go on.' It's the only reference to the 'comic' part and is followed immediately by Scene II of the 'serious'. So we must turn to the *Gentleman's Magazine* for February 1752. In the 1752 revival of the piece, incidentally, Harlequin entered, not in the post-chaise of the original, but 'riding in the air between two witches upon a long pole'.

★ Pinder – an officer of a manor whose duty was to impound stray animals.

The magazine also provides us with small extra production details that are illuminating. Referring to the 'Dance of Witches', for example, it states: 'You may be sure proper use is made of their broomsticks.'

But to the 'comic' interlude. The witches in unison say 'With us 'tis Joy to plague Mankind' and they 'Exeunt Severally . . .'

Next you see the bricklayers and their men going to work, which now marks the time of our drama to be morning. – Harlequin then stands before a balcony, serenading Columbine, who appears to him; but, as he is climbing up, he is surpris'd by Pantaloon, who comes out opening the door, and Harlequin pops in. Hence a warm pursuit ensues of Columbine and our hero by Pantaloon and his servants. The next scene is of an house half built, with real scaffolding before it, and the men at work upon it. Columbine retires behind a pile of bricks: our hero mounts a ladder, and presently down comes the scaffolding, with the men and all upon it.

You next come to a garden wall: where, as Columbine retires under it, Harlequin is turned into an old woman, and the scene converted into a wall with ballads and coloured wooden prints strung upon it, with a large wicker chair, in which Harlequin seats himself, supposed to be selling them. The servant comes in, buys a ballad: and here a slight satirical hint is levelled at the song of 'I love Sue, and Sue loves . . .' introduced in the rival 'Harlequin Ranger' of t'other house.

We have now a most delightful perspective of a farm-house, whence you hear the coots in the water as at a distance. – Several rustics with their doxies come on; and Mr Lowe sings an excellent song, to which all join in chorus, *to celebrate harvest home.* This scene remov'd, a constable comes on, with the bricklayers men, who have a warrant to take up Harlequin: Then you have a distant view of a barley mow and barn; several swains dancing before it, with Harlequin and Columbine. The constable and followers opportunely coming in, Columbine is seized and carried home by Pantaloon.

When they are in the house, the servant after many dumb gestures introduces a large ostrich, which has a very good effect upon the audience; but perhaps would have had a greater, had we not discovered by the extremities, that it was Harlequin, whose legs and thighs appear under the body. This I suppose could not be remedied, as the extremities of this bird are very small in proportion. Besides, Columbine by this means discovers him; and, after having made the whole house ring with applause by playing several tricks (such as kissing Columbine, biting the servant, and the like) they morrice off both together.

We are then carried to a back-part of the farmhouse, which turns into a shed, where in an instant you have the view of a copper with a fire burning under it. Harlequin changes himself into an old washer-woman, and on striking a mound raised of flints mixed with earth, it is immediately turned into a washing-tub and stand; then opening a door, he shows us a horse with real linnen upon it, which is drawn out in many folds to a considerable length upon the stage. Pantaloon and servant come in, and after being soused with the soapsuds, are driven off by the supposed washer-woman with a bowl of boiling-water from the copper, to the no small diversion of both galleries. Columbine then comes forth from her retreat, and goes off with her sweetheart.

But the constable at last catches him; he tumbles down 'midst his guards, and so slips away from 'em. – We then see a fence of boards, as before a building (excellently well painted) which in a moment is converted to a gilt Equestrian statue. Harlequin is discovered to bestride the horse, as I remember by his sneezing: Pantaloon's servant goes to climb up by the head, which directly bends its neck and bites him: he next tries to get up by the hind-leg, which in springing back gives him a most terrible kick, and the poor dog is carried off with his face all over blood and beaten to pieces.

After this, a scene drops, and gives us a prospect of ruinous rugged cliffs, with two trees hanging over them, beautifully executed. The same witches come in again, and, after singing a little while, retire. Then Harlequin appears disconsolate and prostrate upon a couch in an elegant apartment: lightning flashes; and four devils, in flame-coloured stockings mount through trap-doors, surround him with double-tongued forks, and the whole stage with the scenery and all upon it, rises up gradually, and is carried all together into the air.

For details of the rest of the entertainment we now have to turn once again to the published 'book'. This tells us that as the demons bear Harlequin away they are 'triumphing' in the following Chorus:

CHORUS   With our prey let's take our Flight;
                Then Hell will be in full Delight.
(*As they disappear, the Palace of Pluto is discover'd, where several Shades and Infernal Spirits are rang'd on each Side, waiting the Approach of Pluto.*)

After that a machine descends with Pluto and Proserpine and 'fixes on the stage'. News is bought that Harlequin has been captured and has 'reach'd th' infernal Ground'. Pluto proclaims a general celebration. Now, the *Gentleman's Magazine* informs us, 'the stage is extended to a prodigious depth, closing with a prospect of fine gardens and a temple', and we are 'entertained awhile with the agility of Messrs Cook, Grandechamps, Mademoiselles Camargo, Hilliard, and others'. They performed 'A Dance of the Furies' the piece ending with Proserpine agreeing to become Pluto's wife, and the Grand Chorus:

In new delights, for ever join
    Great Pluto and lov'd Proserpine;
Thus let applauding Triumph rise
    Till Jove with Envy quits his skies.

And with a low bow from the performers 'so down drops the curtain'.

Very noticeable at this stage is the almost total lack of connection between the 'serious' and the 'comic' parts. This, after Rich's day, would change. It is interesting, though, to note that kitchens and washerwomen and jokes of a domestic nature are already an established part of the 'comic business' and, indeed, to see an early 'splosh' scene being played with the soap-suds and boiling water. Interesting, too, to note that this was one of the scenes apparently most enjoyed by the galleries. The other was that in which Harlequin, pretending to be an ostrich, ran round 'kissing Columbine, biting the servant, and the like'. Shades of Rod Hull and Emu! Thus do elements of the *commedia* survive to this day.

As long as Harlequin remained a magic-worker, his most important attribute would be the 'wonder-working bat' by means of which his tricks were performed. (It was usually presented to him at some early point in the action as a 'gift from the immortals'.) This bat, which had replaced Arlecchino's wooden sword, was a sword-length lath of flat wood, narrow at the handle and broadening towards the end, which was pliant enough to create a good, sharp crack when tapped on an object prior to its 'transformation'. This crack was vital. It was the signal to the stage crew to effect the change. It thus had to be heard above the stage, below the stage, behind the scenes, or from wherever the trick was being worked, and above the sounds of music and audience.

The immense success of *Harlequin Sorcerer* was equalled at the Lincoln's Inn Fields Theatre two years later with a piece called *The Rape of Proserpine; with, the Birth and Adventures of Harlequin*. This again was the joint work of Rich and Lewis Theobald, the music and songs being written by the eminent composer Johann Ernst Galliard. The printed 'book' of this piece (which by 1727 was already in its fourth edition!) was dedicated by Rich to his friend Thomas Chambers. It was, he says, while a guest at Chambers' country house near Twickenham in what was then rural Middlesex, that he came to 'project and perfect the whole plan'.

That Rich's hand extended to every department of production in the preparation of these pieces is plain. In his letter of dedication to Chambers, written on 10th February 1726, he states that he 'could not then forbear recommending to my friend Mr Lambert, to borrow the Design of two Scenes (the Gardens of Ceres, and the Solitude) in the following entertainment from your own most delightful Garden at Hanworth'. Mr Lambert, whom Rich goes on to describe as 'so early and fine a Genius', was his principal scene-painter, George Lambert, who was, no doubt, despatched with all haste and a sketch-pad to Mr Chambers' garden!

The Rape of Proserpine was one of Rich's most celebrated and spectacular pieces. It was set in the palace and gardens of Ceres; in Sicily; and in the Elysian Fields. The first three scenes of the 'serious' part ran uninterrupted, and subsequently 'serious' and 'comic' scenes alternated, there being in all seven 'serious' scenes and four 'comic'.

45

The stage directions (we have them only for the 'serious' part) read like a catalogue of special effects. First we have Ceres 'in the air in her Chariot drawn by Dragons' ...

> See! see! aloft, advanc'd in Air,
> She rides upon the Clouds.

Then we discover an army of nymphs at Ceres' palace who 'erect a Trophy, in honour to Jupiter, that is form'd of the Spoils of the Giants whom Jupiter overcame'. As they work, 'an Earthquake is felt' and part of the Palace falls. Through the ruins Mount Etna is seen belching flames, and from beneath the rubble of the fallen palace, a giant begins to rise, only to be 'dash'd to pieces by a Thunder-bolt hurl'd from Jupiter'. Later, 'the earth opens; and Pluto's chariot rises'. He forces Proserpine (Ceres' daughter) into it, and it sinks again. One of the most famous of all the scenes was that in which Ceres burned the corn in revenge:

> Rage on the Wings of Fire shall ride!
> And flaming Ruin cover every Plain.

The Gods of the Woods, taking Ceres' side, begin to destroy the trees, but 'the people of Sicily' enter and oppose them, pleading:

> O sacred Ceres, spare the Land,
> Nor thy own gifts in rage Destroy.

But Ceres is adamant. She 'fetches flaming Branches from her Train, and sets the Corn, etc., on fire'.

It was *The Rape of Proserpine* that Alexander Pope was describing when, in the *Dunciad*, he wrote deprecatingly:

> All sudden, Gorgons hiss, and Dragons glare,
> And ten-horn'd fiends and Giants rush to war.
> Hell rises, Heav'n descends, and dance on Earth:
> Gods, imps, and monsters, music, rage, and mirth,
> A fire, a jigg, a battle, and a ball,
> 'Till one wide conflagration swallows all.

Pope singled the piece out for special attention in his wide-ranging attack on pantomime entertainments, because he'd been irritated by a stingingly bad review that Lewis Theobald had written of his edition of Shakespeare published the previous year. Such entertainments as the Rich-Theobald *Rape of Proserpine* ('Not touched by nature, and not reached by art', as he put it) Pope considered typical of the sort of low-brow dross that 'Dulness and her sons' then so much admired. Thus Rich secured his immortal place in Pope's gallery of pilloried 'Dunces'.

Thence a new world to Nature's laws unknown,
Breaks out refulgent, with a heav'n its own:
Another Cynthia her new journey runs,
And other planets circle other suns.
The forests dance, the rivers upward rise,
Whales sport in woods, and dolphins in the skies;
And last, to give the whole creation grace,
Lo! one vast Egg produces human race.

Joy fills his soul, joy innocent of thought;
What pow'r, he cries, what pow'r these wonders Wrought?
Son; what thou seek'st is in thee! Look, and find
Each Monster meets his likeness in thy mind.
Yet would'st thou more? In yonder cloud behold,
Whose sarsenet skirts are edg'd with flamy gold,
A matchless Youth! his nod these worlds controls,
Wings the red lightning, and the thunder rolls.
Angel of Dulness, sent to scatter round
Her magic charms o'er all unclassic ground:
Yon stars, yon suns, he rears at pleasure higher,
Illumes their light, and sets their flames on fire.
Immortal Rich! how calm he sits at ease
'Mid snows of paper, and fierce hail of pease;
And proud his Mistress' orders to perform,
Rides in the whirlwind, and directs the storm.'

Here, Pope provides a marvellous picture of Rich, the 'sable sorcerer' master-minding his theatrical effects. He also, in the line 'Lo! one vast Egg produces human race', describes Rich's first entrance in *The Rape of Proserpine*, an entrance in which he enacted 'the birth of Harlequin' referred to in the full title of the piece. This was one of Rich's most brilliant routines, and people who saw it never forgot it. It took place at the opening of the first 'grotesque' interlude. The scene showed the exterior of a farmhouse with its farmyard, and in it a dung-hill on which there lay an egg 'the size of an ostrich's'. In the heat of the sun, as one spectator described it, 'this egg ... grows gradually larger and larger; when it is of a very large size it cracks open, and a little Harlequin comes out of it. He is of the size of a child of three or four years old, and little by little attains a natural height.' Another who saw Rich demonstrate the piece described it as 'a master-piece in dumb-show. From the first chipping of the egg, his receiving motion, his feeling the ground, his standing upright, to his quick Harlequin trip round the empty shell, through the whole progression, every limb had its tongue, and every motion a voice, which "spoke with most miraculous organ", to the understandings and sensations of the observers.'

As the years went by, the devisers and writers of pantomime were to find themselves increasingly racking their brains for new and original ways of bringing Harlequin onto the scene. He might be conjured up from the depths of a well or a lake, out of a bower, or even from a furnace, forged in fire. In a piece called *Harlequin in his Element; or, Fire, Water, Earth and Air*, the spirits of the four elements, arguing about their respective powers, are finally stopped when Terrena, the Genius of Earth, demands:

> Rather than quarrel, let us join our powers,
> And gift with magic aid some active sprite
> To foil the guardian and the girl to right.

Whereupon she strikes the ground with her wand, a mound opens, 'and Harlequin, the motley hero, is discovered as a corpse'. The Spirits of Water, Air and Fire then breathe life into him and he is 'produced from a bed of parti-coloured flowers' and handed his magic bat with the words 'this powerful weapon your wants will provide'.

In the 1780s, one theatre manager, pondering the problem of how best to create his Harlequin in a story about King Arthur, Merlin and the Saxon Wizards, wrote to his principal scene-painter:

> The pantomime might open with three Saxon witches lamenting Merlin's power over them, and forming an incantation by which they create a Harlequin, who is supposed to be able to counteract Merlin in all his designs for the good of King Arthur. If the Saxons came on in a dreadful storm, as they proceeded in their magical rites, the sky might brighten, and a rainbow sweep across the horizon; which, when the ceremonies are completed, should contract itself from either end, and form the figure of Harlequin in the Heavens: the wizards may fetch him down how they will, and the sooner he is set to work the better.

The manager added the important rider, 'If this idea for producing a Harlequin is not new, do not adopt it.'

By the end of the 1720s, pantomime entertainments were the rage. These 'monstrous medlies' as Colley Cibber called them, 'arose upon one another alternately at both houses, outvying in expense, like contending bribes on both sides in an election, to secure a majority of the multitude'. Poor old Cibber! There we see him, like so many theatre managers before and since, writhing under the sharp necessity of having to be popular! And forced to admit that, were anyone to ask him why he staged such pieces when his loathing of them was so intense, that he did it against his conscience because he 'had not virtue enough to starve'!

Like all truly popular forms of entertainment when new and at their most virile, pantomime was criticised, attacked, vilified, ridiculed, and parodied, in verse and prose and in pieces written for both study and performance. Alexander Pope was by no means alone. One long poem called *British Frenzy; or the Mock-Apollo* (described as 'A Satyr'), lashed into Harlequin-Rich himself, complaining bitterly, 'The sneering Knave usurps Apollo's Crown' and urging the British people to 'pull, pull the parti-colour'd Tyrant down'! Another piece (like most of them anonymous) parodied pantomime's all-embracing titles by calling itself *Dido and Aeneas; or, Harlequin, a Butler, a Pimp, a Minister of State, Generalissimo, and Lord High Admiral, dead and alive again, and at last crown'd King of Carthage by Dido.* It was held up as an example of 'The English stage Italianiz'd' and carried a note advising that 'for the benefit of the English Quality and others who have forgot their Mother Tongue', it was being translated into Italian and printed for sale 'by the Orange Women and Door Keepers at Six Pence each'.

The novelist Henry Fielding had a number of cracks at the genre. He came at it first (in 1736) with a burlesque staged at the Little Theatre (the French House) in the Haymarket, called *Tumble-Down Dick; or, Phaeton in the Suds*, which he described as 'A Dramatick Entertainment of Walking, in serious and Foolish Characters; Interlarded with Burlesque, Grotesque, Comick Interludes, call'd Harlequin a Pick-Pocket'. It was dedicated to Rich in his guise of Mr John Lun, 'Vulgarly called Esquire', and it took the form of a rehearsal for a pantomime entertainment.

In it Neptune appears dressed like a Thames waterman because the deviser of the show, a character called 'Machine' (and obviously meant for Rich), considers it important that the characters be dressed 'somewhat like people have seen', and he knows full well that none of his audience 'have been nearer the sea than Gravesend'. As a critic sneers: 'So that he is more properly the god of the Thames, than the god of the sea.' Even the writer of the piece is rather surprised when he finds that 'a dance of Watchmen' has been introduced into one of the 'serious' scenes, the introduction being effected by Phoebus himself in an interpolated couplet in which he informs his son, Young Phaeton, apropos of nothing in particular:

> Now you shall see a dance, and that will show
> We lead as merry lives as folks below.

Whereupon enter dancing watchmen. The writer wants to know why the dance was introduced, and is told that it was introduced, 'as all dances are introduced, for the sake of the dance'. It's an element of pantomime we all recognise! The piece even pokes fun at Rich's emergence from the egg in *The Rape of Proserpine* when Phoebus recalls a sun that 'hatches an egg and produces a Harlequin', and Jupiter says, 'Yes, I remember that', and asks, 'Do you know what animal laid that egg?' 'Not I', says Phoebus, and Jupiter tells him: 'Sir, the egg was laid by an ass.'

Fielding returned to the attack in *Tom Jones* (1749) in which he asserts that the two parts of the pantomime should really have been called, not the 'serious' and the 'comic', but the 'duller' and the dullest', for 'the comic was certainly duller than anything shown before on the stage, and could be set off only by that superlative degree of dullness which composed the Serious.' Harlequin, he asserts was only welcomed on the stage because he 'relieved the audience from worse company'.

And so it went on. Not that it can have bothered Rich, for by this time he had long been the most successful theatre manager in London, riding not only on a high tide of pantomime success, but having also staged that timeless triumph *The Beggar's Opera*. This he had opened at the Lincoln's Inn Fields Theatre on 29th January 1728, after it had been turned down by the management at Drury Lane. As we all know, it 'made Gay rich, and Rich gay'!

Rich now undertook to build himself a new theatre. Leasing a parcel of land in Bow Street, Covent Garden, from the Duke of Bedford, he opened a subscription which quickly raised £6,000. Building began in March 1731, and took almost two years to complete, the venture being tagged 'Mr Lun's new Project in Covent Garden for the Advancement of Harlequinery'. It created immense public interest, as people of fashion gathered daily in the Garden to watch the building rise.

Rich's actual move from Lincoln's Inn Fields to 'the new House' is the subject of a satirical drawing by William Hogarth. Called RICH'S GLORY, *or His Triumphant Entry into Covent Garden*, it shows a long procession of costumed actors and a cartful of props and effects snaking across the Piazza of the Garden towards the door of the new theatre. At the head of it, in a chariot, rides John Rich, dressed as a dog, or, as a legend to the picture puts it, 'invested with the skin of the famous Dog in "Perseus and Andromeda"' (Rich had staged a version of this story a couple of years previously at Lincoln's Inn Fields). The chariot is drawn by satyrs and his coachman is none other than Harlequin, using his 'bat' as a whip as they process the Piazza to the cries of 'Rich for ever!'

> Not with more glory through the streets of Rome,
> Returned great Conquerors in Triumph home.

The new theatre opened as the Theatre Royal in Covent Garden on 7th December 1732, with a revival of Congreve's *The Way of the World*. As far as pantomimes were concerned, Rich was from now on in the main content to rely on the repertory of tried and tested pieces that he had originated at Lincoln's Inn Fields. He produced very few new ones at Covent Garden, but devoted himself instead to devising and mounting increasingly spectacular versions of the old.

John Rich was now a man to be reckoned with. In his very first season at the new theatre, there were no fewer than six Royal Command performances. King George II liked pantomime, and Rich made him laugh. 'Excellent Harlequin, Mr Rich,' he would exclaim, 'Excellent Harlequin!' To Rich's private room in the new theatre, where he was accustomed to arrange the comic business and construct the models of tricks for his pantomimes, there now resorted men of fashion, rank and wit, who found his company congenial and his inventiveness and technical wizardry fascinating. But no matter who dropped by, Rich had one immutable rule – he always took his lunch at two o'clock sharp. On one occasion the old and venerable Earl of Peterborough stayed on rather later than he'd planned, talking with Rich about his tricks and transformations, and quite unmindful of the time until he saw Rich 'spreading a cloth, then coaxing his fire into a clear cooking flame, and proceeding with great gravity, to cook his own beef-steak on his own grid-iron'. The old earl accepted Rich's invitation to join him, a further supply of steak was sent for, 'and a bottle or two of good wine from a neighbouring tavern' which, we are told, 'prolonged their enjoyment to a late hour'.

The hot steaks dressed by Rich himself, and frequently enjoyed by Rich and his old friend and chief painter, George Lambert, became a feature of the convivial gatherings that took place among the models and sketches in the little private room at Covent Garden, and it was from such gatherings that there eventually evolved the famous Beef-steak Society, founded by Rich in 1735. As the members would robustly sing, in a verse of their club song:

> First Rich, who this feast of the gridiron planned,
> And formed with a touch of his harlequin's wand,
> Out of mighty rude matter, this brotherly band,
> The jolly old Steakers of England.

The Society, which was dedicated to 'the fostering of good fellowship by the eating of beef-steak', took as its emblem the grid-iron, as its motto the words 'Beef and Liberty', and as its culinary watch-word the lines from *Macbeth*:

> If it were done when 'tis done, then 'twere well
> It were done quickly.

The 'Sublime Society of Beefsteaks', as it came to be known, was to survive for well over a century after the death of Rich and to number among its members over the years (there were never more than twenty-five of them at any one time) William Hogarth, John Wilkes, George Colman, David Garrick, the Prince Regent, a host of dukes, both royal and otherwise, and all manner of distinguished convivials. Rich's role in 'The Steaks' would seem to discount suggestions that he was unpopular, uncouth and friendless.

It was at Covent Garden that Rich introduced to the London stage a young actress who was to cause a sensation in those 'breeches' parts that were eventually, long after Rich's day, to find their way into pantomime and give it its 'Principal Boy'. The actress was Peg Woffington. She was twenty-two years old when she met Rich, and newly arrived from Ireland where she'd been on the stage since the age of twelve. She had come to London with one object in mind – to get a job at the Theatre Royal, Covent Garden, and she decided to set about this task by bearding Rich at his home in Bloomsbury Square. She had heard of Rich's reputation for not giving interviews to any stranger below the rank of baronet, but she was undeterred and, hiring a sedan chair, headed for Bloomsbury. She was to call at the house nineteen times in all before the rather imperious manservant finally agreed to inform Mr Rich that she was there. Peg Woffington never forgot her first meeting with John Rich, and has left us a wonderful description of him, then nearly fifty years old, relaxing at home:

> I saw the great man lolling in an ungraceful ease on a sofa, around him about seven and twenty kittens, tortoiseshells, Maltese, brindles, white, black and yellow cats of every description. Some frisking on the floor, others asleep; one licking the buttered toast on his breakfast table, another drinking the cream for his tea, two laying on his knee and another sitting demurely on his head ... so different an environment from my conception of a Covent Garden theatre manager, that I was embarrassed to speak.

Rich had no hesitation in employing her. As he was later to confide to Sir Joshua Reynolds, 'A more fascinating daughter of Eve never presented herself to a manager in search of rare commodities.' Peg Woffington thrilled London as Silvia in *The Recruiting Officer* and Sir

Harry Wildair in *The Constant Couple*,' both by Farquhar, but after only one season she went to Rich for more money, was refused it, and in consequence marched off to Drury Lane, where she was to meet and have a famous affair with the young David Garrick.

Like Doctor Johnson, Garrick hailed from Lichfield, though he was actually born at the Angel Inn in Hereford where his father, an army captain, was leading a recruiting campaign. For a while, when he was nineteen, he was a pupil (one of only three!) at Johnson's short-lived private academy at Edial, near Lichfield, and the two of them had finally set out for London together. Garrick went first into business as a wine merchant, but soon turned instead to the stage. He made his London debut at the little theatre in Goodman's Fields in the October of 1741, being billed anonymously as 'A Gentleman who never appeared on any stage'. Because of the licensing laws, the Goodman's Fields theatre advertised the evening's entertainment as 'A Concert of Vocal and Instrumental Music, Divided into Two Parts' and added the note: 'Between the Two Parts of the Concert will be presented an Historical Play called "The Life and Death of King Richard the Third"', this being 'performed Gratis'. Garrick (he was only 5 foot 4 inches tall) played Richard, was a huge success, and was soon the most talked-of actor in London, so much so that Drury Lane and Covent Garden got the Goodman's Fields theatre closed for being in breach of the law by performing straight plays, 'gratis' or not. Garrick then joined the company at the Theatre Royal, Drury Lane. Later, during a brief period of disenchantment with the Lane, he was to play for Rich, and it has been said that he might easily have been persuaded to continue his association with the Garden had Rich not been so fond of pantomime and similar spectacular entertainments, and so contemptuous of 'straight' plays and of those who acted in them. In the event, Garrick was offered a partnership in the management of Drury Lane, which he eagerly accepted, finally signing the agreement on 9th April 1747.

From then on the pantomime 'war' was to be waged between Rich and Garrick. Not that Garrick had any real desire to enter the lists. He did not like pantomime. But like so many before (and since) he soon discovered that if he wanted to keep his audiences he had to lay aside his own prejudices and give the public what they wanted. So, having resisted staging a pantomime for three years, he finally, on Boxing Day 1750, produced 'An Entertainment with Italian Grotesque Characters' called *Queen Mab*. Like Cibber, he made his apologies for resorting to the form:

Sacred to Shakespeare was this plot designed,
To pierce the heart and humanise the mind,
But if an empty house, the actor's curse,
Shews us our Lears and Hamlets lose their force,
Unwilling we must change the nobler scene,
And, in our turn, present you Harlequin;
Quit poets, and set carpenters to work,
Shew gaudy scenes, or mount the vaulting Turk.★
For though we actors one and all agree
Boldly to struggle for our vanity,
If want comes on, importance must retreat;
Our first great ruling passion – is to eat.

Queen Mab (to most poets, following Spenser, she was Queen of the Fairies, though Shakespeare gave the role to Titania) was the work of a thirty-year-old actor/comedian called Henry Woodward, who had been trained by Rich himself and was, indeed, known to the town as 'Lun, Junior'. He was to provide a number of pantomimes for Garrick during his long association with Drury Lane and was one of the first pantomime writers to glance in the direction of the fairy tale as a source of pantomime plots. *Queen Mab* was an enormous success. It was to remain in the repertory for a quarter of a century. Rich was piqued. So much so that he withdrew his own pantomime and replaced it with a production of King John. From now on he was under pressure. Garrick, having bitten the bullet, was to prove an expert at the staging of such pieces, and with Woodward as an ally, Covent Garden found itself pitched against remorseless competition in the pantomimic field.

So popular had pantomime now become that in 1753 a writer in *The World* ironically suggested that theatre managers should dispense entirely with tragedy and comedy and entertain the town with pantomime alone, people of taste and fashion having given sufficient proof that they thought it the highest entertainment the stage was capable of. 'The most innocent we are sure it is,' he concluded. 'For where nothing is said and nothing meant very little harm can be done.'

The biggest success of Garrick's management, however, came in December 1759 with a piece 'after the manner of the Italian Comedy' called *Harlequin's Invasion; or, A Christmas Gambol.* (Despite its reference to Christmas, the piece did not actually open until 31st December.) It was the joint work of Garrick and George Colman the elder,

---

★This was 'the famous Turk' who 'exhibited on the wire'.

and told the tale of the invasion, by Harlequin, of 'King' Shakespeare's august realm. As one commentator put it: 'The parti-coloured marauder and his satellites are utterly routed and repulsed by invincible Shakespeare.' (Well, in a Garrick show it could hardly have been otherwise!)

It was, incidentally, for this same pantomime, staged in the patriotic fervour of a 'Year of Victories' that had included Wolfe's capture of Quebec in September and Admiral Hawkes' victory over France's Brest Fleet at the Battle of Quiberon Bay on 20th November, that Garrick wrote one of the most famous of 'pantomime' songs. It was set to music by the Lane's musical director, William Boyce. (Dr Boyce, Master of the King's Music, had been brought in by Garrick to replace Dr Arne. The music for Garrick's pantomime was his last work for the theatre.) That New Year's Eve, and in the days that followed, audiences enthusiastically joined in its rousing chorus:

> Heart of oak are our ships,
> Heart of oak are our men,
> We always are ready,
> Steady, boys, steady!
> We'll fight and we'll conquer again and again.

Harlequin's Invasion is famous in the history of pantomime not only because it contained 'Heart of Oak', but also because in it, by way of a novelty, Garrick endowed Harlequin with the power of speech, something he had not enjoyed on the English stage since the revivals of Aphra Behn's play. It was to prove little more than a gimmick, but Garrick added a prologue (spoken by Harlequin himself) which paid a graceful tribute to the memory of old Lun and also put forward the reasons for making the experiment:

> But why a speaking Harlequin? – 'Tis wrong,
> The wits will say, to give the fool a tongue;
> When Lun appear'd with matchless art and whim,
> He gave the pow'r of speech to ev'ry limb;
> Tho' mask'd and mute, convey'd his quick intent,
> And told in frolic gestures all he meant.
> But now the motley coat, and sword of wood,
> Require a tongue to make them understood.

The essayist and critic William Hazlitt, who saw a revival of the piece in 1820, definitely thought it was wrong 'to give the fool a tongue':

> It is called a speaking pantomime. We had rather it had said nothing. It is better to act folly than to talk it. The essence of pantomime is practical absurdity keeping

55

the wits in constant chase, coming upon one by surprise, and starting off again before you can arrest the fleeting 'phantom': the essence of this piece was prosing stupidity remaining like a mawkish picture on the stage, and overcoming your impatience by the force of ennui. A speaking pantomime such as this one is not unlike a flying waggon.

By Hazlitt's time the whole shape of pantomime had changed and Harlequin's position in it had been usurped. *Harlequin's Invasion* must, indeed, have seemed sadly out of date. Rich died in 1761 (he was buried in Hillingdon Churchyard close to his country house at Cowley in Middlesex) and although there were to be many more Harlequins, and although the role was to be constantly tinkered with, it would never again be blessed with the sort of powerfully creative imagination that he had brought to it.

During the Christmas–New Year period of 1781–2, young Charles Lamb, then aged six, was taken to see a pantomime (one of his first) in which he remembered the 'Ghost of Lun' appearing. To the small boy, Lun was already 'as remote a piece of antiquity as Lud', merely 'the father of a line of Harlequins – transmitting his dagger of lath (the wooden sceptre) through countless ages'. But there was one moment in that pantomime that he was able vividly to recall in later years when he wrote: 'I saw the primeval Motley come from his silent tomb in a ghastly vest of white patch-work, like the apparition of a dead rainbow. So Harlequins (thought I) look when they are dead.'

FOUR
SEND·IN·THE·CLOWNS

I n the years that followed the death of Rich, the initiative for innovation in pantomime passed to the Theatre Royal, Drury Lane. It was here that the emphasis first began to shift from the figure of Harlequin towards that of Pierrot and, subsequently, of Clown. Both these characters were *zannis* (servants), as indeed Harlequin had originally been, and both appear off and on in the cast lists of the earliest English pantomime entertainments. Pierrot, for example, appears in Rich's *The Jealous Doctor*, staged at the Lincoln's Inn Fields Theatre in 1717, and again in *The Necromancer* of 1723; and both Pierrot and Clown (described as 'the Squire's Man') are among the 'pantomime' characters in John Weaver's *Perseus and Andromeda* (1725).

The person chiefly responsible for bringing these two characters forward was Carlo Delpini. Delpini, who was born in Rome, had joined Garrick at the Lane in the 1770s, playing Pierrot, and had gone on to become a famous Clown. In January 1781 he took the part of Crusoe and Pierrot in Sheridan's 'Grand Pantomime' of *Robinson Crusoe; or, Harlequin Friday*, the first piece to put Daniel Defoe's hero on the stage. For this piece (in which both Pierrot and Clown appeared) Delpini also arranged the Harlequinade. *Harlequin Friday* is the only pantomime that Sheridan wrote, although he had contributed a new topical interlude dealing with the storming and taking of Fort Omoa a now forgotten incident, to a revival of *Harlequin Fortunatus; or, the Wishing Cap* staged at Drury Lane in December 1779. So loath are some historians to see such a distinguished writer as Richard Brinsley Sheridan (with *The Rivals, The Duenna, School for Scandal*, and *The Critic* already behind him) dabbling in the common rough-and-tumble of pantomime that it has been suggested that *Harlequin Friday* was, in fact, written by a team consisting of his wife, his wife's sister, and his wife's sister's husband; Sheridan himself, when all was done, having merely 'given a lift to it'. Either way, the piece was different from the pantomimes of Rich's day in that instead of the 'serious' and the 'comic' scenes being interwoven, they were separated out to give the piece two distinct parts. The first, or 'opening', part dealt with the adventures of Robinson Crusoe; the second, the Harlequinade, dealt with the comic and knockabout adventures of Harlequin and his cronies. Furthermore, the two parts were linked in that the principal characters of the first part were, at its close, 'transformed' into the principal characters of the second.

It was this device which inspired Horace Walpole to write: 'How unlike the pantomimes of Rich, which were full of wit, and coherent, and carried on a story! What I now saw was "Robinson Crusoe": how Aristotle and Bossu, had they ever written on pantomimes, would swear! It was a heap of contradictions and violations of the costume. Friday is turned into Harlequin, and falls down at an old man's feet that I took for Pantaloon, but they told me it was Friday's father. I said 'then it must be Thursday', yet still it seemed to be Pantaloon. I see I understand nothing from astronomy to a harlequin-farce!'

Nevertheless, this was the pattern that pantomime was to follow for the next century and more, with structural change being limited to altering the relative lengths of its two parts. First, the 'opening' would contract to allow a longer Harlequinade. Then, as the Harlequinade declined in popularity, the reverse would happen and the 'opening' become, as we shall see, the dominant, and finally the only, part.

Although *Robinson Crusoe; or, Harlequin Friday* was held up by one journal as proof that 'even the greatest genius' could 'sink beneath contempt', it proved immensely popular, running at its first showing for thirty-eight nights, a long run for those days. In view of the energetic nature of the Harlequinade it is, perhaps, surprising to find that the original role of 'Harlequin Friday' was taken by a man who was then in his late sixties. But this was a most remarkable man – Guiseppe Grimaldi, sometimes called 'Iron Legs'. Two years earlier, he had caused something of a back-stage sensation at the Theatre Royal, Drury Lane, when, just as the pantomime rehearsals were reaching their chaotic climax, news had arrived that he had just been presented by his 25-year-old mistress with a son, Joseph. The announcement had caused a good deal of ribald merriment among the members of the company, who had seen the event as a great tribute to the old man's continuing virility. It had long been common knowledge that he'd 'littered the Town with bastards'. There had also been considerable admiration for his timing of the birth – right on cue for the pantomime! – and some sombre speculation as to what the future might have in store for the child; after all he'd been born to a curiously ill-assorted couple.

In fact, the future was to prove a bitter-sweet mixture of triumph and tragedy, merriment and pain, but Joseph Grimaldi was to become one of the greatest and best-loved figures in the whole long history of English pantomime. Subsequent generations of Clowns would continue to borrow his catch-phrase ('Here we are again!'), his jokes, his routines, and his songs right up to the 1930s when the Harlequinade (and with it the character of Clown) finally vanished from pantomime, and his name was to become part of the very language of entertainment. Clowns are still called 'Joey' after him, and slapstick comedy is known to this day as 'Joey-Joey' because of him.

Joe's mother, Rebecca Brooker, was an ebullient, quick-witted Londoner, Cockney through-and-through, and a chorus dancer at the Lane. As a child, her father (a carcase-butcher, and keeper of the Bloomsbury slaughter-house) had rented her to David Garrick as an 'occasional fairy', and she was to spend the rest of her days in the *corps de ballet*. Joe's father, Guiseppe Grimaldi, had come to England from the fairgrounds of Italy and France, to become Garrick's ballet-master and, subsequently, a popular pantomimist, playing not only Harlequin, but also Pantaloon and Clown. In the latter role he was to score a major triumph at the age of seventy-one! He was a highly gifted man, but eccentric and licentious with a cruel streak and a melancholy nature that on occasion turned to the morbid. He was, for example, in the habit of wandering about churchyards and similar burial places for hours on end 'speculating on the diseases of which the persons had died, and wondering how many of them had been buried alive'. To his compatriots at the theatre he was known as 'Old Grim'.

On that December day on which his son had been born, 'Old Grim' had boasted to his friends in the green room that he would have the boy on the stage as soon as he could walk. And he did. Young Joe made his first appearance at the Sadler's Wells theatre, when he was only two years and four months old on Easter Monday 1781. The child's upbringing was harsh. The beatings were regular. Strangely enough, Joe was to claim later in life that he owed his first real success to one such beating. It had been a particularly harsh one, and he was still sobbing bitterly when he was called for his entrance. The tears had washed deep channels in his thick make-up, giving him a grotesquely comic appearance, and he entered to a general roar of laughter. This infuriated Old Grim who promptly set about the unfortunate child again, and the audience, taking it all as part of the performance, were delighted. Shouts of laughter and peals of applause shook the house. Next morning one newspaper declared that it was perfectly wonderful to see a child perform so naturally, and highly creditable to his father's talents as a teacher.

By the age of nine, when his father died, Joe was already a veteran, engaged in regular supernumary and occasional character work. He would spend each winter on the stage of Drury Lane and, with the coming of spring, move out to Sadler's Wells, then a summer theatre standing beside the New River in the then rural surroundings of the fields beyond Hoxton, and licensed to be open each year from Easter Monday to the end of September for the production of dancing, singing, and musical pieces. Sadler's Wells was described by Mary Lamb as 'the lowest and most London-like of our amusements'. It was a famous place of resort for Cockney apprentices and sailors, the gallery being sometimes almost solely occupied by blue-jackets and their female companions.

Joey Grimaldi was to spend all but one of his summers here for the rest of his working life; the exceptional year being 1817 when, following a disagreement with the management, he was replaced. There was a public outcry. The words 'Joey for Ever' appeared scrawled in chalk on walls all over the area. There was a demonstration of support outside his home. And the Sadler's Wells Theatre lost £2534!

But that lay in the future. At the time of Giuseppi Grimaldi's death, the Wells was facing difficulties and the management, taking advantage of the old man's passing, immediately slashed his son's salary from fifteen shillings a week to three. When his mother remonstrated, she was told that 'if the alteration did not suit her, she was at perfect liberty to transfer his valuable services to any other house'. As Grimaldi himself was to write: 'Small as the pittance was, they could not afford to refuse it.' His salary was to remain three shillings a week at the Wells for the next three years and, in addition to his stage appearances, his duties were to include 'occasionally superintending the property-room, sometimes assisting in the carpenters, and sometimes in the painters, and, in fact, lending a hand wherever it was most needed'.

His first taste of success was to come at Sadler's Wells which came under the management of Charles Dibdin Jnr (son of the songwriter) in 1799. Dibdin was then thirty. Grimaldi was twenty and already well acquainted with Dibdin's younger brother Tom who'd spent three years at the Wells between 1794 and 1797 as actor, writer, designer and stage manager. Tom had now moved on to pastures new, but he and Charles were destined to play a considerable part in bringing the comedic talents of Joey Grimaldi to full flower. In his *Memoirs* Charles was later to recall how, when he first entered upon management at the Wells, Grimaldi was a mere youth 'promising what he so inimitably performed'. His attention had been particularly drawn to the young man by the theatre's principal director, Richard Hughes. 'Mr Hughes had told me that I should find him to be a very clever lad, and begged that I would cultivate his talents as much as I possibly could.'

It was Charles Dibdin who gave the young Grimaldi his first chance in the role of Clown, on Easter Monday 1800. The bill at the Wells that day consisted of a musical bagatelle called *Old Fools; or, Love's Stratagem* (by Charles Dibdin); an Historical Ballet of Action called *Boadicea; or, the British Amazon* (by Charles Dibdin); some comic songs (by Charles Dibdin); and the pantomime *Peter Wilkins; or, Harlequin in the Flying World* (by Charles Dibdin). Also on the bill, but not by Charles Dibdin, were a Pastoral Ballet and 'Richer's performance on the Rope, clowned by Dubois'. In the pantomime, Grimaldi played Guzzle 'the drinking Clown' with Baptiste Dubois, a stage veteran of some forty years' experience, opposite him as Gobble 'the eating Clown'.

The following year Dubois left the Wells. According to Charles Dibdin he went because he was jealous of young Grimaldi. Elsewhere it has been suggested that it was because he was refused a higher salary. In that case it probably indicates that Dibdin saw little point in paying more to retain the services of an old Clown when he had such a potentially brilliant young one waiting in the wings. Of Grimaldi, Dibdin was to write: 'As a clown, and singer of Clown's songs ... I despair of looking upon his like again. I never saw anyone to equal him. There was so much *mind* in everything he did. It was said of Garrick that, when he played a drunken man, he was 'all over drunk', Grimaldi was 'all over Clown'.

At Christmas 1800, Grimaldi played Clown in the Drury Lane pantomime, *Harlequin Amulet; or, the Magic of Mona.* It is a piece famous in theatrical history as the one in which James Byrne, the Lane's Ballet Master and a famous Harlequin, created the costume in which, to this day, Harlequins are always portrayed. In Rich's day, the character had worn virtually the same costume as that in which Arlecchino had dressed, all those years ago in Italy. It had consisted of a loose-fitting, parti-coloured thigh-length jacket, buttoned from top to bottom and belted, with matching, tapered trousers and a black vizard. Byrne now replaced this with white, skin-tight, silk fleshings, 'fitting without a wrinkle', and covered all over with small diamond-shaped, variegated silk patches, sewn with tinsel and profusely covered with spangles. A black eye-mask replaced the vizard, and he added a bicorn hat. As Harlequin's biographer, Thelma Niklaus, has written: 'The Bergamask yokel was now a very fine gentleman indeed, as he flashed about the stage, a glittering quicksilver figure that caught every eye.' Nevertheless, and despite the very best efforts of Byrne and his successors, the battle was to prove an unequal one. The principal figure of the Harlequinade was henceforth, until it finally disappeared in the early years of the twentieth century, to be Clown. Grimaldi would see to that.

After almost a quarter of a century of playing winter seasons at Drury Lane, relationships with the management began to sour. And in the autumn of 1806 Grimaldi moved over to the rival Theatre Royal in Covent Garden. Here, his old friend Tom Dibdin was working. Tom had, in fact, been trying to get Grimaldi to the Garden for some years. As he was to write in his *Autobiography*: 'Our last three pantomimes had suffered much for want of a good clown: Delpini, Dubois, and Bologna senior, were all on the decline.' But the Garden's management had refused to make an approach to Grimaldi as it would have breached an agreement between the two theatres not to 'poach' each other's artists.

When he finally went to the Garden, Grimaldi sought a three-year contract on terms that Tom Dibdin considered 'so very modest, and so much beneath his value' that he personally intervened, advising the management to offer a pound a week the first year, two the second, and three the third, 'more than the sum Mr Grimaldi had mentioned'. The deal was done, and as Tom was to write: 'The best Clown ever seen on the stage was retained for *Mother Goose*'.

FIVE

GOLDEN·EGGS·AND·HOT·CODLINS

I.

Harlequin and Mother Goose; or, the Golden Egg (it bore very little relationship to the *Mother Goose* pantomime we know today, which was not devised until the turn of the nineteenth century) opened at the Theatre Royal, Covent Garden, on Monday 29th, December 1806. It was preceded by a performance of the favourite forepiece *George Barnwell!* The bills described it as 'a new pantomime, which has long been in preparation', and it was the work of Tom Dibdin, though his name was not billed. In the manner of the day, the bills named the composer (Mr Ware), the director (Mr Farley), the dance arranger (Mr Bologna, Jnr), the scenic artists (Messrs Phillips, Whitmore, Hollogan, Grieve, Hodgings, 'and their Assistants'), the machinists (Messrs Sloper, Bologna, Jnr., Creswell, and Goostree), the dress-makers (Mr Dick and Mrs Egan), and the cast right down to the 'Villagers, Fairies, etc.'. But no writer or deviser, though we are told that the scenes were 'entirely new'.

The piece had, in fact, been written and mounted in a frantic six weeks, because of a last-minute managerial change of plan about the pantomime. But Dibdin and Farley had had the idea in mind for some years, and had long tried to interest the management in it without success. As a last-minute substitute, however, it had considerable advantages. Unlike some previous pantomimes, it was set entirely in England; its scenes were the everyday ones of village green, village inn, the grocer's shop, and London's streets and pleasure gardens, which meant that costumes and scenery could probably to an extent be adapted from stock and would, in any case, require no special, time-consuming research. The English setting was not a new idea. Covent Garden had, some thirteen years before, staged a piece called *Harlequin's Museum; or, Mother Shipton Triumphant*, which had introduced a sporting country squire (Squire Foxchase) and been advertised as including 'for the first time, a Fox Chase, with Real Hounds and Horses'. Among its familiar scenes of town and countryside had been Sir Gregory's country house, a baker's shop, and the dock yard at

Devonport. For the latter the stage was 'completely filled with performers', 'God Save the King' was sung, three huzzas given, and a
ship was launched, followed by 'the firing of a cannon and every
demonstration of joy', during which a naval lieutenant entered to sing
the song described as 'undoubtedly the most popular ever introduced
on a stage'. It was 'Heart of Oak', and every member of the audience
was presented with a copy.

But English domestic settings were by no means the norm. There
was a strong tendency towards the exotic. The Covent Garden pantomimes of 1804 and 1805 (both the work of Dibdin and Farley)
illustrate the point. The 1804 one was *Harlequin Quicksilver; or, the
Gnome and the Devil*, and its scenes had included a Spanish seaport, a
Spanish square at Carnival time, a Masquerade in Madrid, a Fairy
Palace and a Silver Mine. And in the 1805 *Harlequin's Magnet; or, The
Scandinavian Sorcerer*, the comic adventures of the Harlequinade 'were
pursued through various parts of Russia, Siberia and Grim Tartary',
even to Moscow itself. The costumes 'of the Ancient Scandinavian
Mythology', we are told, had been taken 'with some necessary stage
alterations' from Mallet's *Northern Antiquities*. Such things took time.

Mother Goose was probably one of the simplest and plainest pantomimes that had so far been seen. It had 'neither gorgeous processions, nor gaudy banners, nor splendid scenery, nor showy dresses'.
Even the last scene, which was customarily the most spectacular and
lavish of all ('the great question with the majority of the town being
which pantomime had the finest conclusion') was 'as plain as possible'.
It is even said that Harlequin himself would have been denied his
spangles had not Grimaldi stepped in and drawn the line.

Grimaldi himself had very little faith in the piece. Nor did anyone
else (with the exception, one imagines, of Tom Dibdin and Charles
Farley). It was noticeable that the Garden's manager, usually in regular
attendance during the preparations for the pantomime, looked in only
once. However, in the manner of such things, *Harlequin and Mother
Goose* was a tremendous success. It ran for ninety-two nights and is
said to have put more than £20,000 into the pockets of the management. The very plainness of the setting had permitted the jewel, Joey
Grimaldi, to shine at last with unimpeded brilliance.

Mother Goose marks a turning point in the history of pantomime,
because from this point on Clown was set fair and square as the
principal character of the Harlequinade. But beyond that it established
in its opening scenes a style that is recognisable to this day as the
authentic voice of pantomime. The principal characters were Mother

64

(Above) *John Rich 'lolling in an ungraceful ease on a sofa', as Peg Woffington first saw him when she visited his home in Bloomsbury Square in 1740. This detail from an engraving shows just a few of Rich's cats that Peg estimated numbered 'about seven and twenty' in all*

The 61-year-old John Rich as Harlequin in 1753, shortly before he retired. In this engraving from a watercolour by an unknown artist Rich is portrayed without his black mask

Harlequin. Zany Corneto. Il Segnor Pantalon.

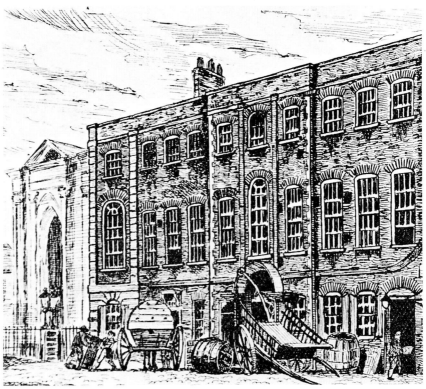

II

(Above facing) *A scene from the* Commedia dell'Arte, *16th century*

(Below facing) *The birthplace of English pantomime, the Theatre in Lincoln's Inn Fields opened in 1714 by John Rich, and used by his company until he moved to Covent Garden in 1732. It was finally pulled down in 1845*

(Above) *Harlequin takes a header through a shop window. Such acrobatic dives through apparently solid objects were a favourite 'trick' of the Harlequinade*

(Right) *A 'Big Head' and over-dress as worn by the actor playing Humpo in the opening of Tom Dibdin's 1812* Harlequin and Humpo; or, Columbine by Candlelight. *He was later transformed into the Dandy Lover*

III

IV

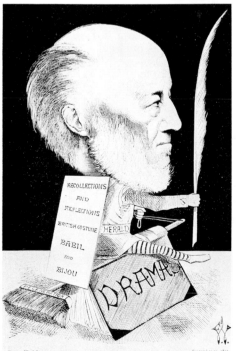

(Above facing) *'Oh, Joey! What Have You Done?' A John Leech cartoon from the mid-19th century which illustrates another favourite pantomime 'trick'*

(Below facing) *The Theatre Royal, Drury Lane, in the early part of the 19th century*

(Above) *The 'moulder of grotesque masks' putting the finishing touches to the 'Big Heads' in preparation for an 1870 pantomime*

(Left) *J. R. Planché, 'antiquarian, dramatic author, man of the world, and honoured officer of the Herald's College', from whose 'fairy extravaganzas' the modern pantomime is directly descended*

Nº 11.

MR GRIMALDI AS CLOWN.

Price Halfpenny

ILLUMINATING THE ENTRANCE TO OLD GUTTER LANE.

London, Pub. Feb. 1ˢᵗ 1823, by J.K.Green, 3, George Street, Walworth new Town.

VI

(Facing) *Grimaldi in his famous 'Night Watchman' scene uses a lantern to guide the wine-bottle into his mouth*

(Above right) *Madame Vestris in one of her most famous 'breeches parts' as Don Giovanni in the comic extravaganza entertainment* Giovanni in London *(1820). Of her it was written: 'Oh, please us long till midnight hour/Either in petticoat or breeches/For none like Vestris has the power/In everything to "run through stitches"'*

(Below right) *Lydia Thompson as Robinson Crusoe. Equally famous on the burlesque and pantomime stages, she, according to Sir Frank Burnand, 'played boys' parts so charmingly, that to "go and see Lydia Thompson", in no matter what the piece might happen to be, was an incentive to the very laziest habitué of the theatres.' Lydia caused a sensation in America in the late 1860s when she horse-whipped a Chicago editor who'd written deprecatingly of her touring troupe 'Lydia's Blondes'. She was fined over $2000, but is said to have considered it well worth it!*

MADAME VESTRIS as DON GIOVANNI.

The real Dick Whittington. This 'true portraicture' was published in the early 1600s. The original version showed him with his hand on a skull, but the public refused to buy it without a cat in it, so a cat was quickly substituted

(Left) The story of Little Red Riding-Hood portrayed in a series of woodcuts which appeared in an English children's book of 1777. As early as 1754 George Colman the elder had recommended the story to pantomime writers, but it was 1803 before the first pantomime version (written by Charles Dibdin, Jnr. for Sadler's Wells) appeared

Goose herself (the 'Benevolent Agent'), played by Mr Simmons; Colin (afterwards Harlequin), the young suitor for the hand of Colinette, played in the opening by Mr King and following his transformation into Harlequin by Mr Bologna, Jnr; Avaro (afterwards Pantaloon), Colinette's aged guardian, played by Mr L. Bologna; Squire Bugle (afterwards Clown), the Squire to whom Avaro has promised his ward's hand, played by Mr Grimaldi; and Colinette herself (afterwards Columbine), played by Miss Searle. There were four scenes in the 'opening' and no less than fifteen in the Harlequinade, plus the customary 'grand finale'. Music ran throughout the piece and there was no spoken dialogue.

The curtain rose on the now familiar pantomime scene of an English village. The 'book' of the piece describes the opening, thus:

SCENE FIRST

A village with storm, etc. Sunset; on the R. are the entrance gates to Squire Bugle's Mansion, adjoining to it Colin's Cottage. A Church with the Churchyard in front, L; the perspective a distance view of a river and a bridge over it, moving objects both on river and bridge. During the storm Mother Goose has raised, she is seen descending from the skies mounted on a gander; after the storm the clouds disperse and a rainbow is seen, the Sun rises gradually, etc., etc. Its golden beams are finely reflected on the window of the Church.

A crowd of Male and Female Peasants assemble, decorated with favours, to celebrate the nuptials of the Squire and Colinette; some dance while others sing the following:

CHORUS OF PEASANTRY

Neighbours we're met on a very merry morning,
Lads and Lasses dress'd in all their pride so gay
Celebrate the happy hour, longer shyness scorning
Sweet Colinette is married to the Squire this day.
Old and young
Join the throng
Cutting nimble capers;
Haste to Church,
In the lurch
Leaving care and vapours.
No one sad
Hey, go mad,
Man and maiden seem to say:
'If I know who
Prove but true,
The next may be my wedding day.'

Enter Avaro leading Colinette. Bugle solo. Enter the Squire from the mansion, equipped for hunting, preceded by huntsmen, jockeys, grooms, and servants. Avaro presents Colinette to the Squire; she turns from him and welcomes Colin, who appears at the window of the cottage; the Guardian interferes; Colinette approaches and points at the tomb of the Squire's late wife, which is seen in the centre of the churchyard. It bears the inscription:

65

"OH, YES IT IS!"

In Memory of
Xantippe
wife of
BULLFACE BUGLE
Esqr

The Squire sings the old air:
>First wife's dead,
>There let her lie;
>She's at rest,
>And so am I.

The procession to the Church commences, but Colinette breaks away and runs to Colin for protection; they are separated by Avaro, and all sing the following:

SESTETTO AND CHORUS

COLIN:	When Guardians break a promise due,
SQUIRE:	Who dares our progress stop?
AVARO:	When richer suitors come to woo,
SQUIRE:	Such Folks as you may hop.
COLINETTE:	Yet listen to this injur'd Youth
AVARO:	Your dignity he mocks,
COLIN:	I Claim her Hand
SQUIRE:	Indeed! Forsooth
	I'll put him in the Stocks,
	Then merrily, merrily march away,
	For this shall be my Wedding Day.
CHORUS:	Then merrily march away,
	It is the Squire's wedding day.
	Then merrily, merrily, merrily, merrily,
	march away,
	It is the Squire's Wedding Day.
	Then merrily, merrily, merrily, merrily,
	march away,
	It is the Squire's Wedding Day.

The Beadle now enters with Mother Goose in Custody

BEADLE:	So please your Worship 'ere you go
	Punish this wicked witch;
M. GOOSE:	O fie!
	Good neighbours why d'ye use me so?
	Indeed, no wicked witch am I;
COLINETTE:	Pity her age;
M. GOOSE:	Pray let me loose,
	Don't hurt poor harmless Mother Goose.
BEADLE:	Out of the way officious fool,
SQUIRE:	Go, take her to the Ducking Stool.
COLIN:	Shame, Neighbours, shame!
SQUIRE:	Don't list to him,
	But try if she chance to sink or swim.
	Meantime, we'll merrily march away,
	Because this is my Wedding-Day.

66

CHORUS: Merrily, merrily, March away
           And keep the Squire's Wedding-Day.

While they are singing this chorus, Colin rescues Mother Goose from
the Beadle and she, retiring, prepares a little surprise for Squire Bugle.
The Squire, approaching his late wife's tomb, strikes it with his whip.
The tomb immediately opens and the Ghost of Xantippe appears
'which Mother Goose has raised, clad in white satin and poppy ri-
bands'. She follows the Squire, shakes her hands at him, 'and descends
through a trap'. The Squire, terrified, runs off, right, and Colin and
Colinette, 'conversing with one another', exit left.

We now go to Mother Goose's 'Retreat'. 'The front a thick wood,
on one side an entrance, on the other thick foliage, etc., an Owl seated
on a branch, very prominent; in the perspective, a clear blue sky with
moon, and stars, etc.' Mother Goose enters 'followed by urchin Spirits, most fantastically habited'. As they dance about her, she sings:

> The grasshopper chirrups, listen, listen!
> The cricket chimes in with the sound;
> On water and windows the moonbeams glisten,
> And dewdrops bespangle the ground.
>
> Then haste from dogrose, briar, and bell,
> From dingle, brake, or daisied dell,
> Collect each potent fairy spell,
> Our magic, magic, can produce.
>
> To plague yon Squire, and to aid
> Young Colin to obtain the maid,
> And when my orders are obey'd
> You'll laugh with Mother Goose.
> Ha, ha, ha! Ha, ha, ha!
> Will laugh with Mother Goose!
> Ha, ha, ha! Ha, ha, ha!
> Will laugh with Mother Goose!
>
> Nay, softly, see Aurora's blush
> Bids swiftly vanish, hush, hush, hush.
> Hush, hush, hush.
>   Hush, hush, hush.
>   Hush, hush, hush.
>   Hush,
>   Hush,
>   Hush.

The wood stage right opens and presents Mother Goose's Dwelling.
Colin enters 'in a very desponding state'. Mother Goose approaches,
followed by her favourite or Golden Goose, and 'addresses Colin in
these lines, with action appropriate'.

M. GOOSE: Youth, why despair? The girl thou shalt obtain,
This present shall her guardian's Sanction gain.
(She gives him the golden goose.)
Nay, doubt not. While she's Kindly used, she'll lay
A golden egg on each succeeding day.
You serv'd me - no reply! - there lies your way.

And we change to Scene Three, which shows 'A Hall in Avaro's House'. The stage direction reads: 'Avaro and Colinette enter, and are followed by Colin and Goose. Avaro endeavours to turn Colin out, when Colin shows him the Goose and Golden Egg, and explains what wealth he may possess; avarice gets the better of Avaro's promise to the Squire, and he joins Colin and Colinette's hands, but presuming he shall gain all the gold at once by destroying the Goose, he draws his Knife, and is preparing to murder her, which Colin prevents. The Squire enters, when Colin, fearful of losing his prize, consents rashly to the Sacrifice of the bird.' The Goose now makes her exit through a panel in the back scene, which turns round and presents Mother Goose, who addresses Avaro as follows:

Thou avaricious, selfish, ingrate elf,
Like other fools, too cunning for thyself;
Thy ward shall still perplex thee by her flight –
Lo! thus I change the lovers

Colinette is changed to Columbine and Colin to Harlequin

- motley white *(addressing Harlequin)*
Thou too shall wander till this egg of gold,
Which in the sea I cast, you once again shall hold.

The Scene opens and discovers –
SCENE FOURTH – The Sea.
Mother Goose throws the Golden Egg into the Sea. The Scene changes back to Avaro's Hall.

M. GOOSE: Stop fool! Some recompense is yet thy due.
(To the Squire) Take that. *(Changes him to Clown.)*
While thou *(to Avaro)* shalt wear my livery too.
(Changes him to Pantaloon).

AIR

For slighted Kindness take your due,
Yet mirth shall with your toils entwine
Be Harlequin while you pursue
Not Colinette, but Columbine.
This gift receive *(she gives Harlequin his bat)*
Amend what's past
And guard it better than the last,
Regain the Egg and happy be,
'Till then, farewell, remember me.
Farewell, farewell,

Remember me.
Farewell, farewell,
Farewell, remember me.
   Farewell,
      Farewell,
         Farewell.

Here, Mother Goose retires 'and is seen to ascend mounted on a Gander'. The comic business then commences and runs through to the 'dark scene', at Scene Nineteen, which takes place in a 'Mermaid's Cave'. Harlequin finally retrieves the Golden Egg from the sea, but at the very moment of triumph is cornered by Pantaloon and Clown, at which point Mother Goose enters. Harlequin gives her the Golden Egg, and she 'reconciles all parties' with the lines:

> The egg returned, receive thy lovely choice,
> The gift is sanctioned by her guardian's voice;
> You, soon restored to person, house, and lands,
> Shall, like a hearty English Squire, shake hands;
> Meanwhile his magic dwelling you shall view
> Furnished by fairy hands to pleasure you.

The final scene is set in 'A Submarine Palace', though not an especially lavish one. It is decorated only with dolphins ('in the perspective a tripod of them'), and has two recesses 'in each of which is seen a mermaid, busily employed in combing their hair'. Dancers approach 'habited to correspond with the scene', and the finale is sung.

FINALE

M. GOOSE: Ye patrons kind, who deign to view
             The sport our scenes produce,
             Accept our wish to pleasure you
             And laugh with Mother Goose.
             Ye patrons kind, etc.

SQUIRE: And let no critic stern reject
             What our petition begs,
             That we may from your smiles collect
             Each night some golden eggs.

CHORUS: Ye patrons kind who deign to view
             The sport we'd fain produce,
             Accept our wish to pleasure you
             And laugh with Mother Goose.
             Who humbly begs
             On bended legs
             That you, good lack,
             Her cause will back,
             And scorn to crack
             Her Golden Eggs.

FINIS

2.

The Harlequinade in Mother Goose got off to a flying start when Harlequin, trying to elude Pantaloon and Clown, 'leaps through the face of the clock, which immediately presents a Sportsman with his gun cocked. The Clown opens the clock door, and a little Harlequin appears as a pendulum. The Clown says "Present! Fire!". The Sportsman lets off his piece, the Clown falls down, during which period Columbine and Harlequin, who had previously entered through the panel, escape. After some tricks, the Clown runs off in pursuit with Pantaloon on his back.' (Harlequin was still to be found leaping through clock faces in the 1890s.) At this stage in the development of pantomime, the story of the lovers' fate was never in any degree forgotten or relaxed during the entire Harlequinade, the two sections of the pantomime remaining firmly linked. Once the Benevolent Agent had intervened (at the end of the 'opening'), had transformed the lovers in order to enable them to escape their enemies, and had bestowed upon Harlequin the gift of his magic bat, they were sent out into this new world to work their way on their own resources, and to baffle their enemies as best they might. All the tricks and changes that were introduced along the way had a purpose, that purpose being to aid the escape of Harlequin and Columbine, when too closely followed by their enemies, until their final entrapment in the 'dark scene'. This logical and positive connection between the two parts was eventually to be severed, and it was that severance that was finally to kill the Harlequinade.

While it flourished, and as it peaked in Grimaldi's day, the Harlequinade marvellously provided what Leigh Hunt considered 'the three general pleasures of a pantomime', its bustle, its variety, and its sudden changes. 'The stage is never empty or still,' he wrote. 'Either Pantaloon is hobbling about or somebody falling flat, or somebody else is receiving an ingenious thump on the face, or the Clown is jolting himself with jaunty dislocations, or Columbine is skimming across like a frightened pigeon, or Harlequin is quivering hither and thither, or gliding out of a window, or slapping something into a metamorphosis', and all the while the music plays with 'unceasing vivacity', running merrily through the piece 'like the pattern in a watered gown'.

In most of these pieces, Harlequin (by now considered by some to be 'the worst part in a pantomime') performed prodigiously energetic feats. It was written that he was 'a thing of shreds and patches, without a single point to get applause except when he jumps'. And jump he did. Indeed, many of the 'leaps and jumps' that he would perform were actually advertised in the press beforehand. We find *The Times* announcing a pantomime called *Mirth's Motley; or, Harlequin at Home* in which were promised 'a Leap through a Hogshead of Water; a Flight across the stage from Balcony to Balcony; an escape through a Cask of Fire; and the astonishing Leap through a Hoop of Daggers, by Mr Simpson in the character of Harlequin, who will likewise introduce the Celebrated Dying and Skeleton scenes.' Harlequin's indestructability seemed to have become his sole attraction. In one Drury Lane pantomime he was 'crammed down a pump, pumped out into a pail, rolled flat, fired out of a cannon, decapitated', had his head thrown into the pit, and was 'otherwise marvellously ill-treated', but, we are told, 'always came up entire again'.

Harlequin's plight was satirised by Tom Dibdin in his comic extravaganza *Harlequin Hoax; or, A Pantomime Proposed* (Theatre Royal, Lyceum, 1814), in which Harlequin, handed his part by the author, reads with mounting horror: 'Harlequin is carried on the tail of a kite to the very top of the theatre and is then dropped back onto the stage, falls through an open trap door, and is shot out of it again enveloped in flames as if blown from the crater of a volcano . . . In order to meet Columbine at the street door, he throws himself out of a three-pair of stairs window, and is caught with his head in a lamp-iron. The lamp-lighter pours a gallon of oil down his throat, sticks a lighted wick in his mouth, and a set of drunken bucks, having no better business on earth than to break lamps, knock his nob to shivers and all go to the watch-house together.' As the writer remarks gleefully: 'Delicious, eh? Delicious!'

Poor Harlequin! And if he was not thus leaping and tumbling, he was reduced to mere posturing; to signalling, albeit with grace and style, the tricks and changes of the chase. All the real fun had passed to Clown.

The Harlequinade of *Mother Goose* contains some typical jokes. Pantaloon at the Inn, cuts open a pie and a live duck flies out. It walks forwards on the stage and Clown waddles down behind it in imitation, then grabs it and runs off. (Theft, especially of food, was a prominent trait in the character of this mischievous rogue.) Again at the Inn, Clown sits at a table and is about to eat when Harlequin waves his bat and the table flies up into the air. The Clown cannot work out what's happened to it. He wanders about beneath it, searching the ground where it stood for clues. Then, looking up, he sees it. He 'utters a shout of surprise', and quietly seats himself again, 'when the table descends' – and Clown on his chair goes up, propelled on a pole that rises through the stage. He yells. Pantaloon is heard knocking at the door. The Landlord enters and opens it. Pantaloon is amazed when he sees Clown sitting on his chair in mid-air. So, too, is the Landlord, and looking at the pole on which the chair has risen, he rushes out and returns with a saw. The scene builds to a climax in which Clown, Pantaloon and the Landlord are each seated at separate cloth-covered tables complete with wax candles and all three are rising and falling 'in a line some six or seven feet'. At this point, Harlequin and Columbine enter and a fourth table is brought on. Harlequin touches it with his bat and a complete supper appears on it, lit up with six candles, 'at which instant the candles on the other three tables disappear'. The scene ends with the exhalted Clown pelting the inn servants with plates and donning a cocked hat in which he proclaims himself 'President Oddfellow' of the 'high though not exactly free and easy situation'.

In fact, Grimaldi himself was never very happy with his role in *Mother Goose*, claiming that there was not a trick or a situation in it to which he had not been accustomed many years before. (The rising table gag, incidentally, can be traced back to the *commedia dell'arte*.) His own favourite pantomime was *Harlequin in His Element* staged at Covent Garden in December 1807. It contains a famous scene in which the Pantaloon character (Sir Feeble Sordid), staying at a hotel, and partaking of his evening meal, instructs Clown to take some wine out to the watchman in the street, who has been prevailed upon to call him early in the morning and to warn him if Harlequin and Columbine appear. Clown enters to the watchman, carrying a bottle and a glass. But the watchman is already fast asleep in his box. (Weren't they always, those 'Charleys'?) So Clown 'makes free with the wine himself, till being quite inebriated, he determines on a frolic'. This involves stripping the watchman of his greatcoat and hat, and dressing himself in them. By now, well drunk, in the dark, and hampered by the voluminous sleeves of the watchman's greatcoat, Clown attempts to take another sup of his wine. 'After many fruitless attempts, he at last gets hold of the bottle, but not being able to guide it to his mouth, he with the other hand feels for his mouth, and tries again, in vain, to put the neck of the bottle into it – being vexed he takes up the watchman's lantern, and holding it to his cheek, affects his wished-for purpose. He then shuts the Keeper into his box, and with the lantern and rattle parades the stage, crying the hour in a ludicrous tone.'

3.

To his contemporaries, Joey Grimaldi was 'The Garrick of Clowns'; 'The Jupiter of Practical Joke'; 'The Michelangelo of Buffoonery'. It was said that he could achieve more with one look than any of his rivals could with the most elaborate transformations. Every limb of him had a language. He seldom spoke, except at some rich rare interval when an overwhelming sensation seemed to force the words out of his mouth. And then it was usually no more than one word or a monosyllable. And all the more effective for being so. To a mob of fellows putting him to some horrible torture, it would be simply – 'Don't!' When eating gingerbread, just – 'Nice!' And after standing silently contemplating the moonlight for several minutes, merely – 'Nice moon!'

Grimaldi clowned his way through the Napoleonic Wars and the days of the Regency, and with boisterous irreverence perfectly mirrored the patriotism, the gluttony, the dishonesty, and the violence of those momentous years, when lords thought it a fine thing to hob-nob with pugilists, marquises grew famous for practical joking, and gentlemen on a night out as a matter of course beat the watch. 'Whether he was robbing a pieman, opening an oyster, grasping a red-hot poker, devouring a pudding, picking a pocket, beating a watchman, sneezing, snuffing, courting, or nursing a child, he was always so extravagantly natural.' Yet, this man who was universally loved, often felt that the whole world and a malevolent Fate were conspiring against him, and was frequently plunged into the deepest melancholy. As he himself once said, in a pun on his own name: 'I am grim all day – but I make you laugh at night!'

It is sad that, whereas endless and detailed descriptions of the work of second and third-rate tragedians regularly filled the columns of the daily press and the periodical publications of the time, precious little was written about our greatest Clown. However, by piecing together snatches from the handful of contemporary and near-contemporary accounts of Grimaldi's performances, it is possible to build, jigsaw-like, a picture that affords us a glimpse of Joey at work. Joey – the genuine droll, the grimacing, filching, irresistible Clown who, as Charles Dickens has written, 'left the stage with Grimaldi, and though often heard of, has never since been seen':

> There he stands, the cunning, round-faced rascal, knock-kneed, yet as agile as if he had not a bone in his body, staring at the young lovers.
> He appears always like a grown child, waking to perception, and wondering at every object he beholds.

73

I see him now. His amazement and awe of Harlequin; his amorous glances at Columbine; and his winks at the imbecility and dandyism of that doting pair.

He watches them intently, his nose screwed to one side, his eyes nearly closed, though twinkling forth his rapture, and his tongue vibrating in his capacious mouth in the very fullness of his enjoyment.

He watches. The lovers leave.

The coast is clear!

He sees on the table, the dinner that was laid for Harlequin and his Mistress. He will eat a Sussex dumpling or two. Down he sits, inviting himself with as many ceremonies as if he had the whole day before him. But when once he begins to eat – it seems as if he has not a moment to lose. The dumplings vanish at a cram; the sausages are abolished; down go a dozen yards of macaronis; and he is in the act of paying his duty to a gallon of rum – when in come Pantaloon and one of the Inn servants, at opposite doors, looking for the glutton.

But no, they've not seen him. For the moment, he's safe. And away goes the monstrous booty into that leviathan pocket of his, that receptacle of all sorts of edibles and occasionally of kettles of boiling water and even of lighted candles.

But Pantaloon and the Inn servant now spot him, and resolve to pounce on him headlong. They rush forward – and he slips from between them, with a – 'Hello, I say . . .!' And the two poor devils dash their heads against one another, like rams, and fall back fainting to the sides of the stage!

The Clown, laughing with all his shoulders, nods a health to each, and finishes his rum. He then holds a great cask of a snuff-box to each of their noses, to bring them to; and while they are sneezing and tearing their souls out, jogs off at his leisure.

What did Grimaldi offer? Fun, pure fun. Thomas Hood summed it all up when he wrote:

> Thou didst not preach to make us wise –
>   Thou hadst no finger in our schooling –
> Thou didst not 'lure us to the skies' –
>   Thy simple, simple trade was – Fooling!

The picture fades, the Clown's very muteness making him all the more ephemeral. Nothing is left us but the pen portraits of those who saw him; the bald unfleshed descriptions of a few Harlequinades; and the songs that once he sang.

Most of these songs were written by Charles Dibdin Jnr, working with composers like William Reeve, William Ware, and John Whitaker. The two most famous were 'Tippity Witchet' written for Sadlers Wells' 1810 pantomime *Bang Up!, or, Harlequin Prime*, and 'Hot Codlins' which Grimaldi first performed at the Wells in *The Talking Bird; or, Harlequin Perizade* in 1819. This latter piece was a re-vamp of an 1805 original with the new song added. 'Tippity Witchet' was described by Dibdin as a set of 'Nonsense Verses (as the Classical school boys say)' and was, he explained, written 'to enable

Mr Grimaldi to exhibit several of his peculiarly whimsical character-
istics'. It began:

> This very morning handy
> My malady was such,
> I in my tea took brandy
> And took a drop too much.

Then followed a 'tol, lol, lol, lol' chorus punctuated by hiccups, and
four more verses that took him through yawning, sneezing, crying
and finally, laughing.

> I'm not in mood for crying,
>   Care's a silly calf.
> If to get fat you're trying
>   The only way's to laugh.
>
> Tol lol lol lol (LAUGHS)
> Tol lol lol lol (LAUGHS)
> Tol lol lol de rol de lay.
> Tol lol lol lol (LAUGHS)
> Tol lol lol lol (LAUGHS)
> Tol lol lol de rol de lay.

'Hot Codlins' was just about as simple. It told a story of those London
streets that Grimaldi knew so well, of the old woman who sold baked
apples in them, and of the street arabs who tormented her.

> A little old woman her living she got
> By selling hot codlins hot, hot, hot:
> And this little old woman who codlins sold,
> Though her codlins were hot she felt herself cold,
> So to keep herself warm she thought it no sin
> To fetch for herself a quartern of . . .

And the drum would bang; and the audience would roar 'Gin!' And
Grimaldi would look at them in utter amazement and exclaim: 'Oh!
For shame!' before going into the chorus:

> Ri tol iddy iddy iddy iddy
> Ri tol iddy iddy ri tol lay.

This was the song that was to be called for again and again from
other Clowns in other pantomimes for years after Joey had quit the
stage. In 1832, Sadlers Wells actually printed a note on its bills warn-
ing the audience that 'no song, or performance of any description,
will be allowed to be introduced, but such as is announced in the bills

75

of the Day'. In 1842, some of those in the gods at Drury Lane 'were somewhat dissatisfied that their attempt to induce Tom Matthews to sing "Hot Codlins" proved abortive'. In 1847, audiences were still calling for it, despite the reluctance of other Clowns to sing it. We are told that Richard Flexmore, at the Princess's Theatre, 'was called upon for "Hot Codlins", according to immemorial custom' but that 'he remonstrated, and was excused'. *The Times* reported that at Sadler's Wells, too, in that year of 1847 the pantomime was 'interrupted at one period of the evening by a universal cry for "Hot Codlins", but that the Clown, Mr C. Stilt, 'excused himself for not complying with this demand by pleading the fatigue and anxiety consequent upon the production of the pantomime.' *The Times* seemed rather surprised that the audience 'with a self-denial and consideration hardly to be expected, unhesitatingly accepted the apology'. By 1855, 'Hot Codlins' was *still* being 'clamorously demanded'. And A. E. Wilson recalls it being used in pantomime as late as 1926.

'Tippity Witchet' and 'Hot Codlins' were the simplest and most easily remembered of Grimaldi's songs. But the great majority of the songs he sang were both musically and lyrically of a far higher quality. Many of them have a musical vivacity and a sinewy tunefulness as interesting as anything in eighteenth-century popular music. And Charles Dibdin's words have a refreshing liveliness that still leaps off the page. They are satirical and comic songs which in the hands of an artist like Grimaldi must have been superb. Here, for example, is 'A Peep at Turkey', the 'favourite comic song' sung by Grimaldi in *Dulce Domum; or, England the Land of Freedom* which was staged at Sadler's Wells in 1811.

> I peep'd in the grand Seraglio,
> Where the Turks their ladies keep snugly, O;
> The ladies there
> Are fat and fair,
> But the gemmen are monstrous ugly, O:
> A bearded bashaw a score wives controls
> For their law says women have no souls!

Spoken: O, it's a bouncer! But these Turkish Foreigners are a different kind of stuff to our English, ladies, for they, bless 'em! are all pretty *souls*, and don't want for *spirit*, as we all know, when 'the grey mare is the better horse' – and if the Ottomy-ladies had but a little *hed*ification at Billingsgate, the *flat fish* would soon prove themselves fine *soles* and make it all *hot cockles* with the *muscle-men*.

> Of Turkey much they have boasted, O,
> But since I here have posted, O,
> No Turkey, see,

76

Say I for me,
Except it is boiled or roasted, O,
The Mighty Grand Turk, when he likes, ne'er fails
To cut off their *heads*, but he gi's 'em *three tails*.

Spoken: In Turkey, heads and tails depend all upon the toss up of a ha'penny; and, when the Sultan wants the mopusses, he orders them to strangle the first bashaw they can catch, who dutifully sends him his head in a hand-basket, and keep his three tails for his own consolation – O, give me little England, where a man's head is his own freehold property, and his house is his castle; and whoever touches a hair of the one, or the latch of the other without leave, is sure to get the door in his face and his head in his hand.

CHORUS
Tang tang tang a tang
Tang tang tang a tang
Tang tang tang a tang
Tang tang tang.

Belligerently nationalistic songs were one of Grimaldi's fortes during the Napoleonic Wars, but he was equally at home hymning the simple delights of ordinary everyday English life. For the pantomime *Gnomes and Fairies* Charles Dibdin wrote him a song called 'The Clown's Bazaar' (music by John Whitaker). Bazaars were then something new in England, and Grimaldi must have got enormous fun out of imagining one run entirely to suit the child-like tastes of Clown.

Bazaars all the fashion are grown,
    Where ev'ry stand plenty of money brings,
I'll have a Bazaar of my own,
    And sell all faragoes of funny things.
Barley sugar and Elecampane,
    For bull's-eyes and lollipops lot a Shop,
And in a snug corner maintain,
    A nice little sheep's head and trotter shop.

Polonies and Cow heel consarves,
    Prince's Mixture and Blackguard and Backy, O!
And for Ladies who've delicate narves,
    A stand, all enclosed, to sell Jacky, O!
With Parliament cakes and peg tops,
    And squibs to fright folks in dark passages;
Nice pigs fry and peppermint drops,
    And a stand to fry Bartelmy Sassages.

Them queer things the Chinamen sell,
    Little men whose heads go niddy noddy, O,
For grown gentlemen learning to spell,
    I'll have gingerbread letters a body, O.

77

> But, pray, of deceptions beware,
>> For counterfeits each day are bowling in;
> So ask for Grimaldi's Bazaar,
>> At the sign of the Rag Mop and Rolling Pin.

The elecampane he intended selling was a sweetmeat flavoured with a preparation made from the root of the elecampane plant. 'Prince's Mixture' and 'Blackguard' were types of snuff, and the 'Jacky' which was to be sold in a stand 'all enclosed' to the ladies with 'delicate narves' was gin. Parliament cakes were thin, crisp rectangular ginger-breads, and a peg-top was a wooden spinning top, set spinning by the pulling of a string.

The Rag Mop and Rolling Pin were apt symbols for Grimaldi. From such domestic utensils he could create whole characters, entire worlds, in what became known as his 'tricks of construction'. In an ale-house garden, for example, he would stand on end and in line a number of wooden beer barrels; mount each on two tankards, serving as legs; provide each with arms made of bottles, or brushes, or various kitchen utensils; devise for them necks and heads from upturned funnels stuck with tobacco pipes, or shallow bowls (collars these!) with bottle and candle, or a stone jar with a ladle stuck in its neck. And here was an army, marching. He would then lay another barrel on a stand, give it a funnel for a tail, a hand-saw for a neck, from which hung a kitchen sieve of a head, and sitting astride his mount in a rattling, shiny uniform of saucepan lids and dish-covers, he would head his troops to battle.

One famous scene in *Harlequin and the Red Dwarf*, staged at Covent Garden in December 1812, opened in a street with a farrier's shop and beside it a blacksmith's. As Clown stood contemplating the scene, a Hussar officer 'in all the extravagant and foolish finery of the corps, passed thundering by'. As *The Times* was to write:

The spirit of imitation instantly took possession of the Clown, and, not unwisely judging that the secret lay in the dress, he determined to be a hero and a Hussar in his own person. A pair of red pantaloons, which he put on before the audience with the happiest play of blushing modesty, was the only thing which he condescended to borrow of his model; two black varnished coal-scuttles formed his boots, two real horseshoes shod the heels, and with jack-chains and the help of large brass dishes or candlesticks for spurs, he equipped his legs in a uniform almost as clattering, unwieldy and absurd, as the most irresistible of our whiskered propugnatores. A white bear-skin formed his pelisse, a muff his cap, and a black tippet finished his toilet, by giving him a beard, whiskers and pendant moustaches. The whole house, in the spirit of general contempt of these miserable imitations of foreign foppery, roared with laughter, as they saw the buffoon of a Theatre turn the favourite invention of the mighty, and the wise, and the warlike, into merited ridicule. The satire was made more pointed, and more intelligible, by the presence of genuine Hussar Officers in the stage box, covered *de cap à pied* with chains and catskins.

Such pieces of satire sometimes got Grimaldi into trouble. On one occasion, it is said, he commanded his stage regiment with 'such an air of hauteur, and in such unintelligible tones' that a private message was sent from the mess-room of the Horse Guards to the manager of the Covent Garden Theatre, threatening withdrawal of patronage if Mr Grimaldi was permitted to continue 'his damned infernal foolery'!

In a send-up of the fashionable mania for driving four-in-hand, Grimaldi in one pantomime created a complete carriage using a baby's wicker cradle, four cheeses, a small fender, two paper lamps, blankets for a great coat, and 'a sheet of garters for a Whip'. The motive power was one small dog! And in *Harlequin Whittington; Lord Mayor of London* (Covent Garden, 1814) *The Sunday News* tell us that 'much mirth was excited by transforming Pantaloon into a wheel-barrow. This was effected not by Harlequin, but by the Clown, who forces a mop stick through a cheese, to make a wheel, and placing this between his hands, he piles several cheeses on his back, and using his legs as the handles of the barrow, fairly wheels the load off the stage.' The newspaper's evident surprise that Clown rather than Harlequin should be responsible for such tricks would seem to indicate that the finality of the shift of power in the Harlequinade was not yet universally understood. A similar wheel-barrow joke had, in fact, been used in the 1793 *Harlequin's Museum; or Mother Shipton Triumphant*. In this, Harlequin changed Punch into a wheel-barrow and himself into a barrow woman. The published synopsis of the piece contains the note: 'This is one of the best tricks now on the stage and was the invention of the late Mr Rich.'

Grimaldi delighted in bringing live animals onto the stage, and was so well-known for this that, on one occasion, when he arrived at a Birmingham theatre to take part in a benefit performance and asked for some 'props', the manager at once sent to the local market for a small pig, a goose and two ducks – all alive. Grimaldi's imagination had no difficulty in finding a use for them. He arranged that Pantaloon and Columbine should enter as though they had just returned from shopping, and that he, as Clown and their servant, should follow bearing their purchases. He entered with a basket full of carrots and turnips on his back, a duck in each pocket, its head hanging out, under one arm the goose, and under the other the pig. He was greeted with roars of laughter.

But Grimaldi's exertions, entered into so early in life, and so whole-heartedly, soon began to take their toll. Sometimes at the close of a performance he was so exhausted and worn out that he could scarcely stand. The applause of an audience, however, merely spurred him to fresh and even more punishing efforts. Before the second decade of the nineteenth century was over, life was turning sour. Within a few years of the victory at Waterloo, recession hit England. Theatre business generally plummeted. And Grimaldi, who now had a financial stake in Sadler's Wells, began to lose money. He was thus driven to fresh exertions, frequently playing two, sometimes three theatres a night. The strain was too much for a body already weakened. And gradually but surely, during the whole of the year 1819, he felt his health sinking. He would stagger off the stage as soon as the act-drop fell on the first scene, crying aloud in pain, his whole frame convulsed with violent spasms. Men were obliged to be kept waiting at the side-scenes to catch him as he staggered off, and to support him while others chafed his limbs, until he was called for the next scene. He was just forty years old. It was about this time that King George IV visited Covent Garden to see Grimaldi and laughed so uproariously that he burst his stays! A witness wrote: 'I saw him trundle downstairs and I never saw anything look so happy.'

In 1824 Grimaldi was forced to retire from the stage. Four years later, he made his very last appearance at a special farewell benefit performance on the stage of Drury Lane. It was a lovely June evening, and the theatre was packed to suffocation. The Clowns of England, among them his own son, turned out that night to pay their homage to Joe. The stage was a sea of motley. Joe was wracked with pain and almost unable to stand. So a chair was placed centre stage and appearing for the last time in the familiar red, white and blue livery of Clown, with his whitened face, red painted cheeks and blue cockscomb, he sat to play his last scene and to sing his last song. And they went as well as ever.

The song they demanded that night was, of course, 'Hot Codlins'.

Joey Grimaldi died, aged fifty-nine, on 31st May 1837. Less than three weeks later a new age began with the death of William IV and Queen Victoria's accession to the throne. Within ten years it was being suggested in the press that Clown and his companions had had their day and should be abolished from the pantomime.

SIX
HERE·WE·ARE·AGAIN!

There were, in fact, to be a lot more Clowns, some of them in their time considered 'great'. There was Tom Matthews, Grimaldi's pupil and assistant, to whom the crown passed when Grimaldi died. Matthews, who was principal Clown at Drury Lane for the best part of forty years, 'waddled about bow-legged, did no acrobatic tricks, never danced, and was always pilfering in the most innocent manner possible'. Sir Frank Burnand (dramatist and for twenty-five years Editor of *Punch*), who saw him, recalled that he

> knocked frequently at shop doors, hiding himself twice, but immediately after the third knock lying down in front of the threshold so as to ensure the tripping up of the incautious irate tradesman over his prostrate body, when he, the artful, comic, mischievous Clown, would slip into the shop and reappear with all sorts of stolen goods, hams and turkeys, under his arm and sausages hanging out of his pockets, just in time to come into a violent collision with the now furious trades-man, whom he would incontinently floor with one of his own hams, and at the watchword 'Look out, Joey; here's a policeman coming!' given by his faithful but weak-kneed ally old Pantaloon, he would rush off the stage and on again, followed by a mob, when, in the middle of a regular 'spill and pelt' while everybody appeared to be assaulting everybody else, he would somehow or other manage to escape the hands of several constables, as the scene changed and light and airy music ushered in the Harlequin, masked, with pretty Columbine, to execute some graceful pas de deux.

Then there was Robert Bradbury, daring and reckless, a tumbling rather than a humorous Clown, who would jump from the flies to the stage floor, and always wore nine strong pads about his person for protection - one on his head, one round his shoulders, one round his hips, two on his elbows, two on his knees, and two in the heels of his shoes. 'Thus armed', as Charles Dickens relates, 'he would proceed to throw and knock himself about in a manner which, to those unacquainted with his precautions, appeared to indicate an in-tense anxiety to meet with some severe, if not fatal accident.'

There was Redigé Paulo, son of La Belle Espagnole and 'the Little Devil', well-known artists at Sadler's Wells. The latter died as a result of striking his head on an iron screw because the stage-hands failed to have the customary carpet held ready to catch him when he made a Harlequin leap through a window. Paulo was one of Grimaldi's main rivals. He died in 1835.

The Clowns, with their red-hot pokers, strings of sausages, and butter-slides, tumble on right through the nineteenth century, and into the twentieth. Nimble George Wieland displayed 'a flexibility of limb and an elasticity of heels that made him apparently a creature of whalebone and rubber'. Harry Boleno (real name Mason) began his career in the theatre as one of a gang of boys employed to jump up and down under a painted canvas to simulate waves in a nautical melodrama; he was a grave and rather peculiar-looking man whose physiognomy in repose, we are told, 'gave little indication of the rollicking humour which he displayed on the stage'. 'Jefferini', in real life plain Jeffreys, and the proprietor of a Clerkenwell tobacconist's shop which was also a gambling den, was very tall, and his long legs made his leaps through shop windows in the Harlequinade extremely perilous. He was a 'talking' Clown who told jokes and performed comic monologues. In December 1843, *The Times* castigated him as being 'too noisy, too obstreperous. He talks too much,' it objected. In the 1850s there was even a female Clown, a Miss Cuthbert, described as 'spirited and lively' though, one newspaper commented, 'it is difficult to dispossess oneself of the idea that a lady Clown is out of place.' There was James Huline of whom it was written: 'A more dextrous and nimble Clown was never seen. His performance on two chairs and four bottles was little short of wonderful.' Huline also played a comic scene with a performing dog, danced a hornpipe, and performed a dance on stilts with a gigantic effigy of a negress, which was described as 'quite as droll as it was difficult and dangerous'.

For a while in the later nineteenth century there was a Clown called Wattie Hildyard, but he was diverted from the path of clowning when an aunt, in her will, left him three pounds a week on condition that he renounced the motley. He is said to have gone to live at Deptford 'with an aged female relative to guard against backsliding'. He is also said to have kept his Clown's costume in a drawer in his bedroom and to have proudly produced it for visitors when the coast was clear.

And then there was the brilliant and pathetic Richard Flexmore, described in his day as 'a Clown whose fun and frolic never cease', and whose vaults, leaps, falls and dances are said to have 'kept all alive to the very end'. He was particularly noted for his skilful imitations of the leading dancers of the day, especially of the Spanish dancers so popular in the London of the 1850s. Poor Flexmore (he died when he was only thirty-four, weakened, as Grimaldi had been, by physical exertion) was taken ill while playing the Wolf (afterwards Clown) in *Little Red Riding Hood* at the Theatre Royal, Covent Garden, early in 1859. Behind the scenes his 'skin' was stripped from him and handed to the company's twenty-nine-year-old Harlequin, who had never before played Clown. This was Harry Payne, and now the long line of Clowns was all but complete, for Harry Payne's father, W. H. Payne, a celebrated pantomimist, had played with Grimaldi, and Harry himself was eventually to be dubbed 'the last of the great Clowns of Drury Lane'.

Payne, like his predecessors in the role, invented the business of the Harlequinade himself. In this scene taken from a pantomime manuscript written in the 1890s we see Clown in his declining years. The word 'Trip', incidentally, indicates a dance.

SCENE – BUTCHER'S SHOP

Enter Harlequin and Columbine. Trip. Clown and Pantaloon. Business. Various promenaders cross – blacking-box. – Man with paste-can – small brush – bottle and ladder. Man with basket of candles. Man with Pie-can. Man with Ice-Cream. Truck – Boys come on – Man serves them with ice. One boy bolts without paying – Man runs after him – the other boys follow laughing. Clown, who has stolen the man's apron and boy's cap, puts them on and says: 'I'll show you how to make ice-cream'. Empties paste-can and blacking-bottle into ice. Pantaloon asks: 'What are you doing?' – 'Colouring it, old'un' – Clown stirs the mixture with a bundle of candles and calls out: 'Ice-cream'. – Swell and boys enter. 'Have a Hice?' asks Clown. Swell says: 'What sort is it?' 'Rasperry', replies Clown, and serves him one – black. Swell: 'You don't call this raspberry?' Clown replies: 'You called for *black*-berry'. Swell pays for it and pulls a long face. Boys do also and cry, 'We're poisoned!' and exit shouting 'Police!' – 'We'd better hook it', says Clown. About to do so, meet Policeman, swell and boys – Business – A Tinker enters with soldering-iron hot in can. Clown steals iron and burns Tinker off. Clown has now candles in one hand and the hot iron in the other. He comes forward eating a candle (made of turnips), saying 'How nice', when he makes a mistake and puts the red-hot iron into his mouth. – Business – Pantaloon says: 'Give me a bit'. Clown says: 'Open your mouth and shut your eyes', and then puts the hot iron into Pantaloon's mouth. Policeman walks on. Clown puts the hot iron into one of his pockets, and candles into the other. Clown begins dancing as the iron burns him. – Business. – Ending with the transfer of the iron to the Policeman's pocket.

Even at that late stage in the history of the Harlequinade, Payne could claim that 'the children always look for the sausages and the red-hot poker. They like to see the policeman burned,' he said in the course of one interview, 'And they like to see the little boy burn the clown in return. I know it is very wrong to teach boys this kind of thing, but if you are going to do away with joking of this sort, you might just as well stop clowning altogether.'

In the 1860s it had been argued (in *Chamber's Journal*) that Clown and the Harlequinade generally were getting too soft. The writer particularly regretted the decline in the Spill and Pelt. In an open letter to Clown he wrote:

> To what has that degenerated? Why, once in an evening a knot of long-striding youths and screaming maidens, all in sad-coloured attire, hurry pell-mell from wing to wing, pursued by a policeman or two, and a mere handful of high-flying carrots. What a falling off is here! We have now no longer the organised mob – imagemen, fishwomen, greengrocers, crockery sellers, bakers, police – running in Indian file across the stage, out at one wing, round at back of flat, and in again at the other, for you and Pantaloon to spill and pelt, and bring every scene to a conclusion amid a protracted eruption of vegetables, crockery, images and fish.

The letter went on to urge Clown to be cruel – 'brutally, increasingly, perpetually cruel', and in a spill and pelt, to take care that people really were hit. 'Never mind hurting the supers – supers have no more right to feel pain than eels have.'

Here was still the authentic voice of Georgian England, looking nostalgically back. Some of the supposedly comic antics in the pantomimes of those days had been too strong even for the gentlemen of the press. Describing a scene in an Adelphi pantomime of 1827, the *Morning Herald* had written:

> An effigy of a child was flung towards the pit. It appeared to the whole theatre, at the moment, to have been a living one. Everybody was terrified for the consequences. The people in the pit lowered their heads, when a sudden check was given to the fall of the child, which was then seen quickly to ascend through the ceiling of the proscenium. This incident was loudly applauded. The manner in which the child in the cradle was managed, cannot be too reprobated. No one can view the stifling of an infant, even in jest, and the supposed flattening of its body by the pressure of a superior weight, even though that weight should be the riduculous person of Pantaloon himself, without an unmixed sense of pain. But a still worse violation of the decorum which should ever be preserved on the stage, is to go through the Ceremony of putting the corpse into a stewing-pan for broth, and to turn up the skull and brains with a ladle.

That such scenes were not uncommon in the Harlequinade is evinced by Charles Dickens' reference to a pantomime which was 'not by any means a savage pantomime, in the way of burning or boiling people, or throwing them out of window, or cutting them up. . . .'

The violence was an integral part of the 'comic' business, but that it survived for so long into the Victorian era is perhaps curious. It seems so antipathetic to the spirit of the Victorian Christmas, with its accent on the revered values of family life and its re-dedication as a children's festival. Perhaps it was not just the length of the pantomime that inspired so many families to put on their hats and coats and head for home and supper as soon as the Harlequinade began.

It was the custom in the latter half of the nineteenth century to include in the book of words sold in the theatres a synopsis of the action of the Harlequinade. A typical example is the following one taken from an *Ali Baba and the Forty Thieves; or, Harlequin and the Magic Donkey* staged at the Alexandra Theatre, Liverpool, in 1868. Note the 'blowing up' of the policeman and the 'murder' of the baby.

SCENE I – A WELL KNOWN SPOT

Trip.... Harlequin – Columbine & Harlequina – Clown and Pantaloon on for a lark – Look out, Joey – All right – Clean your boots – Swells and Blacking – Three boxes a penny – Dark Kids – Division of plunder – Explosion extraordinary – 'He was a Policeman, now he's a whole division' – Billstickers beware – Turning heads – An easy way of making money – Crutches that can run – Clown turns soldier – 'Lewis' and 'Hyam' outdone – Halt, attention, stand at ease – Discipline and its effects – The Magic circle – Dancing taught here: Polkas and Old Women, Quadrilles and Policemen, Waltzes and Fishmongers, Schottisches and Bakers, Mazourkas and Butchers – Clown and Pantaloon in trouble, bolt to

SCENE 2 – EEL PIE HOUSE & PROVISION SHOP

Wanted a 'Smart young man' – Pantaloon too old – Clown goes fishing, gets more than he can cook – Pork at a discount – Clown in difficulties – Shopman objecting – Policeman interfering – Pork pies and barber's poles – Fair halves – Two for you, and 'two' for me 'too' – Customers as well as goods 'sold' – Fishmongers and sweetmeats – Policeman always on hand when 'not' wanted – General scrimmage, and off we go to

SCENE 3 – 'BED – FORDSHIRE'

Trip.... Harlequin, Columbine & Harlequina – Quiet spot for invalids – Clown turned nurse – Flying cloths – Supper disappearing in a most remarkable manner – Reading made 'difficult' – Music hath charms – Unpleasant dreams – Useful chains – Clown commits 'Manslaughter' by murdering an infant – Ghosts and hobgoblins – Table-moving extraordinary – Coopers and blacksmiths – Pleasant neighbours – Useful furniture – Housemaids and nightmares – Ghost of Slanoshallmygloghen, who sends Clown and Pantaloon to

SCENE 4 – A DISMAL CAVERN

At which point, and with just the final dance to come, the synopsis ends.

'Harlequina', as the name indicates, was a female Harlequin who was quite frequently added to the Harlequinade. It was also common practice in the second half of the nineteenth century to have a 'double' Harlequinade – two Harlequins, two Columbines, two Clowns, two Pantaloons, *plus*, perhaps, a Harlequina or even a 'Harlequina-à-la-Watteau'. It was proving impossible to be very original at this end of the show, so quantity was frequently tried as a substitute for quality. Mind, the double Harlequinade could complicate things when it came to the transformations, but the writers usually managed to come up with some surprisingly simple solutions to the problem. In one 1866 pantomime, for example, the Benevolent Agent, having created the first Harlequin, Columbine, Pantaloon and Clown, is then faced with a chorus of 'What's to become of me?' 'And me?' 'And me?' To which, with wonderful fairy imperturbability she replies: 'Ditto repeated *all* of you shall be!'

But to follow the violence on. . . . Even in the 1870s we find scenes like this:

> Enter Soldier. Clown steals his sword. Soldier remonstrates. Clown runs Soldier through with sword, sings 'He like a soldier fell'. Pantaloon alarmed. They put Soldier in letter-box. Flap falls: 'Dead Letter-Box'.

A decade later, James Johnson, in *An Account of Pantomime* (covering the London season of 1882-83), could give this description of the Clown's 'How to Nurse' routine:

> Toss the baby to Pantaloon, crying 'Catchee, catchee!'. Snatch it away from him, and hit him with it over the shins, knocking him down. Squat upon the ground with the baby in your lap and begin feeding it out of a large pan with a great dripping ladle. Ram the ladle into the mouth of the baby, and scrape the lips with the edge of it, then lick them clean. Now wash the baby by putting it in a tub, pouring hot water on it from the kettle, and swabbing its face with a mop. Comb its hair with a rake; then put the baby into a mangle and roll it out flat. Set the baby in its cradle, and tread it well down. Make the baby cry; then take it out of the bed to quiet it, and give it to Pantaloon to hold whilst you administer poppy syrup. Smear the syrup over its face. Take it away again, catch hold of its ankles, and swinging it round your head by its legs, thrash the Pantaloon off the stage with the baby, and throw it after him.

There were, however, some people who could see nothing remotely amusing in such antics, and lovable, laughable old Joey came to be described in print as 'a demon in baggy breeches', and even as 'one of the most detestable beings ever set before a juvenile audience'. Victorian susceptibilities (so carefully cultivated) were being offended. In 1879 a writer in *The Theatre* magazine declared: 'When Clown sits upon the baby the anguish of the infant's suppositious mother wrings my heart. When the leg of mutton is purloined from the butcher's tray, I see in my mind's eye a respectable family left dinnerless.' He also, incidentally, considered Columbine's costume 'unbecoming in the extreme', and her conduct 'far from praiseworthy'.

But by this time the Harlequinade was doomed anyway. In the early years of this century it vanished from the principal London pantomimes, though it was to drag on in some parts as late as the Second World War, and even to surface as a curious prologue to a 1953 *Cinderella* at the London Palladium. In the final years of its long, slow, inevitable decline it was to be reduced to a one or two-scene appendage, lacking rhyme or reason, and used mainly as an advertising medium for local shopkeepers who paid to get their names onto the canvas shop-fronts of the painted street-scene and donated sausages in return for 'plugs'. Harlequin posed, and slapped things with his bat (mainly Clown, for there were no tricks left). Columbine rushed upon the stage, minced to the footlights, corkscrewed across the front, twirled up the wing and across the flats and down to the floats again, stood erect on her toes, kissed both hands to the audience, and ran off breathing heavily. The Clown smacked the face of the Pantaloon, and the Pantaloon smacked him back, and somebody fell over. And, finally, after a few more feeble falls and a tired attempt at knockabout in which the customary policemen were assaulted, the steps ritually buttered, the red-hot poker ritually exhibited, and a real live pig let out of the basket, the Clown and Pantaloon might throw a few bon-bons to the handful of people who had stuck it out to the end. Most would by now have gone. Yet still, this sad remnant would begin with Clown poking his head through the curtain and shrieking Grimaldi's old phrase: 'Here we are again!'

As Bernard Shaw wrote in 1937: 'Sham Grimaldi was dying an intolerably slow death.' And as the theatre critic Ivor Brown had complained before him, 'Joey is of use only to ritualists and the high-brows who moan away about a grand philosophy of clowning.' Pantomime, he pointed out, had successfully reflected the taste of the average urban adult of several generations, but 'the Harlequinade would not change and the price of its pedantry was death.'

SEVEN
ANOTHER·OPENING·ANOTHER·SHOW

I.

By the time the Harlequinade died, the 'opening' had become the pantomime. It was a move that had started back in the second decade of the nineteenth century when, as we have seen, the pantomime still had something like three scenes in its opening and as many as fifteen in the Harlequinade, the opening being sung or chanted in recitative and the Harlequinade, with the exception of the odd word, being mute. Writers had already attempted adding speech to the Harlequinade, but such experiments had tended not to work, and were not generally persisted with. Perhaps William Hazlitt was right. Perhaps a speaking pantomime *was* rather like a flying waggon. Certainly the addition of dialogue would slow it down and interrupt that 'quick succession of incidents' that had been so carefully devised 'to keep the eye constantly engaged'. (We've seen the effect of dialogue on comedy in our own time in the cinema.) It seems that the Harlequinade was immutably set and virtually unchangeable well before Grimaldi left the stage. Attention therefore began to be paid to what had hitherto been considered the least important part, 'the opening'.

On 11th August 1814, a piece called *Dr. Hocus-Pocus; or, Harlequin Washed White* opened at the Little Theatre in the Haymarket. It was described as 'An Anomalous, Multiloquacious, Indicro-Magico, Absurdo-Ratiocinatio Pantomimical Entertainment', and the first scene consisted of 'a dialogue between the Chief Necromancer and Scaramouch, touching ingeniously on some prominent absurdities of the day, and opening the plot'. Not only had spoken dialogue been introduced into the opening, but topical allusions, customarily made visually and strictly reserved for the Harlequinade, had been brought forward as well. (The Haymarket, incidentally, held a Summer Patent only to stage spoken drama, which explains the August opening.)

The plot of the piece centred upon efforts to turn the black-vizarded Harlequin white, Columbine having otherwise refused to marry him. Harlequin was first plunged into a tub, from which he was subsequently dragged out 'still of his original hue, but fearfully bloated by his long immersion'. He was then put through the mangle (a favourite joke, and one still used in pantomime) to emerge 'signally compressed', but with a 'fair skin', which says a great deal for the old-fashioned mangle. As one critic wrote: 'What this might promise it is useless to conjecture.' Down the ages there has always been somebody looking for logic in pantomime!

The experiment was way ahead of its time, and there was no great rush to follow it. Indeed, it was to be another sixteen years and more before the 'speaking opening' became general. In 1830, however, Covent Garden staged *Harlequin Pat and Harlequin Bat; or, The Giants Causeway*, the opening of which was entirely in prose. It was set on the 'Island of Celtic Myth' and dealt with Brian Boru's quest to find his abducted bride, a fine example of pantomime laying its hands on an historical character and stirring him, willy-nilly, into the mix. Brian Boru, the great Irish chieftain who became king of Munster and subsequently king of all Ireland, and who, in 1014, had defeated the Danes of Dublin at the Battle of Clontarf, only to be killed afterwards in his tent, was at Covent Garden Theatre that December duly transformed into Harlequin and, with his Columbine, set running, with Pantaloon (previously King O'Rourke, the abductor), and Clown (previously 'a Comic Piper') in hot pursuit. The Benevolent Agents, incidentally, were the Fairy Mealy Moth and Saint Patrick himself, and the Irishness of the piece was completed at the transformations when Harlequin rejected the offer of a bat and asked instead for a magic shillelagh!

Harlequin Pat and Harlequin Bat was not a success. And the much-proclaimed 'speaking opening' seems to have done nothing to help it. As *The Times* wrote: 'The advertisements in the playbills that there was to be a speaking opening and the emphatic large letters in which that advertisement was printed had led us to believe that some attempt was to be made which would revive these entertainments.' It went on to accuse the writers of dullness and lack of invention. This, indeed, was to prove a plaguing deficiency in the attempt to revive pantomime's flagging fortunes in the post-Grimaldi years. It was one thing to make the characters of the opening speak, it was quite another to find writers capable of making what they said worth listening to. In the event, pantomime would have to turn first to other forms of entertainment for its lessons and its salvation, principally to burlesque and extravaganza.

2.

Exactly a week after the opening at Covent Garden of *Harlequin Pat and Harlequin Bat*, there had opened at the little Olympic Theatre in Wych Street a 'Grand Allegorical Burlesque Burletta' in One Act (and 'Not translated from the French') called *Olympic Revels; or, Prometheus and Pandora*. Unlike the Covent Garden pantomime, it was an immediate and enormous success, and it heralded the opening of a new era in London theatrical entertainment.

Wych Street, which ran off the lower end of Drury Lane towards what is now the Strand (it vanished with the Strand improvements of the early 1900s) was at that time one of the dirtiest and most disreputable of London's streets and the Olympic stood surrounded by brothels, drinking dens and thieves' kitchens. However, this, 'the most depressed nook in the dramatic world', was to become one of the most fashionable theatres that London had ever seen. The transformation was to be achieved by the remarkable combination of the theatre's actress-manageress, Madame Vestris ('Missis Westris' to her Cockney public, 'Madame' to her company), and the writer James Robinson Planché (known to the stage staff at the Olympic simply as 'Plank').

Madame Vestris, singer, theatrical innovator, and 'remarkable for the symmetry of her limbs', had been born Lucy Elizabeth Bartolozzi (her grandfather was the eminent engraver Francesco Bartolozzi) into the London of 1797. Her father was a commercially indolent Italian with a passion for music and a talent for the tenor violin; her mother a German, vain and tending to corpulence, who indulged a liking for flowered hats and provided for the family by giving piano lessons. When she was sixteen, Lucy entered into a short-lived marriage to a French dancer, ballet-master and rake named Armand Vestris, and two years later, in 1815, made her debut (as an opera singer) at the King's Theatre in the Haymarket, when her husband put her on in his own benefit performance. She was a considerable success, and was thus launched upon a stage career.

In April 1820 Vestris played Dolly Snip (afterwards Columbine) in *Shakespeare versus Harlequin*, a revival of Garrick's old speaking pantomime, *Harlequin's Invasion*, at the Theatre Royal, Drury Lane. Among the audience at the first performance was Garrick's widow. *The Times* proclaimed Vestris's acting and singing 'delightful', and was pleased to add that she 'exhibits gracefully in one scene as a dancer'. Elsewhere she was lauded as 'one of the most pleasing actresses it has ever been our enjoyment to applaud'. A few weeks later she essayed a 'breeches part', playing the ultimate rake and libertine Don Giovanni in a short after-piece described as a 'comic extravaganza entertainment' and called *Giovanni in London*. The plot of the piece was simple: Giovanni, sexually too hot for Hell, moves on to a wickeder place, London, where he is finally redeemed by a good woman. It doesn't sound much, but with its 'devil effects', its cheery songs, its firework finale, and more important than any of these, Vestris's legs, it took the town by storm.

For more than a century and a half, since the days of Nell Gwyn, the town had enjoyed the theatrical sight of women showing a leg in breeches, and Vestris went on to play a succession of famous 'breeches parts', among them Captain Macheath in *The Beggar's Opera* and Don Felix in *Alcaid*. The more she showed her legs, the more the town loved her. With one or two exceptions, that is. The *Theatrical Inquisitor*, for instance, described Giovanni as 'a part which no female should assume till she has discarded every delicate scruple by which her mind or her person can be distinguished', and went on to warn darkly that the road Vestris was treading was 'fraught with viler consequences than we shall venture to describe'. Another journal was subsequently to declare angrily: 'This theatrical system of putting the female sex in breeches is barbarous and abominable.' But such prudish voices were rare, and the *London Magazine*, reviewing Vestris' performance in *Alcaid*, wrote glowingly: 'Madame Vestris enacted Don Felix in a good loose dashing rake-helly fashion. She is the best bad young man about town, and can stamp a smart leg in white tights with the air of a fellow who has an easy heart and a good tailor.'

Vestris was by now placarded on every wall and her likeness stuck in every window of every print shop. Songs and verses were written about her famous legs, and one enterprising modeller is said to have made a 'capital speculation' out of selling plaster casts of them. There is even a song, about a pair of such casts having been stolen:

> Have you heard about this piece of work
>   All over London Town, sir?
> It's all about an actress,
>   A Lady of renown, sir;
> The case was heard at Marlborough-street,
>   The truth I will tell you now, sir,
> A man had stole the Lady's legs,
>   Which caused a pretty row, sir.

> CHORUS
> Some villain stole my Lady's legs,
>   We hope he will get justice,
> Handsome just above the knee,
>   The legs of Madame Vestris.

Madame Vestris, incidentally, was still playing breeches parts when she was fifty, and was, according to one biographer, 'still able to show a neater leg than any other performer'. She was not, however, just a pretty leg. She was a highly gifted performer in all manner of parts and a noted singer (she is said to have had 'one of the most luscious of low voices'). One song that will be forever associated with her is 'Cherry Ripe' which she introduced in the musical play *Paul Pry*. When she opened the Olympic Theatre in Wych Street, Vestris became the first woman ever to manage a London theatre. She was later to become the first manager to introduce realistic settings to the stage. As her second husband, the actor Charles Mathews, was to write: 'Drawing-rooms were fitted up like drawing-rooms, and furnished with care and taste. Two chairs no longer indicated that two persons were to be seated, the two chairs being removed indicating that the two persons were not to be seated.'

The Vestris-Mathews management, first at the little Olympic Theatre and later at the Lyceum, was to become one of the most famous and progressive in the history of the London stage. It was to become known particularly for the production of extravaganza. And the principal writer involved was to be James Robinson Planché. As Planché himself has written, in his *Recollections and Reflections*: 'I believe I made my first appearance in Old Burlington Street, Burlington Gardens, on the 27th of February, 1796, about the time the farce begins at the Haymarket, that is, shortly after one o'clock in the morning.' His parents were Huguenot refugees, his father practising the trade of a watch-maker. His mother, who had herself undertaken her son's education, died when he was only nine years old, and he was then 'im'perfected' at a boarding school, where he was 'untaught' the French he'd spoken so fluently as a child, and 'made to resemble Shakespeare in the solitary particular of "knowing little Latin and less Greek"'.

An early interest in the theatre had manifested itself when, as a bribe to take some 'nasty stuff', he had been presented with a complete Harlequin's suit, 'mask, wand, and all'. Later had come 'a miniature theatre and strong company of pasteboard actors, in whose control I enjoyed all the roses without any of the thorns of theatrical management.' Professionally, Planché made a number of false starts in life. His father tried, without success, to turn him into a watch-maker. A French landscape painter attempted to teach him geometry and perspective ('He died before I could discover the quadrature of the circle, and his death was the vanishing point of my line in perspective.')

Finally, he was articled to a bookseller, during which time his 'theatrical propensities began to develop themselves'.

Planché's first piece written for the theatre was a 'serio-comick bombastick operatick interlude' called *Amoroso, King of Little Britain*, which was staged at the Theatre Royal, Drury Lane, in April 1818, when he was twenty-two years old. *Blackwood's Magazine* described the piece as 'an imitation of Bombastes Furioso, which is an imitation of Tom Thumb, which is an imitation of nothing at all'. It added: 'It inculcates the morals of St James's in the phraseology of St Giles's. The author – (*author!* what *will* the term be applied to next? But the shoe-blacks of Paris call themselves *Marchands de Cirage!*).' Nevertheless, *Blackwood's* did say that the piece was a 'complete success'. Its plot was simplicity itself. Amoroso is in love with Mollidusta, Mollidusta with Blusterbus, and the Queen with Roastando. 'The King sees Roastando and the Queen salute: he discharges Roastando. The Queen sees the King and Mollidusta together: she stabs Mollidusta. The King stabs the Queen, Roastando stabs the King, the King stabs Roastando.' At the end all of them come to life again. In the course of the play the King declares his passion for Mollidusta thus:

> When gooseberries grow on the stem of a daisy,
>   And plum-puddings roll on the tide to the shore,
> And julep is made from the curl of a jazey,
>   Oh, then, Mollidusta, I'll love thee no more.
>
> When steamboats no more on the Thames shall be going,
>   And a cast-iron bridge reach Vauxhall from the Nore,
> And the Grand Junction waterworks cease to be flowing,
>   Oh, then, Mollidusta, I'll love thee no more.

Planché went on to become a prolific writer, mainly of extravaganzas, though he also wrote a number of pantomimes, comedies and melodramas. It was in his melodrama *The Vampire; or, the Bride of the Isles* (adapted from the French and produced in 1820) that he introduced the so-called 'Vampire trap' that was to become such a feature of the English pantomime.

There was a scholarly side to this modest and unassuming man that seems curiously at variance with his writing for the theatre. He was, for example, a student of art, especially of costume, and was responsible for the design and supervision of the costumes in Charles Kemble's *King John* (1823), which was the first such production to approximate to historical accuracy. Planché's *History of British Costume*, published some ten years later, remained for a long time the standard work on the subject. Among his many other interests he numbered archaeology (he helped to form the British Archaeological Association), and heraldry (he was Rouge Croix Pursuivant at Arms at the Royal College of Heralds and was subsequently created Somerset Herald). His non-theatrical writings include an edition of Strutt's *Regal and Ecclesiastical Antiquaries of England*.

Planché was also a good musician, and from 1826 to 1827 was musical director at Vauxhall Gardens. During this period he wrote the libretto for Weber's opera *Oberon; or, The Elf King's Oath* which was staged at the Theatre Royal Covent Garden, in April 1826, with Madame Vestris playing Fatima. Thus, did 'Missis Westris' and 'Plank' begin a professional relationship that was to have far-reaching effects on the future of pantomime.

3.

Some four years after the production of *Oberon*, Planché was passing through Long Acre when he encountered Madame Vestris riding in her carriage:

> She stopped it, and informed me she had just taken the Olympic in conjunction with Miss Foote; that they had engaged Mrs Glover, and several other performers, and would be glad if I had anything ready for immediate production, and would assist them in any way by my advice or interest. I readily consented; and remembering a classical burlesque I had written shortly after the production of 'Amoroso', but could never get accepted at any theatre, mentioned the subject to her; and it was agreed that I should immediately make such alterations as time and circumstances had rendered necessary, and that she would open the season with it and in it.

The piece Planché had in mind was a burlesque on a story called *The Sun Poker* which had been written by George Colman the younger. Planché induced his friend Charles Dance to collaborate with him in brushing the piece up, and in two or three evenings the pair of them had completed the work and given to it what he described as the 'locally-allusive title' of *Olympic Revels*.

Olympic Revels was one of four pieces announced on the bills for the opening night of 'Madame Vestris' Royal Olympic Theatre'. All four of them were described as burlettas of one sort or another – either 'historical', 'comical', or, 'burlesque'. This was a subterfuge made necessary by the licensing laws. The situation in London at that time (and until 1843) was that the Theatres Royal at Covent Garden and Drury Lane still enjoyed, by their Patents, the exclusive privilege of being open all year round (if they so desired) for the performance of any species of dramatic entertainment. The Little Theatre in the

Haymarket had a limited licence, which entitled it to produce drama during the summer months only, and no other theatre in the whole of London was permitted to stage any drama in which there was not a certain amount of vocal or instrumental music. The Lyceum was specially licensed for the performance of English opera and musical dramas, and the Adelphi and Olympic Theatres had the Lord Chamberlain's licence for the performance of 'burlettas' only. There had been a good deal of controversy 'both in and out of court' over the exact legal definition of the word 'burletta', but it had finally been determined that it described 'dramas containing not less than five pieces of vocal music per act'. Astley's, the Surrey, the Victoria, Sadler's Wells and the rest had licences for 'music and dancing' only. This originally had meant public concerts and balls, but was gradually extended to cover ballets, pantomimes and equestrian performances. 'But', as Planché himself reminds us, 'no one had a legal right to open his mouth on a stage unaccompanied by music; and the next step was to evade the law by the tinkling of a piano in the orchestra throughout the interdicted performances.'

So successful was *Olympic Revels* that later the same year Planché provided Madame with a companion-piece, called *Olympic Devils; or, Orpheus and Eurydice*. Vestris herself essayed a breeches part as Orpheus (described as 'the Thracian thrummer'), and the piece opened at the Olympic on Boxing Day. It was generally held to be livelier than its predecessor, its dialogue and lyrics being even more amusing. As an example of its exhuberance and literary 'funning' one might take the scene in which Charon, the Ferryman of the River Styx, discovers that Cerberus, the three-headed guard-dog of the Infernal Regions, has suddenly started speaking and ends up singing a quartette with him:

CHARON: Why, Cerberus! You've found a tongue I vow,
              And can say something more than 'bow-wow-wow!'
CERBERUS: Ay, thanks to Orpheus, I've three tongues found.
CHARON: One of 'em talks dog-Latin, I'll be bound.
              But wherefore Orpheus thank? Responde cur?
CERBERUS: Why, ere he came and made this mighty stir,
              I was a three thick wooden-headed dog,
              With but a bark like any other log.
              Now as I am described - and by no dunce -
              I really feel 'three gentlemen at once!'
              And ever since I heard him play and sing,
              I've sat and warbled, sir, like anything.
CHARON: You mean you've howled some doggrel to the moon.
CERBERUS: No, sir; I sing I say - and sing in tune!

95

CHARON: A *bark*-a-role of course.
CERBERUS: No, sir, a glee.
CHARON: You take the *treble*, then?
CERBERUS: I take all three
My voice is tenor – counter-tenor – bass.
CHARON: Let's try a quartette then, if that's the case.
CERBERUS: With you, forsooth?
CHARON: Oblige me by beginning one –
I've seen a dancing dog, but never heard a singing one!

QUARTETTE – CERBERUS & CHARON – 'Begone Dull Care'
CERBERUS: Begone, dull Charon! pry'thee begone from me!
Thou'rt too dull, Charon, ever to sing a glee.
Long time thou hast been ferrying here,
And souls from far dost bring;
But thou know'st, dull Charon,
Little of sol-fa-ing.
I range with care through all the keys –
My compass – octaves three!
My voice can rove from A above,
Down, down to double D.
CHARON: Begone dull cur! shall such a land-lubber as thee,
Pretend, dull cur! to talk of a compass to me?
I'm the son of Nox,
And a compass could box,
When thou wert a blind puppy.
So avast, dull cur! I'm a vast deal 'cuter than thee.
For I will bet my crazy bark
Against your own crack'd three,
That no one can go to the D below,
If I didn't go to C.

In the cast list for the published version of *Olympic Devils*, incidentally, we find Charon described as 'a Wherry Ferry Funny Fireman-Waterman, and *Imp*-orter of Spirits', and Pan as 'a *pan*-to-mimic Character'. Such jokey character descriptions were to be taken into the programmes of the pantomime and to survive, albeit in a pretty emaciated form, even down to our own day. In a piece called *The Deep, Deep Sea; or, Perseus and Andromeda* (produced in 1833, with Madame Vestris as Perseus), Mr James Vining, who played 'The Great American Sea Serpent' was described as 'A Yankee-Doodle come to Town – "half man", with a *sea*-gar in his mouth – "half horse", with an azure *mane* – and "half alligator", with an endless *tale*.' The jokes continued right down the programme to give 'The *Sea*-nery by Mr Gordon. The sea-breezes and other *Airs*, *sea*-lected by the Authors, and arranged by Mr Tully', and included the information that 'in the Overture will be introduced Handel's celebrated Water Piece'.

Although Planché's pieces were of necessity usually billed as 'burlettas' most of them were, in fact, extravaganzas, and this is what he called them when he was able to (as, for example, when they were staged at one of the Patent Theatres). The passing of the Theatres Act in 1843 'freed' the London theatres, permitting all of them to play whatever they liked, subject only to a scrutiny of the script by the Examiner of Plays at the Lord Chamberlain's office, and so Planché from then on could call his pieces what he would. Earlier, though, he was more cautious. In his introduction to the published text of *High, Low, Jack, and the Game*, which he described as 'A Most Extravagant Extravaganza or Rum-Antic Burletta', he wrote: 'This piece, produced at the Olympic at the opening of the season 1833–34, is the first which was entitled an "Extravaganza", the necessary precaution, however, being taken to add to the novel term that of "Burletta".'

These entertainments are nowadays frequently lumped together as 'burlesques', which they very definitely were not. V. C. Clinton-Baddeley, in *The Burlesque Tradition*, has defined both forms with blazing clarity. Burlesque, he points out, 'employs laughter as criticism' although, unlike satire, it is 'never angry', its criticism being directed 'not against faults of virtue, but against faults of style and of humour'. He goes on to define extravaganza as 'burlesque without an object ... a whimsical entertainment conducted in rhymed couplets or blank verse, garnished with puns, and normally concerned with classical heroes, gods and goddesses, kings and queens. The central idea might be a burlesque one: the interpolated songs might be parodies: but as a whole the extravaganza was pure travesty. It had no critical purpose. It was not aimed at any dramatic absurdity of the contemporary stage. The only burlesque element was the wide contrast between style and subject.'

Planché's *Riquet with the Tuft*, written in 1836, was described as 'A Grand Comical, Allegorical, Magical, Musical, Burlesque Burletta'. In it Madame Vestris played the Princess Emeralda, the suitors for her hand being Prince Riquet, played by Charles Mathews, and Prince Finikin, played by Mrs Anderson. The final scene of the piece was set in the Palace of Queen Mab in Fairyland and 'the Denizens of Fairyland' were processionally introduced. They included Jack the Giant Killer, who entered bearing the Giant's head; Cinderella, who came with the Prince (Miss Jackson), a page, and the two sisters (the Misses Norman and Goward) to perform 'the slipper business'; Little Red

Riding Hood; Beauty and the Beast; Valentine and Orson; The White
Cat (Miss Kendall); and Puss in Boots (Master Hutchinson). The party
was completed by the arrival of the Seven Champions of Christendom. For the Finale the entire company came forward and the Princess Emeralda led them in the final song, which was sung to the tune
of 'The Old English Gentleman':

> Old friends, I've the old prayer to make, before it is too late,
> With your old kindness please to view this change in our old state.
> Our old mythology, we thought, was getting out of date,
> And so we've left Olympus old, and all its gods so great,
> For a fine old English fairy tale, all of the olden time!
> Now winter old brings frost and cold, we open house to all,
> For while we strive to please the *large*, we don't forget the small.
> Then 'boys and girls come out to play', in answer to our call,
> And with a good old English cheer, Oh, let our curtain fall
> Upon this good old English fairy tale, all of the olden time.

Planché was subsequently taken to task for calling his version of what
was, after all, a French original, a 'good old English fairy tale'. In his
defence, he pointed out that it had been available in translation for
almost two centuries and might therefore, like himself, be considered
'naturalised'.

Riquet was described by Planché as 'a turning point in the history of
extravaganza'. From then onwards he rewrote the old fairy stories in
plays full of charm, humour and gaiety, and these are important in
the history of the theatre as the originals from which the modern sort
of pantomime is directly descended. *Riquet* was followed by the
one-act *Puss in Boots*, which Planché described as 'An Original, Comical, Magical, Mew-sical Fairy Burletta', and in which Madame Vestris played the hero, Ralph, with Charles Mathews as Puss. Later
came *Blue Beard, Beauty and the Beast, The White Cat* (Madame Vestris
as Prince Paragon), and *King Charming; or the Blue Bird of Paradise*
with Vestris in the title role of Charming the First, King of the Fan-
Sea Isles. (In 1849, Planché wrote an Easter piece for the Lyceum called
The Seven Champions of Christendom, in which all seven champions
were played by girls!)

These pieces, which provided a rival holiday entertainment to the
pantomime, did not, of course, have a Harlequinade. They were
staged regularly as Christmas pieces at the Olympic, and subsequently
at the Haymarket and Royal Lyceum Theatres. At the two Patent
Houses, however, the Harlequinade was still sacrosanct, and when the
Olympic Company moved into the Theatre Royal, Covent Garden,
at the close of the Olympic's 1839 season, Planché found himself de-

ferred. 'A harlequinade being unavoidable at Christmas time at Covent Garden', he wrote, 'the fairy piece, which had become an institution under Madame Vestris' regime, was postponed to Easter, and I, who had accepted the position of "superintendent of the decorative department", and was also engaged to provide the Easter piece, had to do so single-handed.'

The piece he provided that year affords a fine example of Planché pre-dating W.S. Gilbert in the creation of a humorous character, something he did on a number of occasions. Called *The Sleeping Beauty in the Wood*, it introduced a character called 'Lord Factotum' who was Lord High Chamberlain, Lord High Steward, Lord High Constable, Lord High Treasurer, Great Grand Cup Bearer, and Great Grand Carver – clearly the model for W.S. Gilbert's Pooh-Bah in *The Mikado*. And as he sang wistfully:

> Verily! verily! – Few could live now
> Under the honours beneath which I bow!!

Of Planché's work, *The Times* was to write: 'Who can weave verse into simpler or happier colloquial forms, or who can better make a fairy talk slang or hit off political allusions, and be of the 19th century without ceasing to be still a sprite? ... It is good to give even the uneducated an opportunity of having something better on Boxing Night than "Hot Codlins". We think a reasonable preference will be shown by all people of taste for such fairy extravaganza.' Planché was to go down as the founding father of Victorian extravaganza and burlesque, though he was to write deprecatingly of some of his followers that they 'plunge themselves into jungles of jingles and shrouds of slang' and to claim as his only demand 'not to be accused of having set the example'.

Most of those who followed Planché (they've been described as 'illegitimate descendants, denounced and denied by their parent'), and who so brilliantly, if gaudily, brought the pun to its extravagantly literary climax, had journalistic backgrounds, and were to write both burlesque and pantomime openings. They were to be dubbed 'the rhyming punsters of Fleet Street'. They included burly, genial, Mark Lemon, of the rich, deep laugh, who was born in 1809, began life in a corn-mill, drifted into a brewery, dabbled in 'prose and worse', and was to admit in later life: 'How I ever came to be editor of Punch is a mystery to me.'

There were the prolific 'Brothers Brough', William and Robert Barnabas (both born in the London of the 1820s). Robert, who has been described by 'Honest John' Hollingshead of 'Gaiety Theatre'

fame, as 'the genius of this little family', died when he was only
thirty-two years old, having started in life with 'one of Nature's
slop-work constitutions'. A bohemian and a radical, his *Songs of the
Governing Classes*, published in 1855, is bitterly anti-aristocratic. It was
said that he could, like Charles Lamb, get drunk on two pennyworth
of gin, yet if asked what his ailment was would invariably reply,
'Devilled kidneys!'

There was Robert Reece, who gave us the lines:

> 'You've got red hair!'
> 'Well, that's *hair-red*-itary!'

and

> You jeer at Pallas 'cos she's strict and staid.
> With all your *railing* you'll need Pallas' aid!

There was Gilbert à Beckett whose gems include:

> They've schools with teachers who from sloth will win her
> They learnt their A B C in ABCynia!

and

> Policeman A got this 'ere pie from Ann,
> Which proves at least that he's a pie-ous man.

Most prolific of them all were Sir Francis Burnand and Henry J.
Byron. Burnand (another editor of *Punch*) is said to have written
more classical burlesques than anyone. Born in 1836, he had his first
piece staged when he was still a schoolboy at Eton. One of his biggest
successes was the 1866 full-length burlesque of the nautical melodrama
Black-Eyed Susan, in which Miss Rosina Ranoe appeared as the hero
William, and 'with a dashing vivacity totally distinct from that which
is generally displayed by the actresses of burlesque gentlemen' delivered, among others, the following lines:

> Shiver my anchors! bless my marlin-spikes!
> If this aint just the sort o' thing I likes!
> Messmates, what cheer? (*They cheer*)
> Another! (*They cheer again*)
> Reef my spars!
> Naval and milit'ry: *sailors* with *Huzzas*.

The piece, incidentally, ran for over a year, and Burnand himself
played the part of Captain Crosstree in several provincial cities.

H.J. Byron (the inventor of a number of characters who were
subsequently purloined by the pantomime) was born in Manchester,
the son of the British Consul at Port au Prince in Haiti. He abandoned
careers in medicine (which he hated) and the law (which bored him),

and joined a provincial theatre company, eventually arriving in London at the age of thirty-five to appear in one of his own plays. He was one of the founders and the first editor of the humourous weekly *Fun*, which began publication in 1861 and was, according to Sir Frank Burnand, outwardly designed 'to look as much like "Punch" as legally possible'. It was Byron who was said to have translated 'Honi soit qui mal y pense' as 'On his walk he madly puns'. Apart from a mass of burlesques, extravaganzas and pantomime openings, he wrote a number of comedies, the most successful of which was *Our Boys* which, in 1875, began a run of 1362 performances, a record unbroken until *Charley's Aunt* came along, almost twenty years later. Here, from his 'original burlesque extravaganza' based on the Aladdin story and staged at the Strand Theatre, London, on Easter Monday 1861, is the first entrance of Abanazar:

ABANÁZAR: Well, after travelling for many years,
I find myself in Pekin, it appears.
At once, perhaps, I'd make admission,
That I am Abanazar the Magician;
Not a mere conjuror, I'll have you know
I keep no caravan, and make no show;
No Houdin, Anderson, Frikel, you see –
There's no deception, my good friends, in *me*.
I am the real thing – a horrid spirit,
A downright British brandy as to merit.
But stay, to business – this fine town of Pekin
I've been – let's see – the best part of a week in;
My magic art informs me that without
The town there doth exist, beyond a doubt,
A cave where lies the wondrous lamp I sigh for,
Cry for, and die for, and exclaim 'my eye!' for;
That lamp all other lights beats out of time,
Camphine and solar, paraffine or lime;
O'er the Electric it has quite the pull,
And beats the Bude light – it's so *bude*-iful.

Bude light, incidentally, was a particular bright light which was obtained from two or three concentric rings of argand gas jets. It was invented in 1834 by Sir Goldsworthy Gurney and was named 'Bude' light because it was first used in the lighthouse at Bude, in Cornwall, near Sir Goldsworthy's home.

These, then, were the men whose work was to have such an influence on the 'opening' of the pantomime, and finally to change the shape of the entire show. Indeed, so thoroughly did the pantomime writers ape their methods that many of these extravaganzas and burlesques sound to us just like pantomimes, with which they are frequently confused, the more so because all three genres frequently dipped into the same well of fairly story for their plots.

3.

By December 1842 *The Times*, reviewing the Drury Lane pantomime, could write: 'Pantomimes are grave matters nowadays. Very little roaring, or giggling, or grinning, or any frivolity of that sort, is to be got out of a modern harlequinade.' It went on to complain that 'when Harlequin, Columbine, Clown and Pantaloon make their appearances the pantomime assumes its gravity.' The following year, the same newspaper, reviewing the pantomime at the Surrey Theatre, described the Harlequinade as 'about as good as such things now are'. It also noted that at Drury Lane 'there was not a single change or trick that was worth recording.' The disenchantment with the old comic business of Clown and his cronies was pretty general.

But the influence of burlesque and extravaganza was already being felt in the openings. Drury Lane's 1842 piece was *Harlequin William Tell; or, the Genius of the Ribston Pippin*. In describing it, *The Times* uses the word 'burlesque' three times.

Now the introduction may be said to begin: Tell's cottage, which is a kind of burlesque on the corresponding scene of the play, is chiefly amusing from the squabbles of Albert, one of those outrageously incorrigible children peculiar to pantomimes, and his mother, to whom he is alternately a torment and a delight. William Tell (C.J. Smith) teaches the youth shooting, but the lesson does not progress well, and repeated trials only lead to the insertion of an unlucky arrow in Tell's ear instead of the target, and this terminates the course of instruction. The arrival of the tax-gatherers has first excited the wrath of Tell, but the appearance of Melchthal, who has had his ears cut off for not paying the imposition, moves him to rebellion. The following scene, which is that of the ante-chamber in the Castle of Altdorf, exhibits the toilette of Gesler, who undergoes the process of shaving. It is not very effective until a shower of vegetables comes in at the window from the indignant mob without, and then of course it is diverting enough to see Gesler rolled down with an enormous turnip in his eye. He goes out hunting, and loses his way in a mountain pass, where he would be devoured by a bear, did not Albert Tell briskly come to his assistance, and cut the bear into two pieces, each of which hops off in a different direction. Gratitude is a sentiment unknown to Gesler, and therefore no sooner does he discover that his deliverer is the son of William Tell, who was the thrower of the turnip, than he has him bound and carried off. We are now brought to the market-place at Altdorf, where Gesler's hat is set up, and the people are made to bow to it, Tell all the while contemptuously playing the air of 'All round my Hat' on a hurdy-gurdy. C.J. Smith is sometimes a capital burlesque actor, and this scene was an instance. The calm superiority with which he turned round his instrument, and contemplated the servile crowd, was inimitable, it was a quiet preparation for the noble daring of the patriot, who in a few moments, cast aside his quietness, and, clapping his thumb to his nose, 'took a sight' at the hat, and knocked down the pole. The sentence of shooting the apple off Albert's head was pronounced, and Master Albert, after a world of kicking and screaming, at last consented to stand still. This character was played by Mr Hance with much humour, and by the pertness, the acuteness, the passion, the love of mischief, which he displayed in the broadest burlesque spirit, he made Tell, the younger, the most amusing of the *dramatis personae*. Tell selects an apple so large that it would be considerably easier to hit it than to miss it. Gesler will not stand this, but chooses an apple so exceedingly small, that Tell can scarcely see it, and contemptuously swallows it whole. A happy medium is at last found, and Tell achieves his task. The unreasonable Gesler is not satisfied, but orders him to prison, when the Genius of the Ribston Pippin arises, and the transformations take place.

That year the heading *The Times* gave to its three-and-a-half columns of close-typed Christmas reviews was 'The Christmas Pantomimes'. The following year this had been broadened into 'Christmas Entertainments', and by 1846 it had become 'The 'Christmas Pantomimes and Burlesques'. *The Illustrated London News* was by now suggesting that burlesque had entirely superseded pantomime 'as at present constructed', and was advising that, if it was not to 'go out altogether and rank with the Mysteries and other dramatic productions of the past', it should get rid of Clown and his companions of the Harlequinade altogether. 'We think that a great hit might be made by producing a pantomime all opening.' It was to be well over half a century, however, before anything so radical happened.

What the managements did do, trying to have their cake and eat it, was to replace the old 'opening' with a burlesque entertainment, on to the end of which they tagged, as an unexplained second part, the old Harlequinade. The book of one such piece, William Brough's *Conrad and Medora; or, Harlequin Corsair and the Little Fairy at the Bottom of the Sea*, described as 'A New Grand Christmas Burlesque and Pantomime', actually carries a note advising 'country Managers' that if they wish to play it as a burlesque without the Harlequinade, all they need do is drop the word 'Harlequin' from the title and bill it as *Conrad and Medora; or, The Corsair and the Little Fairy*. Small wonder that when the Harlequinade *was* played with it, it made little sense! To quote *The Illustrated London News* again: 'Not one person in one hundred has the slightest idea what the Harlequin and Columbine, Clown and Pantaloon, are running about after. All their connection with the opening legend is entirely lost sight of, and so little is cared what becomes of them or where they go, because there are no motives shown for their various shifts.'

By this time, the reviewers tended to devote most of their reviews

to the 'introductory burlesque' and to dismiss the 'succeeding pantomime' in a few paragraphs. Furthermore, two separate companies were
usually engaged – the actors of the opening, and the pantomimists of
the Harlequinade, and as the humour began to move forward, so did
the comedy actors who increasingly appeared in the first part.

This split was a change that was deeply regretted by some old
pantomime-goers since it denied them the fondly-remembered pleasure of spotting early on who was going to become what. Ever since
the days of Grimaldi, the most common means of 'disguising' the
pantomimists in the opening had been to engulf them in grotesque
'big heads' and over-clothes; the heads being carnival-style affairs
sculpted in papier-mâché or the like, and modelled to suit the various
characters of the opening. These were worn to conceal the fact that
the artists were wearing beneath them the costumes of the Harlequinade. As the time approached to effect the transformations, the characters would be seen trying discreetly to loosen the necessary tapes, ease
the necessary buttons, and unhook the necessary hooks on their dresses
in good time to obey the behest of the chief fairy and transform
themselves. As Dickens has written: 'We all knew what was coming
when the Spirit of Liberty addressed the King with a big face, and
His Majesty backed to the side-scenes and began untying himself
behind, with his big face all on one side.'

> Gamen and Morgiana triumphs win
> As graceful Columbine and Harlequin.
> You Orchobrand will meet your deserts soon,
> Meanwhile appear as tottering Pantaloon.
> And Hassarac, pursue him up and down,
> As Mischievous and laughter making Clown.

And the big heads would be whisked away, and the rest of the
costume of the characters of the opening would be pulled down the
various stage traps over which the actors had carefully positioned
themselves, and the business of the Harlequinade would commence.
And the clever ones in the audience, having already briefly glimpsed
the parti-coloured costume and spangles of Harlequin, or been afforded a chance glance at the motley trunks and hose of Clown, sat
back content in the knowledge that observation could always triumph
over 'magic'. It is said that some pantomimists, unwilling to suffer
anonymity for even a short while, would deliberately expose their
under-dress to view. Mind, anybody who liked to invest in a copy of
the 'book' of the piece could have saved themselves the effort of
identification, but that would have been to spoil the fun.

104

Although no longer used as a device of 'transformation', the big heads were to survive in pantomime for many years to come, being used for animals, gnomes, imps and grotesque characters generally. As late as 1883 *The Theatre* magazine could promise 'There will be some big heads! No pantomime is worth the name without big heads!'

In 1855, at London's Adelphi Theatre there was produced 'A grand coalition of Burlesque and Pantomime' called *Jack and the Beanstalk; or, Harlequin and Mother Goose at Home Again*. In it Madame Celeste appeared as Jack; Miss Wyndham as Mother Goose; Paul Bedford as Grim Griffinhoof, the 'ogre, giant, man-eater, wife-beater, and everything that is bad and bulky'; and Mr J. Bland as Jack's father, Sir Gilbert. The press described the piece as 'an ingenious combination of pantomime and burlesque' and as 'a decided novelty in its kind, being a mixture of the burlesque spectacle and the pantomime proper, with Madame Celeste playing the hero of the first, and dancing through the last as Harlequin.' The opening (which was the work of Mark Lemon), began with a prologue 'fairly sprinkled with puns, points, and hits touching on the war, lodging-houses, fashions, and the topics of the day generally' (the war being the Crimean) in which Mother Goose and a character called 'Burlesque' (the latter dressed in the fashionable Bloomer costume) summoned up the spirit of 'Old Adelphi Pantomime to help amuse the public as the rigorous custom of Christmas requires'.

The opening proper then began. It was set in a village on the English coast, to which the Ogre came devastating the countryside, knocking down castles, and carrying off men, women and children, among them Sir Gilbert, an unfortunate knight who left behind him a wife and infant child. Sixteen years elapsed, at the end of which Sir Gilbert's wife was discovered living in a lonely valley with her son Jack, who had the reputation of being a fool and justified that reputation by allowing himself to be cheated by a card sharp who gave him a bean in exchange for his mother's cow. The benevolent fairy (Mother Goose) directed Jack to plant the bean, which immediately sprung up so rapidly that Jack, using it as a ladder, could ascend to the Snowdown Plains in Cloud-land where the Ogre had his Castle. Here he was re-united with his long-lost father, whom he discovered working as the Ogre's game-keeper. The pair of them made a run for it, shinned down the beanstalk with the Ogre in hot pursuit, and Jack then, true to the story, cut the stalk off at the root, bringing the Ogre down 'in a manner rather sudden than pleasant'. Here, instead of the usual straightforward 'transformations', an argument broke out over who was to play what. The Ogre flatly refused to play Clown on the grounds that 'no trap of Adelphi dimensions would let him through'; and Sir Gilbert refused to play Harlequin because, he claimed, 'hard work in the Ogre's service had brought on rheumatism'. It looked for a moment as if the Harlequinade would have to be abandoned, but Jack stepped forward and volunteered to play Harlequin and Mother Goose 'kindly assented' to appear as Columbine.

The piece was an enormous success, and the following year (1856) a follow-up was mounted with Madame Celeste again essaying the breeches role of Sir Beau. At the Strand Theatre, too, in 1856, the influence of burlesque was in evidence and even spilled over into the Harlequinade itself in which, we are told, the characters were 'no longer restricted to the time-honoured "Here we are!" and words of one syllable, but continue the rhymed dialogue proper to burlesque. ...' (Yet another effort to get the flying waggon off the ground!)

The opening was now firmly established as the most amusing, interesting and important part of the pantomime and when, in December 1857, the Lyceum staged William Brough's *Lalla Rookh and the Princess, the Peri and the Troubadour; or, Harlequin and the Ghibers of the Desert*, *The Times* could write:

> The introduction is a complete burlesque acted by a regular dramatic company without the addition of grotesque masks and so great a stress is laid on the so-called 'Transformation Scene' that when this has been exhibited with all its elaborate glories, the spectators may at once retire, satisfied that they have virtually seen the whole entertainment, without waiting for the two or three scenes in which Harlequin and Company appear for the mere purpose of allowing the Christmas word 'Pantomime' to figure in the bills of the day.

The 'transformation scene' was to survive as a monument to scenic splendour with no other purpose but to be spectacular. It was scenery henceforth that was to be 'transformed' and not characters.

4.

Through having essayed the part of Jack *and* Harlequin in the Adelphi's 1855 *Jack and the Beanstalk*, Madame Celeste is sometimes put forward as the leading candidate for the illusive title 'First Principal Boy'. But she was not by any means the first woman to play a 'breeches part' in pantomime. Such parts originated in the theatre of the Restoration. Samuel Pepys recorded seeing one played in the October of 1661: 'To the theatre, and there saw "Argalus and Parthenia", where a woman acted Parthenia, and came afterwards on the stage in men's clothes, and had the best legs that ever I saw, and I was very well pleased with it.' Later in the same century there was

Mrs (Anne) Bracegirdle of whom it has been said that she was 'as much esteemed for the austerity of her private life as for the excellence of her acting'. It has also been said that when in men's clothes she outshone all the actresses of that age. 'She was finely shap'd, and had very handsome legs and feet; and her gait or walk, was free, manlike, and modest, when in breeches.'

Then there was Peg Woffington who had so determinedly bearded John Rich at his home in Bloomsbury Square that day after her arrival in London from Ireland in 1740. Born into the slums of Dublin in the second decade of the eighteenth century, she had been trained and brought up by the famous rope-dancer Madame Violante, and at the age of twelve was already a member of a children's theatre company. Her most famous breeches roles were Silvia in Farquhar's *The Recruiting Officer* (a girl who 'disguises' herself as a man), and the high-spirited, good-natured rake Sir Harry Wildair in the same author's *The Constant Couple*, a role which inspired all manner of tributary verses, among them:

> That excellent Peg
> Who showed such a leg
> When lately she dressed in men's clothes –
> A creature uncommon
> Who's both man and woman
> And the chief of the belles and the beaux!

There was Mrs (Dorothy) Jordan, of whom Leigh Hunt wrote, 'her leg is reported to have been copied into a model for the statuary, and her foot has rivalled the sublime toes of that modest dancer Vestris.' She had an affair, lasting twenty years, with the Duke of Clarence (later King William IV) and was survived by thirteen illegitimate children, not all his. As one biographer has sweetly put it, 'misfortune rather than lack of moral principle was the main cause of her irregular private life.' According to Tate Wilkinson she 'sported the best leg ever seen on the stage' and Charles Lamb described her as 'a privileged being sent to teach mankind what he most wants – joyousness'.

The 'breeches part' was thus a well-established theatrical convention. But as long as the Harlequinade formed the principal part of pantomime, and consisted largely of dangerous acrobatics, the pantomime, unlike opera, the drama, comedy, burlesque and extravaganza, could offer no suitably dashing male roles that could be safely undertaken by an actress. Nevertheless, in 1819 Eliza Povey undertook the role of Jack in *Jack in the Beanstalk; or, Harlequin and the Ogre,* staged at the Theatre Royal, Drury Lane. However, she flatly refused to climb the beanstalk which reached from the stage floor to the very roof of the theatre. It was thus necessary to find a substitute for this feat, as similar in figure to 'little Miss Povey' as possible. The sex of such a substitute was irrelevant, similarity of build was all. The role was finally offered to a lad who had been spotted by the stage manager working as a waterman's devil on the coach-stand in Bedford Street, Covent Garden. His job was to fetch the water for the horses. He said he believed his name was Sullivan, and was duly employed to scale the giant beanstalk nightly throughout the run of the pantomime, and was never once spotted as a 'double'.

It is written that some years later a company of French dancers appeared at the Lane, among them Madame Duvernay, Monsieur Paul, and a 'Monsieur Silvain, principal dancer from the "Académie Royale" in Paris'. Monsieur Silvain turned out to be none other than little Jack Sullivan, the waterman's devil of Bedford Street, who went on to become principal dancer at the St James's Theatre and, according to one who knew him, 'an artist of considerable merit and a highly respectable member of society'. Surely a great lesson in how to seize a chance! Miss Povey, incidentally, not only did not go up the beanstalk, she did not go into the Harlequinade either; and of the two songs she sung it was said that, though sung in a pleasing manner, they 'might be omitted on a further representation without any considerable detriment to the piece'.

In 1831 Elizabeth Poole played the title role in *Hop o' my Thumb and his Brothers; or, Harlequin and the Ogre* (it was said 'with much cleverness') in Charles Farley's production at Covent Garden. She, in fact, played three 'young boy' roles for Farley: 'Hop o' my Thumb'; Josselin (the miller's son) in *Puss in Boots; or, Harlequin and the Miller's Sons* (1832); and Cupid in *Old Mother Hubbard and Her Dog; or, Harlequin and the Tales of the Nursery* (1838). In none of them did she play in the Harlequinade. Again, in 1847 we find a 'Prince Perfect' at the Marylebone being played by 'Miss Saunders', but at the transformations, another performer was substituted as Harlequin.

Nevertheless, with a breezy tradition of breeches parts stretching back almost two hundred years behind them, and with Madame Vestris and the ladies of burlesque and extravaganza serving as models before them, it is hardly surprising that, as soon as the pantomime openings grew longer and the Harlequinade shorter, the girls should have leapt at the chance to play what is, after all, an ideal breeches role, the fairy-tale hero. By 1865 'Principal Boys' were general.

EIGHT
NEW·TALES·FOR·OLD

As early as 1754 George Colman the elder, writing in *The Connoisseur*, had suggested that the writers of pantomime should abandon the classical myth or legend as the subject of their openings and take a look instead at 'some Old Garland, Moral Ballad, or Penny History Book' as a source of possible story-lines. He particularly recommended *The Children in the Wood*. ''Twould be vastly pretty to see the paste-board robin-red-breasts let down by wires upon the stage to cover the poor innocent babes with paper leaves', he wrote. But if the writers were going to insist upon having their fairies and their genii, then he suggested they should 'take their stories out of that pretty little book, called the "Fairy Tales". I am sure, instead of ostriches, dogs, horses, lions, monkeys, etc. we should be full as well pleased to see the "Wolf and little red Riding Hood"; and we should laugh vastly at the adventures of "Puss in Boots".'

It appears to have been almost three-quarters of a century before all his suggestions were taken up. Most of the stories that continue to this day to hold the stage as pantomime subjects were first pantomimed between the years 1781 and 1832, though many of them (including *Sleeping Beauty*, *Little Red Riding Hood*, *Puss in Boots*, and *Cinderella*) had been available as stories since 1729 when Charles Perrault's *Histoires ou Contes du temps passé. Avec des Moralitez* had first appeared in English translation.

Perrault, poet, essayist, member of the Académie Française, and retired civil servant, was one of the creative elite who flourished at the court of Louis XIV, the 'Sun King'. By collecting and setting down for the first time the eight traditional French fairy tales that comprise the book, Perrault created a masterpiece. It was dedicated to the king's niece, Elisabeth Charlotte d'Orlèans, and the moral of each story was underscored by Perrault in a witty little *moralité en vers*. (Andrew Lang, the Victorian folklorist, was to complain that the moral was not very obvious in the case of the success story of that 'unscrupulous adventurer' Puss in Boots!) The frontispiece to Perrault's collection of stories showed three young people gathered round an old woman seated before a fire and listening to the tales she was telling. Boxed on the wall behind her were the words 'Contes de ma Mère l'Oye'. When this appeared in translation as 'Mother's Goose's Tales', it heralded the start of the Mother Goose legend in England.

As we have already seen, the first pantomime to use Mother Goose (the 1806 Dibdin-Farley one in which Grimaldi appeared), used her solely as a 'Benevolent Agent'. She would have to wait another hundred years before she became the character we know. As late as 1880, when she appeared in Drury Lane's *Mother Goose and the Enchanted Beauty*, she was still the Benevolent Agent, an 'excellent old creature, who little children will be delighted to learn lives in "Lowther Arcadia"'. (The Lowther Arcade, off the London Strand was famous for its toy shops. It closed in 1898.) In this pantomime Mother Goose was pitched against the evil of the witch Malignia, in what was really the story of the Sleeping Beauty. The golden eggs were used as a 'magic' device to rejuvenate a court that awoke from its hundred-year slumber to find that (with the exception of the Princess) they were all a hundred years older.

It was at the Theatre Royal, Drury Lane, on Boxing Day 1902 that the Mother Goose (in the person of Dan Leno) we know made her first appearance. The poor old woman who, given wealth, then desires beauty, and to gain beauty, sacrifices everything (to prove correct the Demon King's assertion: 'Search all the world, and you will fail to find; A man or woman with contented mind'), was the creation of a famous pantomime writer, J. Hickory Wood, working in collaboration with the Lane's manager, Arthur Collins. Theirs was the original from which all subsequent *Mother Goose* pantomimes are derived. The Goose was christened 'Ann Priscilla Mary May', after Mother Goose's grandmother, and was known from the beginning as 'Priscilla'.

The most popular of all pantomime subjects has for many years now been *Cinderella*. A version of the story had, in fact, been published in English even before Perrault's book was translated, appearing as 'The Story of Finetta the Cinder-Girl' in the first volume of a three-volume edition of Madame d'Aulnoy's fairy tales published in 1721. (It was from Madame d'Aulnoy's tales that Planché took most of the stories for his fairy extravaganzas.) The Cinderella story was first taken onto the pantomime stage in a 'New Grand Allegorical Pantomime Spectacle' staged at the Theatre Royal, Drury Lane, in 1804. But in this version, the author, 'for the purpose of heightening the splendour of the scene', dragged in a load of ancient gods and goddesses, among them Hymen, Cupid, Venus, and various Graces, who , we are told, gave 'an éclat to the whole'. The Fairy Godmother's role was transferred to 'the Goddess of Love, who, by her legitimate aids, Cupid and Hymen, accomplishes all the ends of the spectacle, and makes the lovers happy'. There was no Baron, no Baroness, no Buttons (Grimaldi played the fairly straight servant role of Pedro), and no Dandini.

In January 1820, however, Rossini's comic opera *La Cenerentola* opened at the King's Theatre in the Haymarket. This version of the Cinderella story was the first to make Cinderella's father a Baron (the Baron Monte Fiascone). In Madame d'Aulnoy's version he was an impoverished ex-King; and in Perrault's merely 'a gentleman'. It is to Rossini's librettist, Giacopo Ferretti, that we also owe Dandini, who originated in *La Cenerentola* as valet to the Prince of Salerno and who obviously owed something to the Dandy Lover figure of the *commedia*. The sisters in the opera (they were vain, flighty and rather unpleasant, but not yet the grossly ugly figures of fun that we know) were Clorinda and Thisbe, and their step-sister was Angelina, known as 'Cenerentola'. There was still no Fairy Godmother, the 'magic' in this version being, for some unaccountable reason, performed by the Prince's tutor, Alidoro.

A little over twelve weeks after the London opening of *La Cenerentola*, Covent Garden opened its Easter pantomime, *Harlequin and Cinderella; or, The Little Glass Slipper*, and it is this version that is usually accepted as the first real pantomime version of the story. 'The author', wrote one critic, 'deserves boundless credit for having at length restored the genuine fairy to the stage'. Here, too, was the Baron (called Pomposini), and his wife, who was played by Grimaldi. The Cinderella character, incidentally, was called 'Finetta', *à la* Madame d'Aulnoy.

The next most important date in the history of *Cinderella* as a pantomime is Wednesday, 26th December 1860. It was on that day that 'A Fairy Burlesque Extravaganza', written by H.J. Byron and called *Cinderella; or, The Lover, the Lackey, and the Little Glass Slipper* opened at the Royal Strand Theatre in London. In this production the Prince (named Poppetti) was played by Miss Oliver and Dandino by Miss Saunders. The Baron was now 'Baron Balderdash', and his two daughters still Clorinda and Thisbe, as in *La Cenerentola*, though the eldest (Clorinda) was now played by a man, James Rogers. It was in this burlesque version of the story that the sisters came to full ugliness. It was also in this production that Buttons first appeared, suitably Italianised as 'Buttoni', whom Byron described as 'a page of the "last of the Barons"'. (Page-boys had come to be called 'buttons' because of the close-sewn row of small round buttons that fastened their jackets from chin to waist.) Not only did Byron give us the name 'Buttons', he also gave us the basis for the character, the perky, likeable, lad who takes a shine to Cinders:

> CINDERELLA: I dreamt that I was decked in gorgeous dress;
> With gems and jewels - oh! in such profusion!
> And 'midst a scene of glittering confusion,
> A youth, in whose toilet there were no faults,
> Whirl'd me round wildly in the giddy *valse*.
> I wake, alas! to life's far different round,
> In these the dullest vaults that could be found.
> BUTTONI (*aside*): Alas! with all her *vaults* I love her still!
> (*rapturously*) Oh, make me happy, Miss, do say you will.
> Love in a 'Buttons' may appear a riddle;
> I know I'm *but an* 'umble indiwiddle,
> But still my heart's in the right place - I mean
> That you have got it, as you must have seen.
> (*Cinderella turns aside*)
> Oh don't be deaf as *post*, Miss, I beseech you;
> Let the memorial of this sad page reach you;
> Don't stop its course by letting pride prevail,
> Or *wrong de-livery* of this *mourning male*.
> CINDERELLA: Impossible!
> BUTTONI (*severely*): Some rival has your heart! (*Cinderella starts*)
> My sweet - my very *sweet* one - why thus s-tart?
> Come, come - confess - who is it, I entreat?
> *Sweet* girl, come *to't*, at once - in fact, *tout de suite!*

It was, however, to be a long time before Buttons became the indispensable figure he is today, and he was to appear down the years as Chips, Billy, Pimples, Hobbedehoy, and a host of others, before the name Buttons was immutably settled upon him. As late as 1874 he returned to Pedro, and even in 1905 appeared at Drury Lane as Alfonso. In an 1893 *Cinderella* at the Lyceum, he was dropped altogether, the job of comforting Cinders in the kitchen scene going instead to a large black cat. (The trouble with *Cinderella* is that it contains no proper 'skin' parts.)

It was to be a long time, too, before the Prince (somewhere towards the end of the First World War) finally settled for 'Charming' as a name. He'd previously been called Plenteous, Poppet, Roderick, Lovesick Lackadaisy, Ferdinand, Vanilla, Par Excellence, Exquisite, and Prettihop, among other things, and this despite the fact that

Aphra Behn had used a Don Charmante and Madame Vestris played a King Charming in 1850. The names of the Ugly Sisters remain to this day infinitely variable. A recent survey of Uglies produced Euthanasia and Asphyxia; Phoebe and Fanny; Namby and Pamby; Valderma and Germolena; Buttercup and Daisy; and Alexis and Krystle (a popular pair in 1984-5). The idea of using the Ugly Sisters to represent topical characters or types is by no means new. In 1897, for example, we find a Thisbe, who is described as 'a Girton girl' and dressed in 'a gown adorned with figures from Euclid and algebraic symbols', pitched against a Clorinda who's 'a young woman of muscle'. She has taken lessons from Eugene Sandow, the strong-man who had recently exhibited at the Westminster Aquarium, and is 'disposed to challenge all and sundry to "put them up", has a passion for lifting up in her arms every man she meets, and whisks a cottage piano about as if it were a match-box'.

The Baron's name, too, remains fairly flexible, though it is usually chosen to indicate a lack of resources, Stonybroke and Hardup now being favourites. However, it is sometimes chosen simply to add to the fun of the Ugly Sisters' names. In 1934, for example, at Drury Lane, the sisters were played by Ethel Revnell and Gracie West, who always billed themselves as 'The Long and the Short of It', Ethel Revnell being lean and tall, and Gracie West very short. In their *Cinderella*, therefore, the Baron became Baron 'Mumm', so that they could be 'Maxie' Mumm and 'Minnie' Mumm!

There has over the years been a good deal of discussion about Cinderella's slipper. Where did the idea of glass slippers originate? In Madame d'Aulnoy's version they are of 'red velvet braided with pearls', and in other versions they are of silk, satin, or even of gold. Because of the similarity of the French words *vair*, meaning 'fur' (now obsolete, except in heraldry), and *verre*, meaning 'glass', it has been suggested that a mistake crept in and that either Perrault heard it wrongly or that his English translator translated it wrongly. It certainly was not the latter. In the 1697 *Contes du temp passé*, Perrault's tale is clearly titled 'Cendrillon, ou la petite pantoufle de verre'. So, if the oral tradition had a 'fur' slipper, then the mistake (or the master-stroke) of changing it to 'glass' was Perrault's. The advantages of a glass slipper are obvious and enormous. For one thing, it is rigid and unstretchable. For another, it enables the perfectness of its fit on Cinderella's foot to be clearly seen. It also immediately exposes any attempt to *make* it fit by the cutting off of toes or heels, a trick tried by the sisters in some versions of the story.

In 1958 the Rodgers and Hammerstein *Cinderella*, which had started as a TV spectacular in America, was staged as a pantomime at the London Coliseum, with Yana as Cinderella, Tommy Steele as Buttons, Jimmy Edwards as the King, and Kenneth Williams and Ted Durante as the Ugly Sisters. The following year the Coliseum staged an *Aladdin* with music and lyrics by Cole Porter. (Bob Monkhouse was Aladdin.) At the time it was thought that pantomime might as a result of such productions be nudged permanently into something more akin to the stage musical, but the trend was short-lived.

Aladdin ranks second only to *Cinderella* as a popular pantomime. It originated as a story in the Arabian Nights and was first performed as a pantomime at the Theatre Royal, Covent Garden, on Boxing Day 1788 in a version written by John O'Keefe with music by William Shield, the former boat-builder's apprentice from County Durham who was composer to the Garden for almost twenty years, and one of the most memorable melodists of his day. In 1813 Covent Garden staged another version of the story (it was not a pantomime) as an Easter piece with Mrs Charles Kemble playing Aladdin and Grimaldi as Abanazar's dumb slave, Kasrac. It was in this version, produced by Charles Farley, that the anonymous 'African Magician' of the original story became 'Abanazar'. In March 1822 *Blackwood's Magazine*, noting a performance of *The Marvellous Lamp of Aladdin* staged at the French Opera, wrote: 'I shall tell you nothing new by informing you that the subject of the Wonderful Lamp is very well known. Different theatres have long since taken possession of this ingenious fairy tale.'

Four years later, in 1826, both Drury Lane and Covent Garden mounted versions of the story. The Lane's version took the form of a one-act 'Fairy Opera' by Sir Henry Bishop; the Garden's of 'A Grand Romantic Spectacle' by James Blood with Miss Vining as Aladdin and Grimaldi's son (J. S. Grimaldi) as Kasrac. Blood's version of the story (it was a revival of the one first seen in 1813), was in prose, and Aladdin's mother in the piece still bore her original name 'the Widow Ching Mustapha'.

MUSTAPHA: I'll tell you what, Aladdin, you are a lazy good-for-nothing fellow! The life you lead is a shameful one, and I will no longer endure it, that I wont!

ALADDIN: Why, lord, mother, you do nothing but scold, scold, scold! chatter, chatter, chatter! from morning till night! Can I help it if I feel such new, such pleasing sensations? and that my mind delights in nothing but love stories, and, what's more, that I am in love with a great princess, and, what's more, that a great princess is in

love with me? I dare say, mother, you were the same at my age.
MUSTAPHA: Ungracious varlet! I delight in love stories? I defy you to say that I ever heard a love story in all my life! Such nonsense was not the fashion when your·poor dear father, Ching Mustapha, the tailor, courted me. Oh, that he were now alive! or your poor dear dead uncle, Quam Mustapha, who left us, and died in foreign parts. They would make you stick to trade! but the business of a tailor, forsooth, is not good enough for you.

In December 1856 another pantomime version of the story was mounted at the Royal Princess's Theatre under the title *Aladdin and His Wonderful Lamp; or, the Genie of the Ring*. In this version, in which we are told, the events of the 'Arabian Nights' story were 'pretty closely followed, or rather burlesqued', Aladdin's mother was played by a man (Redigé Paulo, afterwards Pantaloon), so was Aladdin, and so, too, was the Princess Badroulbadour who was represented as 'a young lady some seven feet high' and 'played very cleverly by Mr Daly on stilts'. Burlesque versions of the story were numerous but, as in the case of *Cinderella*, it was to be H. J. Byron who was ultimately to have the most lasting effect on the pantomime versions of the story, for he was to change the widow's name from 'Mustapha', or 'Ching Mustapha' or 'Ching-Ching' to 'Twankay'. Byron's one-act 'Original Burlesque Extravaganza' opened at the Strand Theatre on Easter Monday, 1st April 1861, with Marie Wilton as Aladdin and James Rogers as the Widow, 'Aladdin's mother, who, to quote the Arabian Nights, was rather old, and who, even in her youth, had not possessed any beauty'. These were the days when the great clipper ships (among them *Cutty Sark*) raced each other back from the east across 14,000 miles of ocean laden with tea for the merchants of Mincing Lane. As Philip McCutchan has written in his book *Tall Ships*, 'the China tea run was possibly the most glamorous of all the many aspects of the sailing ship days'. Fittingly, Byron opened his burlesque with a parody of Chevalier Neukomm's famous song, 'The Sea':

> The Tea! The Tea!
>   Refreshing Tea.
> The green, the fresh, the ever free
>   From all impurity.

Twankay tea was a variety of green tea grown in the Tuon Ky District of China. Byron extended the joke to the Vizier's son, to whom he gave the tea-name 'Pekoe'.

The punishment meted out to Abanazar, incidentally, has varied enormously down the years. In James Blood's *Grand Romantic Spectacle* of the 1820s the poor chap is not only poisoned (as per the story) but is also stabbed. In Byron's burlesque he merely gets his face slapped by Widow Twankay and falls burlesquely to the ground. In E.L. Blanchard's 1874 version he is given a poisoned potion which (as he was played by Fred Vokes, who was famous for his dancing), far from killing him, immediately starts him capering:

> Good gracious, what's the matter with my legs?
> They want to dance all sorts of ways, ifegs!

And he performs 'A Dance of Desperation', after which he sinks exhausted onto a couch to be revived just before the Transformation Scene so that he can dance off with Aladdin (who was originally played by Vokes's sister, also famous for her dancing!).

In a 1983-4 *Aladdin* at Bath, Abanazar (played with great relish by actor John Nettles of *Bergerac* and RSC fame – 'I used to be a classical actor,' he quipped as he offered his 'New lamps for old'), ended up having a spell put on him which, to his utter horror and the raucous delight of the children in the audience, 'made him good'. A drum rolled, a cymbal crashed, music tinkled, and birds tweeted as he skipped in his new-found innocence to the footlights and beamed with benevolent delight:

> Oh look! Kiddy-winkies!
> I *love* kiddy-winkies!

But perhaps the most curious of recent Abanazar's was one at Gravesend who, with an inappropriateness unusual even in pantomime, sang 'If I Ruled the World' which, as we all know, continues 'every day would be the first day of Spring'.

Of the other stories taken from the *Arabian Nights*, Sinbad remains in fairly regular, if somewhat limited, production. It was first seen as a pantomime at Drury Lane in 1814 under the title *The Valley of the Diamonds; or, Harlequin Sinbad*. The most curious version is undoubtedly that staged at the Surrey Theatre in 1887 as *Sinbad and the Little Old Man of the Sea or the Tinker, the Tailor, the Soldier, the Sailor, the Apothecary, Ploughboy, Gentleman and Thief*, in which Dan Leno made an early pantomime appearance as Tinpany, the Tinker.

Ali Baba and the Forty Thieves is very seldom seen these days (the forty thieves, no doubt, being the principal deterrent). When a version was staged at Astley's in 1846, *The Illustrated London News* made special mention of the fact that the management had 'turned the old story of the Forty Thieves into a pantomime', and went on: 'The old melodrama has been taken as the foundation of the piece, but the robbers are represented by our most notorious highwaymen.' The piece, which was written by Nelson Lee, was called *The Forty Thieves; or, Harlequin Ali Baba and the Robbers' Cave*, and was described as 'an original grand comic equestrian fairy pantomime', the thieves entering on 'beautiful little ponies'.

Apart from *Cinderella*, the only other fairy tales that remain regularly in use are *Little Red Riding-Hood* (a Perrault tale first pantomimed in 1803); *Jack and the Beanstalk* (1819, with 'little Miss Povey' and Jack Sullivan); *The Sleeping Beauty* (again found in Perrault and used as a pantomime story in 1822); and *Puss in Boots* (1832). In Perrault's version of *The Sleeping Beauty*, incidentally, the Prince, having discovered her, simply kneels at her side and she obligingly wakes up. In an earlier Italian version of the story the Prince is a king who rapes her while she sleeps, and leaves her to wake up nine months later when she gives birth to twins. It was pantomime that invented the simple device of waking her with a kiss.

Riding high in the popularity stakes among modern pantomime subjects are the English 'historical' stories of *The Babes in the Wood* and *Dick Whittington*. The former is based on an old ballad registered on the books of Stationers' Hall in 1595 under the title *The Children in the Wood; or, the Norfolk Gentleman's Last Will and Testament*. It appears in the collection of ballads, sonnets and historical songs collected by Thomas Percy, Bishop of Dromore (and later Dean of Carlisle), published in 1765 as *Reliques of Ancient English Poetry*. A similar story is to be found in the second of *Two Lamentable Tragedies; the one the murder of Maister Beech, a chandler in Thames Street. The other of a young child murthered in a wood by two ruffins, with the consent of his unkle*, written by Robert Yarington and printed in 1601. The story, supposedly true, is that 'a gentleman of good account' (a widower) living in the region of Watton, about twenty miles north-west of Norwich in Norfolk, on his death-bed placed his two infant children in the charge of his brother, bestowing upon them all his worldly wealth. In order to get his hands on the money, the uncle determined to do away with the children.

> He bargained with two ruffians strong,
>   Who were of furious mood,
> That they should take these children young
>   And slaye them in a wood.

The wood was the nearby Wayland Wood that stands today alongside the A1075 East Dereham to Thetford Road, and is now owned by the Norfolk Naturalists' Trust. Once into this wood, however, one of the ruffians ('he that was of mildest mood') took pity on the children, killed his partner-in-crime instead, and, on the excuse that he was going to find food, made off, leaving the children to fend for themselves 'within an unfrequented wood', and obviously late in the year because, according to the ballad, they survived for a time by eating wild blackberries.

> In one another's arms they died
> Awanting due relief;
> No burial this pretty pair
> Of any man receives,
> Till robin redbreast piously
> Did cover them with leaves.

From then on, nothing went right for the uncle. His sons died; his barns were fired; his cattle perished; and he himself ended up dying in gaol. It is said that some seven years after the event, the surviving ruffian was arrested for highway robbery and sentenced to death, when he confessed the whole affair.

On Tuesday, 1st October 1793 a 'New Musical Piece in Two Acts' called *The Children in the Wood* (music by Dr Arnold) opened at the Haymarket Theatre. 'This piece', wrote *The Times*, 'is avowedly taken from the popular ballad, and the story is adhered to as closely as was consistent with those sacrifices which must ever be made to dramatic effect.' In fact, at the end of this version the 'all but famished innocents' were 'restored in safety to their parents'. It was, incidentally, suggested that the 'little opera' might well prove as popular as 'the well known ditty had'.

But if opera had jibbed at permitting the babes to die, pantomime was for a long time to have no such qualms. In 1827 in Drury Lane's *Harlequin and Cock Robin; or, the Babes in the Wood*, they were abandoned to their fate, 'birds of almost every shape and size covering them with leaves' – and then the Harlequinade began. In 1856 at the Haymarket they similarly perished, their bodies being covered by robins 'of more gigantic proportions than those described in the story books'. At Covent Garden in 1874 in *The Babes in the Wood and the Big Bed of Ware*, they not only died and were duly covered with leaves, but were also afforded a 'choir of white-robed angels' to 'celebrate their Heavenly ascent'. In this version, the wicked uncle, Sir Rollingstone, died 'in the big Bed of Ware, haunted with hobgoblins in the most extraordinary manner'.

Not all pantomimes even then, however, were so faithful to the original ballad. As early as 1867 at Covent Garden we find Robin Hood and his Merry Men (all of them, including Robin, played by women) being brought to the rescue through the good offices of Maid Marian who, by a happy coincidence, was Nurse to the Babes. This version (it was called *The Babes in the Wood; or, Harlequin Robin Hood and his Merry Men*) took quite a few liberties. The Babes, for example, were played by comics and blessed with the names 'Milendo' and 'Primrosehilina'. The Robin Hood story, like that of the Babes, had first been taken onto the stage as a subject for opera. Thomas Arne had written one in 1741; and William Shield another in 1784. Then, in 1795, had come the pantomime *Merry Sherwood; or, Harlequin Forester*, 'the incidents principally selected from the legendary Ballads of the 13th Century ... The pantomime invented by Mr Lonsdale; the songs written by Mr O'Keefe; the Overture and the Music (with the exception of a few ancient Ballad Tunes) by Mr Reeve.'

As late as 1888 *The Times* could still express some surprise that the fortunes of the Babes should be 'mixed up with the proceedings of Robin Hood and his merry men in Sherwood Forest, owing to the accidental circumstance, as it would seem, of Maid Marian having been engaged as their Governess'. Surely the most curious version of all, though, must have been the one staged at Drury Lane in 1897 in which the Babes were not murdered, but 'by a sort of Rip van Winkle transformation' were discovered in the second act 'grown up and leading a fashionable and exciting life about Town'. It ended with 'a grand festival' to celebrate their coming of age!

In the 1892-3 pantomime season, when the song 'Ta-ra-ra-boom-de-ay' was already a year old, still going strong, and driving everyone mad, the villains in a *Babes in the Wood* staged at the Crystal Palace were named 'Tarara' and 'Boomdeay'. Equally unusual was the introduction into the Wood Scene of a 1940 version of the story staged at the Theatre Royal, Edinburgh, of a torture rack. It was the invention of Jack Radcliffe, who played the 'good' robber to the 'bad' robber of Bob Merry. During their fight in the wood, Radcliffe stabbed Merry with a banana. He then seized hold of his shoulders, and instructing the Babes to grab a leg each, lifted him onto the rack, strapped his feet and legs in, and began turning a huge handle which duly started to stretch him, to delighted cries from the young audience of 'Another inch! Another inch!' By the time Radcliffe had finished Bob Merry was 'eighteen feet long', the trick having been accomplished by his having worn sixteen-foot long trousers, which had been tucked into his robber's boots and gradually pulled out.

On 21st September 1668 Samuel Pepys wrote in his Diary: 'To Southwark Fair, very dirty, and there saw the puppet show of Whittington, which was pretty to see.' It is the first reference to an entertainment based on the historical character of Richard Whittington who was born, sometime about 1350, the third son of Sir William Whittington, at Pauntley Court, Pauntley, in Gloucestershire, a still remote village standing in the beautiful valley of the River Leadon, some nine miles north-west of Gloucester. (His coat of arms may be seen to this day in the west window of the tower which he almost certainly added to the village's Norman church.) He is first heard of in London in 1379, by which time he appears already to have been a wealthy merchant. His name appears on the roll of the Mercer's Company, indicating that he made his money supplying textiles, especially silks and similar expensive stuffs. He did, indeed, marry Alice Fitzwaryn, daughter of Sir Ivo Fitzwaryn. In 1387 he was a member of the Court of Common Council (the City's governing body), in 1393 was chosen Alderman of the Broad Street Ward and in the same year was elected Sheriff. In 1397, the then Mayor dying in office, Richard II appointed Whittington his successor. He was to be elected Mayor again in 1398, in 1406 and in 1419. And in 1416 he was elected Member of Parliament for the City. His charitable work was legion. As was written: 'This worshipfull man so bestowed his goodes and substaunce to the honor of God, to the relief of the pore, and to the benefite of the comon weale, that he hath right well deserved to be registered in the boke of fame.'

The earliest references to Whittington's cat occur in two plays printed in 1605. Best known of these is the Ben Jonson–George Chapman–John Marston comedy of London life, *Eastward Ho!*, in one scene of which the goldsmith Touchstone says to his former apprentice and newly-acquired son-in-law, Golding:

> Worshipfull sonne! I cannot containe my selfe, I must telle thee; I hope to see thee one o' the monuments of our city, and recon'd among her worthies, to be remembred the same day with the Lady Ramsey and grave Gresham, when the famous fable of Whittington and his pusse shalbe forgotten....

Since then there seems to have been a conspiracy to deny Whittington his 'pusse' and to suggest various more complicated and curious alternatives. In December 1771 a certain Sir Samuel Pegge actually delivered a dissertation on Whittington and his cat to the Society of Antiquaries, thus exposing himself to the satirical pen of Samuel Foote ('Muster Footsey', as John Rich called him) who, in his comedy *The*

Nabob, staged at the Theatre Royal in the Haymarket in June 1772, caricatured him thus:

> The point I mean to clear up is an error crept into the life of that illustrious magistrate, the great Whittington, and his no less eminent cat, and in this disquisition four material points are in question.
>
>   1st. Did Whittington ever exist?
>   2nd. Was Whittington Lord Mayor of London?
>   3rd. Was he really possessed of a cat?
>   4th. Was that cat the source of his wealth?
>
> That Whittington lived no doubt can be made; that he was Lord Mayor of London is equally true; but as to his cat, that, gentlemen, is the gordian knot to untie. And here, gentlemen, be it permitted me to define what a cat is. A cat is a domestic, whiskered four-footed animal, whose employment is catching mice. But let puss have been ever so subtle, let puss have been ever so successful, to what could puss's captures amount? No tanner can curry the skin of a mouse, no family make a meal of the meat, consequently, no cat could give Whittington his wealth. From whence, then, does this error proceed? Be that my care to point out! The commerce this worthy merchant carried on was chiefly confined to our coasts. For this purpose he constructed a vessel, which, from its agility and lightness, he aptly christened a cat. Nay, to this day, gentlemen, all our coals from Newcastle are imported in nothing but cats. From thence it appears that it was not the whiskered, four-footed, mouse-killing cat that was the source of the magistrate's wealth, but the coasting, sailing, coal-carrying cat. That, gentlemen, was Whittington's cat.

It is an idea that has been advanced in all seriousness on numerous occasions. It has also been suggested that the old French word *achat*, or its English derivative acate, meaning 'a purchase', has somehow down the years contrived to become 'a cat'. Whatever the answer, Whittington has been represented since the early years of the seventeenth century as having a perfectly ordinary cat, and as similar stories of cats who bring fame and fortune to their masters are to be found in the folk tales and legends of various countries of the world, it would seem both pointless and unnecessary to deny him his 'Tommy'.

The Whittington story was first taken as the subject of a pantomime on Boxing Day, 1814, when Covent Garden staged *Harlequin Whittington; or, The Lord Mayor of London*. Grimaldi appeared in the opening as Dame Cecily Suet 'whose soul has been compelled to animate the body of the Clown', and the Benevolent Agent was called 'Bizzyboea', the Goddess of Industry, as a reminder that Whittington obtained wealth and fame 'by his laudable industry and perseverance'.

There are two productions of *Dick Whittington* that have earned a special niche in both the history of pantomime and the history of popular song. The first is the 1891–92 production at the Grand Theatre, Islington, in which Lottie Collins sang and danced 'Ta-ra-

ra-boom-de-ay', which she had introduced with electrifying effect at the Tivoli the previous October. This 'paroxysm of motion and emotion', as one critic described it, created a furore. 'It was such an affront to English respectability as had never yet been administered, not only because it flaunted a vision of a high-kicking dancer on a music-hall stage, but because the very sound of the tune was jeering, as well as ludicrous ... it was the voice of the crowd asserting itself.'

It was in another *Dick Whittington* at Drury Lane in 1908–9 that the Cockney music-hall comedian Wilkie Bard introduced the song 'She Sells Sea-Shells', and established a pantomime fashion for tongue-twisting lyrics:

> I've just had a letter to say I'm engaged
> To appear in the pantomime;
> The part I've to play is the Principal Boy,
> So I'm in for a beautiful time.
> The panto's 'Dick Whittington' – I'm Dirty Dick,
> The fellow who once rode to York.
> The manager says I must get a good song
> About which the public will talk.
> I've commissioned some authors to write me a song;
> A very fine chorus they've sent me along!
>
> She sells sea-shells on the sea-shore,
> The shells she sells are sea-shells, I'm sure,
> For if she sells sea-shells on the sea-shore,
> Then I'm sure she sells sea-shore shells.

In more modern times we've seen a *Dick Whittington* pitched into the space-age with Alderman Fitzwarren portrayed as a rocket-inventor and a Dick described as 'The Last Hope of the Universe' who is sent by a bunch of 'witch-cats' to pursue King Rat 'across the galaxy'. If he catches him, he will be made Lord Mayor of London, which seems small enough reward for such galactic efforts on behalf of 'good'! In the mayoral year of London's first lady Lord Mayor there was a Queen Rat at Windsor whose great ambition was to be Lord Mayor. She emerged from among the alley dustbins shimmering in figure-hugging shiny black to cry: 'Eat your heart out, Lady Donaldson!' There was also a modern production in which a local karate school was called in to liven up the fight between the rats and the cats.

Thus do the old tales continue to serve. By the mid-1870s there was already a clear and growing tendency to limit the pantomime stories to those that we still know. A glance down the theatre list for the Christmas of 1874 shows us that at the London theatres that year we could have found: Drury Lane, *Aladdin*; Covent Garden, *Babes in the Wood*; Holborn, *Sinbad*; Surrey, *The Forty Thieves*; National Standard, *Robinson Crusoe*; Pavilion, *Cinderella*; Princess's, *Beauty and the Beast*; Adelphi, *Babes in the Wood*; Crystal Palace, *Cinderella*; Charing Cross, *Aladdin*; New Albion, *Sleeping Beauty*; Sangers, *Aladdin*. Those were the stories, not necessarily the titles. Not all the titles were yet as simple as they are today; not all the stories were as straightforward; and there were still a number of other titles on the list. But *Cinderella* was already 'a favourite theme with pantomimists'.

NINE

THEY·MAKE·A·LOVELY·COUPLET

With the passing of the Theatre Act of 1843, which bestowed on all London theatres the freedom to stage dramas without music, theatre-building received a fresh impetus. Grandiose new playhouses soon began to proliferate throughout the developing suburbs of the rapidly expanding metropolis. Furthermore, many of the old 'minor' theatres that had previously hovered on the borderline between music-hall and legitimate theatre plumped for the legitimate. With pantomime forming a regular part of the fare at all of them, and with the new age exhibiting a developing taste for things 'literary', the pantomime writer came into his own. Many of those who turned to it came initially from the world of burlesque, and continued to straddle both worlds. But pantomime also produced a crop of specialist writers who, between the 1840s and the 1880s, were to raise the quality of its openings to a level never since attained.

Principal among such writers was E. L. Blanchard. From his first professionally staged pantomime of 1844 to his last (sadly mangled by other hands) at Drury Lane in 1888, just nine months before his death, Blanchard treated London to a succession of elegantly imaginative scripts. For the best part of forty years, every single Christmas pantomime staged at the Lane was his. So, too, were a good many staged elsewhere. Indeed, they came to call him 'The Prince of Openings', and he was presented by one journal with a framed Award of Merit proclaiming him 'King of the Pantomime Writers'. Curiously, in later years, Blanchard did not like his pieces being called 'pantomimes' and always referred to them himself as his 'Annuals'. Of him it was written: 'As an exponent of fairy mythology for the little ones, he was the Countess d'Aulnoy, Perrault, and the Brothers Grimm rolled into one.' He was one of the most prolific, the most literary, the most consistently inventive of pantomime writers, and his work stands as a monument to the charm, grace, prettiness and true delights of Victorian pantomime. Furthermore, with its moral overtones and fond use of allegory, it perfectly encapsulates the spirit of its age.

Edward Leman Blanchard was born in Great Queen Street, London (within a stone's throw of the Theatre Royal, Drury Lane), on 11th December 1820. His father, who has been described as 'a useful comedian', was for thirty-five years a member of the company at the Covent Garden Theatre and his mother, too, was on the stage. Indeed, Blanchard claimed that he learned the alphabet from the large Covent Garden playbills. According to the leading theatre critic Clement Scott, he derived much of his inventive talent from his mother who 'used to illustrate by doll models all the nursery stories on which he afterwards founded his pantomimes; and, at a very early age, he used to invent words for Little Boy Blue to speak, for the Old Woman Who Lived in the Shoe, Bluebeard's family, and the like.' It is said that as a child he could always be induced to go to bed by his mother commanding, 'Change into Harlequin!', whereupon he would 'take off his clothes and jump through the dimity curtains'.

Blanchard began writing in his youth, and between the ages of sixteen and twenty completed some thirty dramas, farces, burlesques and pantomimes. He frequently used the pseudonym 'Francesco Frost' and, in later life, wrote also (with T. L. Greenwood) as 'The Brothers Grinn'. A glance at his diary for the year 1851 shows how fast and how hard he worked. On 29th August that year he began work on the pantomime for the Princess's Theatre, making what he called 'very slow progress'. Eleven days later it was finished and delivered. He immediately began work on the pantomime for the Surrey Theatre, and by the 24th of the month that, too, was out of the way. Three days later he sold it for £10, of which he received half. On the evening of 6th October he settled to writing the pantomime for the Marylebone, which he delivered on the 27th; and four days later he was at work on his script for Sadler's Wells. After this he was kept busy attending rehearsals, writing the bills and such like. 'Bills and plots of pantomimes all day,' he writes exhaustedly. On 29th December the manager of the Surrey Theatre called at his house to ask for 'an extra comic scene', and the next day Blanchard wrote an 'extra half flat (china shop)'. His income for the year was £139 14 shillings.

Occasionally Blanchard's diary contains entries like: 'Not a penny in the house, and little prospect of immediate supply'; or, 'Miserable day; nothing done; upset every way; no money from anybody; pushed hard for cash'; or, 'All day brooding over the entertainment. Imagination and inventive powers dormant. No exercise, no enjoyment, no money, no nuffin.' All his life he poured out a steady stream of work, writing not only pantomimes and theatre pieces, but reviews (for forty years he contributed to *The Era*, and for fourteen was drama critic for *The Daily Telegraph*) and, indeed, anything else that might serve to turn him an honest penny – most of his money going to support a host of needy, sponging relatives. As John Hollingshead, founder of the Gaiety Theatre, has written:

> Like a true writer of all work, he shrank at nothing. He was quite ready to edit a financial journal, to write an entertainment, and to revise Sternhold and Hopkins's Hymns; to provide sermons for clergymen of limited literary capacity, and to produce an astronomical almanac like 'Zadkiel'. Comic songs fell from him like rain. He was great in 'Answers to Correspondents'. A book of riddles or a new version of Poor Richard's maxims; an auctioneer's descriptive catalogue, or a sensational advertisement for the three great motive powers of the world - Soap, Pills and Mustard - were all fish for his net. His opinions were so neutral that he could write for any paper without a blush.

The first of the thirty-seven pantomimes that Blanchard wrote for the Theatre Royal, Drury Lane, was *Harlequin Hudibras; or, Old Dame Durden and the Droll Days of the Merry Monarch*. It was described as 'A New Grand Poetical, Historical, Operatical, Dramatical, Anachronistical, Tragical, Comical, Pastoral, Christmas Pantomime', and it opened on Monday, 27th December 1852, with Mr Halford as Dame Durden (afterwards Pantaloon), and Miss Bromley as 'The Genius of Improvement'. The house was full 'from the pit to the highest gallery', and in reviewing the piece, *The Times* affords us a marvellous glimpse of a mid-century pantomime audience waiting for the pantomime to begin:

> Men in shirt-sleeves, women with their bonnets half off, faces ripe for mischief, and the usual complement of those unearthly tones which a Christmas audience seems bound to utter, occupied the interval between the filling of the house and the rising of the curtain. Oranges, too, were eaten with the customary eagerness, and the skins flung upon the heads of the persons in the pit, who sought to return the courtesy, but their performance falling short of their intentions, the occupants of the boxes came in for a share of wet orange-peel.
>
> Standing up fights there were, too, among the occupants of the upper regions, to the signal interest of all those who were lucky enough to get a sight of the combatants. But, on the whole, the audience behaved very decently for a Christmas audience. Never in one instance did a fight lead to a general engagement; and even the conversations across the theatre or between gallery and pit, were full of politeness and good humour.

There was, of course, the customary forepiece to sit (or talk or fight) through first, and then silence fell as the curtain rose to reveal:

SCENE I – THE ABODE OF ANTIQUITY
The scene represents a grotesque curiosity shop, on a gigantic scale, crammed with relics and vestiges of old manners and customs.
The figures of Gog and Magog are on each front wing, and Jack in the Green,

Guy Fawkes, etc. on the second; at the back are introduced an old mail coach, stuffed guard, and coachman; book of 'Joe Miller' open, page 35, old joke, 'two travellers – Irishman – X miles – only five miles apiece'; 1st number of Gentleman's Magazine; Horoscope of Widdicombe, cast by Dr Dee, 'born 1666' – old street lamps, pair of knee breeches, old armour, dresses, and illustrations of by-gone times fill up scene.

A chorus of characters with names like Mildew, Moth, Cobweb and Rust (all attendants on Antiquity) then sang a brief opening number devoted to 'by-gone relics old and musty', at the end of which the centre trap opened and a watchman's box rose slowly onto the stage. Out of it stepped Antiquity himself, 'a grey-haired old man in a purple gown'.

> ANTIQUITY: Moth, Mildew, Cobweb, Rust – my faithful elves –
> For where I am you always show yourselves,
> Know that from earth I've got for your inspection
> A famous stock to add to my collection;
> Blackfriars Bridge is coming very soon,
> And Smithfield will be sent to me by June.
> But ha! What's this? What means this sudden
> movement –
> Who have we here?

The orchestra now struck up a few bars of 'A Good Time Coming', and the Genius of Improvement (Miss Bromley in a yellow-spangled dress) entered in a 'fairy car of progress drawn by two winged steeds, the reins arranged like electric telegraph wires and the whole of the decorations symbolical'. When the car reached centre stage, it stopped, and Miss Bromley alighted to complete Antiquity's couplet by announcing herself: 'The Genius of Improvement!' She then went on:

> GENIUS: To me for all you have had, some thanks are due,
> I clear the way – and rubbish send to you.
> Thanks to a certain Prince, my task, you see,
> Is now much easier than it used to be.
> If there's a prize in science to be won,
> He comes to me – and lo! the thing is done.

This was 1852. The previous year Prince Albert's 'Great Exhibition of the Works of Industry of all the Nations' had been held in Hyde Park, and the spirit of progress it had generated lived on. Blanchard's Genius of Improvement now proceeded to claim: 'Great abuses I have yet to banish/And with them make old prejudices vanish'. But Antiquity felt far from easy about such changes:

> ANTIQUITY: Such wholesale dealings must make some folks
> sleep ill.

GENIUS: I'm full of glorious projects for the people.
          The working man shall find me raise his station,
          I'll give him health – his children education,
          Link the whole world in one vast railway chain,
          Till wiser grown, men never war again.

In that summer of 1852 Joseph Paxton had packed up his Crystal Palace and moved it lock, stock and barrel from its original site in the Park to a new one at the top of Sydenham Hill, in what was then Surrey. The work of re-assembly had commenced in August, and although the building (slightly modified) would not re-open until June 1854, Blanchard provided a preview. The scene changed, by 'rise and sink', from 'The Abode of Antiquity' to 'The New Crystal Palace and Gardens at Sydenham'. Fairies appeared at the entrance, representative of Art, Science, Concord, Progress, Peace, Invention, Wealth, Health, Success, Happiness, Industry and Plenty. They 'struck a Tableau', and an Imp announced:

> Behold my treasures here, there's nought forbid' in 'em,
> And all will be revealed though now *it's hid in 'em*. (*Sydenham*).

This sort of opening sequence which pitted the likes of Antiquity against Improvement; Industry against Idleness; Education against Ignorance, and so on, was a common feature of the pantomime between the 1840s and the 1880s, the disputations between the two parties usually ending in a reconciliation and an agreement, for whatever reason, to stage a Christmas pantomime. In Blanchard's 1856 *See Saw Margery Daw; or, Harlequin Holiday and the Island of Ups and Downs*, for example, the curtain rises to reveal a large terrestrial globe across the top of which is fixed an equally large see-saw. At one end sits a group of people 'significant of wealth and abundance'; at the other a group representing 'squalid poverty and rags'. As one reviewer describes it: 'A clever device of mechanism metamorphoses Wealth into Poverty, and *vice versa*, according to whichever end of the see-saw happens to be uppermost; and thus are shadowed forth the "Ups and Downs of Life".' Into the scene there now enters a character called 'Holiday' who is described as 'The Genius of the Season' (Miss M. Stanley). She comes in an 'emblematical car', interrupting a somewhat prolix dialogue between 'Up' and 'Down'. 'Up', being a snob, of course, snubs her; and 'Down', being a 'werry 'umble creature', approaches her with befitting humility. Holiday suggests that the two of them forget their differences and form a coalition 'for the attainment of the largest possible amount of festive and seasonable recrea-

*The principal characters of the English Harlequinade
– Harlequin, Columbine, Clown and Pantaloon.
From a toy theatre sheet of 1811*

Grimaldi on his 'charger' leads his 'troops' into action, a scene from Harlequin and the Swans *or* the Bath of Beauty *(1813)*

(Left) *Sir Augustus Harris caricatured by Spy. As manager of the Drury Lane Theatre Harris raised pantomime to new peaks of scenic opulence at the turn of the century*

(Facing) *The 'magic' table and chairs joke from* Mother Goose *(1806), and its predecessor as designed almost a century earlier for the* Commedia dell'arte

Comic Scene in Mother Goose.

XI

(Facing) *The below-stage machinery for 'shooting' a character at high-speed onto the stage via the star-trap*

(Above) *The 'Meccanoland' scene from Drury Lane's 1929* Sleeping Beauty

(Right) *A fairy about to 'materialise' through a corner-trap. These were small square traps normally positioned on each side of the stage and used to raise standing figures*

XIV

(Facing) *Dan Leno and Herbert Campbell as the Babes in the Wood, Drury Lane, 1897–98*

(Below) *Topicality. Ada Reeve playing Aladdin in a Bristol pantomime of 1899 adopts the uniform of the Boer War (it had broken out that October) to sing the Rudyard Kipling/Arthur Sullivan 'smash' hit, 'The Absent-Minded Beggar': 'Will you kindly drop a shilling in my little tambourine/For a gentleman in Khaki ordered South?' Proceeds from the song went to the wives and children of servicemen*

(Right) *Dan Leno's Mother Goose as she appeared before and after her visit to the Magic Pool. Drury Lane, 1902–03*

"MOTHER GOOSE" Act I
3055 PHOTO BASSANO   DAN LENO AS MOTHER GOOSE   ROTARY PHOTO. E.C.

MOTHER GOOSE Act II
3056 PHOTO BASSANO   DAN LENO AS MOTHER GOOSE   ROTARY PHOTO. E.C.

(Facing) *Fred Vokes as Baron Moore of Moore Hall 'encounters and subdues the Dragon' in E. L. Blanchard's 1870–71 pantomime* The Dragon of Wantley; or, Harlequin and Old Mother Shipton

(Left) *George Conquest as the Octopus ('the nearest approach to Nature, and a marvel of ingenuity') in the Grecian Theatre's pantomime* Grim Goblin *(1876). In the top part of the picture he's shown being 'shot at an angle of forty-five degrees from the mouth of a Dragon onto a Trapeze'*

(Below) *A satirical drawing of 1808, attacking the Drury Lane management, shows some stage 'animals' in the making*

DRURY LANE

PRINCESS'S

(Right) *George Graves as Dame and Arthur Conquest (third generation of the family) as Priscilla the Cow in Drury Lane's* Jack and the Beanstalk *(1910–11)*

(Below) *The Pender Troupe stilt-walking as 'giant storks each carrying an egg in a nest', surround Mrs Halleybut (George Graves)*

Kay Lyell, in the skin part she has made famous, playing to Danny la Rue's Mother Goose in 1984

(Below) *For this up to the minute haute-couture* Cinderella, *the Emmanuels were responsible for the lavish costumes*

A line-up of Ugly Sisters that includes Euthanasia and Asphyxia, Valderma and Germolene, and Tutti and Frutti

(Right) One of the liveliest of recent Principal Boys, Cilla Black appeared as Jack at the Birmingham Hippodrome in 1983–4

tion'. This good advice is duly accepted; a reconciliation is agreed upon; and just as everything is settled to universal satisfaction, Dame Necessity arrives to claim from Holiday 'her annual tribute in the shape of a Christmas pantomime'.

In the earlier (1843) and anonymous *Harlequin and King Pepin; or, Valentine and Orson*, the opening is set in the 'Abode of Idleness', a dull, gloomy waste with a shattered old house in the foreground where Idleness himself (in a 'long tattered dress' and with 'long matted hair') sets up a school dedicated to the principle of 'all play and no work'. But Industry ('a little muslin-petticoated and silver-wanded fairy'), enters from a bee-hive to demonstrate the happier land in which hard work is the rule, and at a wave of her wand transforms the scene into a beautiful landscape full of turning windmills, rattling trains, and busy reapers, into which, 'from a door at the side', there struts forth a Beadle followed by 'a long string of charity children'. The writer gets into the pantomime story of Valentine and Orson by having Idleness and Industry agree to take one child each to bring up according to their own precepts to determine which way is really best.

On occasion, historical characters, too, are pitched in among the allegorical figures of such opening sequences, as in the case of the Surrey Theatre's 1843 *Harlequin Grammar; or, Lindley Murray and A.E.I.O.U.* By this means was introduced the unlikely figure of Lindley Murray, the American-born grammarian who, in 1784, had settled in England to become 'the father of English grammar', and whose books were for many years used in schools to the exclusion of all others. Murray was joined in the Surrey's pantomime by Aesop and 'old Cocker' (Edward Cocker, the arithmetician), the three of them being pitted against King Ignorance 'and his fiendish crew', which included Vice, Indolence, Folly and Envy. *The Times*, incidentally, while generally applauding the piece, objected that Aesop had not been given his hump!

The historical convolutions contained in some of these plots are extraordinary. At the Princess's Theatre in 1849, for example, the pantomime was *King Jamie; or, Harlequin and the Magic Fiddle*. It opened in the Hall of Evil Spirits, and introduced a character called Alcohol who had been exiled by 'Father Mathew and the Water Cure'. Father Mathew was the great Irish apostle of temperance who had managed to get five million Irish people to 'sign the pledge' before going on to tackle England and America. He was still alive, though getting on in years, when he was appropriated by the pantomime. The broad idea of the piece was that Alcohol sought revenge by 'conspiring against the Peace of King James' and, as the last of many demonic schemes finally came up with the Gunpowder Plot! But even this plot device was comparatively simple compared to the Victoria Theatre's 1855 pantomime which was called *Harlequin and the Five Senses; or, Happy Land and Evil Land, and the Union of the Allied Powers in the Realms of Truth and Light* (the Crimean War was by now in its second year). Of this piece, a reviewer wrote: 'It would be almost as easy to fathom the Eleusinian mysteries as to develop the plot of so complicated a production.'

Although these 'morality' openings were common in the middle years of the nineteenth century, they were by no means universal. Truly imaginative writers like Blanchard devised all manner of fanciful ways of introducing their chosen stories. A good example of Blanchard's work at its best is his 1859 Drury Lane 'annual', *Jack and the Beanstalk; or, Harlequin Leap-Year, and the Merry Pranks of the Good Little People.* This opens in 'The Atmosphere, 45 miles above the Earth's Surface', where Old Moore, Zadkiel, Hannay and three other Almanack-Concoctors ('to be respectively identified as the "Illustrated", "Pocket", and "Nautical"') are each discovered looking through a large telescope. To them enters Weather in her Aurora-Borealis car attended by 'Heat' and 'Cold'. She has to explain to them why it is that they find her so difficult to predict. 'I'm like a woman, changeable, you know,' she tells them. There is then staged 'A Parade of the Months', at the end of which she explains:

WEATHER: They all know me; with them throughout the year,
I'm pleasant, dull, mild, open, or severe.
In short, like someone else described in song,
I'm everything by turns, and nothing long.
Just now I am unsettled.
ZADKIEL: Come, be reasonable!
WEATHER: I think of Christmas –
ZADKIEL: Do so, and be seasonable!
WEATHER: What would you have?
ZADKIEL: What I may safely state
It wants no Zadkiel to prognosticate.
A pantomime, through winter to befriend us.
WEATHER: My ancestor, the past, has got the key
Of all the objects in that realm, you see.
But I'll unlock my cabinet in air,
And what it holds with pleasure you may share.
This we the Don-Jon in great Jackland call,
Where Jacks are packed together, great and small.

Then, as music plays, the scene opens and discovers 'The Don-Jon in Jack-Land' where are found crowded together all the well-known 'Jacks' of legend, history, nursery rhyme and fairy tale.

> WEATHER: Here are the Jacks that all have had their turn,
> Jack Frost, Jack Cade, Jack Straw – besides discern
> Jack in the Box, Jack who would Giants kill,
> Jack Horner, Sprat, and also Jack and Jill.
> ZADKIEL: I prophesy, to banish quite the dumps,
> Jack and the Beanstalk is the Jack of Trumps!

So, Jack of Beanstalk fame steps out, the Don-Jon closes on the rest, and Weather then instructs the months to assist Jack in his allotted task, the first six months being deputed to 'help the magic stalk to grow', the last six the 'after-fun to show'. The remainder of the pantomime is divided into twelve scenes, the first six telling the tale of Jack and the Beanstalk and covering the months January to June; the last six devoted to a Harlequinade composed of scenes representative of the months July to December, with Clown and the rest set loose at the Seaside, the Village Flower Show, in a Kentish Hop Garden and so on. The final scene takes place in 'the Merry Halls of Happy Old Christmas'.

The opening of the story proper in this piece provides a good example of the sort of gentle prettiness that Blanchard brought to the pantomime stage. It is January, and we are outside Jack's cottage, somewhere in a wintry Devon landscape. 'Quick pantomime music plays', and the scene opens with the rapid bustle of boys snowballing and 'engaging in leap-frog, hockey, and other winter games'. Jack enters, rolling a huge ball of snow, and the boys generally fall to snowballing. While they're at it, Jack makes a slide on a little pool that runs off to one side of the stage:

> JACK: Look, here's a slide – to make it I've been toiling;
> Stop! – I go first – you keep the pot boiling.

Jack goes first, slides and falls, and slides and falls again. Soon they're all jostling onto the ice. Finally, one of them pitches through it into the water below, and is rescued 'with the usual pantomimic fun'. It is at this point that Jack's mother enters, just back from market 'with a large market-basket'. Named 'Goody Greyshoes' in this version, she was played by Tom Matthews who sang a version of 'Hot Codlins' that managed to avoid any reference to gin or drunkenness. (The book of the piece, incidentally, announced both 'Hot Codlins' and 'Tippity Witchet' as 'Tom Matthews' Celebrated Songs'.)

The most famous scene in *Jack and the Beanstalk* is, of course, the selling of the cow. This is how Blanchard tackled it:

GOODY: To pay the rent, as I my landlord told,
The time has come; my calf must, then, be sold.
He seems unwilling, and for him I feel;
But, Jack, just put your shoulder to the veal,
And urge him on: It is our fair, you know.
You'll meet a customer ere far you go.
*Music. Pantomime action of the old Dame's
regard for the calf, her injunction to Jack to
get a good sum for it, and his promise of
obedience to her wishes.*

JACK: Was ever boy so much perplexed before?
I don't know what they stand for calves, I'm sure.
(*To calf*) What do you think you are worth?
(*Calf shakes his head*) I perhaps should say
How many pounds do you think are in your weigh?
However, what I ask they must allow –
Folks bait a bull, but never bate a cow.

Blanchard, like the burlesque writers, delighted in carrying his literary jokes beyond the stage and onto the programmes and playbills. In his *Jack and the Beanstalk*, for example, he was not content to let the performers who played the months use their real names, but instead credited January, February, March, April, and the rest as being played respectively by 'Messrs Slippy, Drippy, Nippy, Showery, Flowery, Bowery, Hoppy, Croppy, Poppy, Wheezy, Sneezy and Freezy'. The most extravagant example of his literary ingenuity, however, is to be found in the billing of his *Little Jack Horner; or, Harlequin A.B.C.* (1857) which he described as an 'entirely new Allegorical, Beautiful, Comical, Diverting, Educational, Fanciful, Gorgeous, Hyperbolical, Intellectual, Jovial, Keen, Laughable, Merry, Novel, Original, Peculiar, Quizzical, Romantic, Splendid, Transcendent, Unobjectionable, Volatile, Waggish, X-travagant, Youthful, and Zig-Zaggy Grand Comic Christmas Pantomime.'

Blanchard's greatest rival as a pantomime writer was Nelson Lee. Born at Kew on 8th January 1806, he was the son of a Lieutenant-Colonel Lee, and was christened 'Nelson' because on the day he was born his father was performing duties connected with the funeral of Lord Nelson which took place the following day. Lee began his theatrical career as a conjuror and juggler. For a time he was one of the company in the original Richardson's Show which toured the London and country fairs, and later he became joint proprietor of its successor, Richardson's Travelling Theatre. Charles Dickens was to recall 'the pantomime which came lumbering down in Richardson's waggons at fair-time' to the 'dull little town' in which he was brought up. He was to recall, too, the long row of small boys, 'with frills as white as they could be washed, and hands as clean as they would come', who were taken to see the performance. At Greenwich Fair, Dickens remembered, Richardson had once presented a melodrama (with three murders and a ghost), a pantomime, a comic song, an overture, and some incidental music, all in the space of twenty-five minutes!

Lee went on to become a distinguished actor and pantomimist, playing Pantaloon, Clown and Harlequin. He subsequently and successively managed several London theatres, finally settling at the City of London. Like Blanchard's, his pantomimes were highly literary and moralistic in style, as may be judged from such titles as *Industry and Idleness; or, Harlequin Little Tommy Tucker – Red Rufus; or, Harlequin Fact, Fiction, and Fancy – Knife, Fork and Spoon; or, Harlequin Breakfast, Dinner, Tea and Supper* – and *Romeo and Juliet; or, Harlequin Queen Mab and the World of Dreams.*

Then there was Thomas Longden Greenwood (the T. L. Greenwood who, with Blanchard, formed 'The Brothers Grinn'). He was a fourth-generation theatre man. His father, his grandfather and his great-grandfather had all been scenic artists at Sadler's Wells Theatre, an unbroken line that stretched back through the days of Grimaldi to the 1750s when Rich was still at Covent Garden. Thomas Longden himself became assistant manager and writer at the Wells, eventually going on to manage it with Samuel Phelps for the sixteen years up to his retirement in 1859. Greenwood, too, in the manner of the day, liked the allegorical opening scene. His 1852 pantomime for Sadler's Wells, *Whittington and His Cat; or, Old Dame Fortune, and Harlequin Lord Mayor of London* opens with a moonlight view of the 'mismanaged abode' of Old Dame Fortune's daughter, 'Miss' Fortune, who with her associates Miss Hap, Miss Anthrope, and 'other evil spirits', is found lamenting the fact that the 'good time' which has been so long a-coming seems finally set to arrive. She views with dismay the prospect of a future in which there is no cause for grumbling. But that good old lady Dame Fortune has a sure cure for her daughter's *ennui* – a grand Christmas pantomime 'which shall illustrate the wonderful history of Richard Whittington!' In this version of the story, the ill-natured Cook was a 'Dame Dorothy Drippington' (played by Nicolo Deulin, afterwards Clown), and Whittington's arch-enemy was 'the designing clerk, Inkpen'.

During the forepiece on the opening night, incidentally, we are told, 'a jacket was accidentally dropped from the gallery into the pit, and very cleverly fished up again by a rope composed of a choice collection of neck-ties and pocket handkerchiefs, which were cheerfully volunteered for the occasion.'

There were so many other writers – among them, Frank W. Green, of whom one critic declared, 'we readily forgive him for his inveterate habit of mutilating the Queen's English for the sake of the fun'; then there was that formidable pair, George Conquest and Henry Spry, whose pantomimes for the Grecian and Surrey Theatres were so sensationally successful between the years 1858 and 1901. Asked how he conceived them Conquest once said: 'What I generally do is to run down to Brighton for about four months and worry, worry, worry.' He claimed that he got some of his ideas from shop windows, and 'obtained many a notion from toys and pieces of china'. The names run on: Horace Lennard, Charles Millward, J. F. McArdle, and J. Hickory Wood who, finally, at the turn of the century, got rid of the rhyming couplets for all but the 'Immortals', abandoned the Harlequinade, and cleared the way for the pantomimes of our own day.

There was even, for a brief while, W. S. Gilbert. Gilbert wrote just one pantomime on his own, though he wrote two others with various collaborators. His solo effort, commissioned by the Lyceum Theatre for the 1867–68 season, he called *Harlequin Cock-Robin and Jenny Wren; or, Fortunatus and the Water of Life, The Three Bears, The Three Gifts, The Three Wishes, and The Little Man who Woo'd the Little Maid.* The dramatic high-point of the piece comes when the Little Maid arrives at the House of the Three Bears who immediately take her prisoner and declare their intention of making a meal of her, to which she sings:

> Oh, dear me!
> Oh, hear me!
> You couldn't come for to go for to cook such a particularly
> Nice little girl as I?
> Oh, spare me!
> Don't tear me!
> You mustn't come for to go, if you please, sir, for to take and put me in a pie!
> Oh, sir, please spare me
> Don't in pie prepare me!
> Don't come for to go, sir, for to put me in a pie.

Whereupon the bears seize her and put her in the pie!

Gilbert did not enjoy working in pantomime, and a few weeks after his Lyceum opening, he said of the pantomime writer:

He writes simply to order, and his dialogue is framed upon the principle of telling as much as possible in the very fewest words. He is ready to bring in a 'front scene' wherever it may be wanted, and to find an excuse at the last moment for the introduction of any novelty in the shape of an 'effect' which any ingenious person may think fit to submit to the notice of the manager. From a literary point of view his work is hardly worth criticism.

He went on to describe his essential qualifications. He must be quick at weaving a tale that shall involve a great many 'breeches parts'; he must accept the fact that his work will be 'cut up and hacked about' by the stage-manager; and he must be prepared 'to "write-up" this part and cut down that at a moment's notice'. Furthermore, if one song won't do, he must be able at once 'to extemporise another'.

Many writers were similarly and increasingly to complain as the century wore on, none more so than E. L. Blanchard. Gilbert himself had earlier lampooned pantomime in a Bab Ballad which appeared in *Fun* on 2nd December 1865, in one verse of which he wrote:

All the stockings gone in ladders – then the sausages and bladders,
And the chromes, and greens, and madders, that I've seen five thousand times;
And the glitter, gauze, and spangle, and the Clown turned in the mangle,
And the everlasting jingle of the mutilated rhymes.

T E N

THERE · NEVER · WAS · SUCH · TIMES

From the very beginning the pantomime was acutely aware of the world around it and eager to exploit the comic or emotional possibilities of whatever was topical. Indeed, no other form of entertainment has ever devoted itself so wholeheartedly to holding up to the public, for its approbation, censure, or mere amusement, the events, manners, whims and fancies, fads, crazes and absurdities of its time. 'Allusions to current events are the life of a pantomime', wrote Henry Morley in his *Journal of a London Playgoer* in 1853. Over thirty years before *The Times* had declared: 'The effect of a pantomime very much depends on the introduction of the reigning follies or extravagant inventions of the day.'

In the nineteenth century particularly, pantomimes tended to be judged by the number of 'raps' or 'hits' at passing events that they managed to include. A critic reviewing the Olympic's 1848 pantomime *William the Conqueror; or, the Sack of the Saxons*, wrote in high glee that it sported a Harlequinade which 'hits at everything. The Sea-Serpent, and the National Guards, Louis Philippe, M. Soyer, emigration, gutta percha, the state of the drama, the baby jumpers, our national defence, and many other topics', he raved, 'were all introduced in rapid succession.' At Sadler's Wells, always famous for its 'hits', 1848 was similarly a vintage year. 'Everything and everybody is shown up', wrote a delighted reviewer in *The Illustrated London News*. A couple of years earlier this same periodical had taken the Lyceum sharply to task, even going so far as to suggest that it should never produce another pantomime, because it had 'unaccountably overlooked' such topicalities as 'the Gun Cotton, Free Trade, Cattle Shows, Montpensier Marriages, Cheap Steamers and Omnibuses, the Rival Operas, and a host of other subjects'. Topicalities could even compensate for deficiencies in other areas. We are, for example, told (by *The Morning Herald*) that Drury Lane's 1827 pantomime, *Harlequin and Cock Robin; or, The Babes in the Wood*, left a good deal to be desired scenically, but that 'some caricatures of the follies and extravagances of the day made up for the defect'.

A certain amount of topicality could be included in the original scripting of the pantomime, but if it was to remain bang up to date new material would need to be written in later, and the printed 'books' that were sold in the theatres frequently carry the note: 'The Libretto is subject to alteration from time to time for the introduction of topical allusions.' In our own time it is common enough practice for the comics to 'gag' topical lines inspired by a reading of the daily papers, but in earlier times whole new scenes might be devised on the strength of a news report or a press paragraph. In December 1779, with the pantomime preparations well under way at Drury Lane, the *London Gazette* carried a despatch from the war with Spain reporting the storming and capture by British sailors of Fort Omoa and the town it defended, Puerto Omoa on the Gulf of Mexico in Honduras. As we have seen, Sheridan immediately 'dramatised' the despatch and inserted it as a three-scene interlude into his revival of *Harlequin Fortunatus; or, The Wishing Cap*. And it was not only 'major' news stories that got written in as scenes. On 23rd January 1831, the *Sunday Times* revisited the Sadler's Wells pantomime and reported:

> A very whimsical addition of a scene has been made, founded upon a Mansion House report, which was published in most of the papers, relative to a man being caught by the City police for stealing pies from Billingsgate, and upon whose person so many were found secreted; also the incident mentioned to the Lord Mayor, of the fellow placing a live lobster in his pocket, and, when accused of the theft, after enduring the greatest torment from the attack of the lobster, imploringly looking his accuser in the face, with tears of agony in his eyes, and exclaiming, with an oath, 'Here's the lobster, master – I have been punished enough!' Both incidents are given with the happiest effect.

At its best, then, the pantomime has traditionally found its topicality equally in great national or international events and in the humble occurrences of day-to-day life. Hence, pantomime scripts read in conjunction with the newspaper reviews, provide a rich, frequently amusing, and always informative guide to the events that stirred the public imagination and also to the minutiae of social history over some two-and-a-half centuries.

In John Rich's time, topical allusions tended to be contained mainly in the interpolated songs. For example, *The Magician; or, Harlequin a Director* which, as we have already seen, was staged in the wake of the bursting of the South Sea Bubble when so many people were facing financial ruin, there was a song called 'A New South Sea Ballad' which not only poked fun at the 'Bubble' and its bursting, but even made special mention of 'Mr Knight', in the lines:

Let every trick be a clean one
Fat sorrow is better than lean one,
Then frisk it about, and Jerk it away;
For here's no sign of sorrow
Unless Mr Knight shou'd darken the day.

Mr Knight was the Treasurer of the South Sea Company and as such had been 'entrusted with all the dangerous secrets of the dishonest directors'. During the Parliamentary enquiry into the affair that year he had 'packed up his books and documents and made his escape from the country', embarking in disguise in a small boat on the Thames and 'proceeding to a vessel hired for the purpose' which conveyed him to Calais.

These very early pantomimes, just like all those that succeeded them, also tilted at smaller issues, and their songs especially serve to remind us of some of the fads and fashions that prevailed in their time. In a song called *A Raree Show*, which was sung by Mr Salway (no doubt in the then popular guise of a Savoyard!) in the Rich/Theobald *Rape of Proserpine* in 1727, it was theatrical London's obsession with foreign artistes that came in for ridicule. Among those singled out in the words are 'De Italian Opera' at the Haymarket Theatre; 'De troupe Italien'; and Mademoiselle Violante who 'jump upon de rope ten story high, and never break her neck'.

But Rich didn't confine his topical allusions entirely to the songs. In December 1726, for example, he added a 'Rabbit Scene' to his production of *Harlequin a Sorcerer* in order to take advantage of a story, then current, that a woman in Guildford, known as 'The Rabbit Woman', had given birth to nine rabbits!

There can seldom have been a more topical pantomime than John Thurmond's *Harlequin Sheppard*, which was staged at the Theatre Royal, Drury Lane, in November 1724. Jack Sheppard, the notorious thief, had been arrested at the end of July and, after a number of sensational escapes from Newgate, had finally gone to the gallows on 16th November. He was twenty-three years old when he died, and 200,000 people turned out to watch the execution. Thurmond's pantomime, which was first staged twelve days later, opened in Sheppard's cell in Newgate (the scenes, we're told, were 'painted from nature'), showed his escape, his pursuit through London, and his final re-arrest at an ale-house where he was found cavorting with one 'Frisky Moll'. One journal, reviewing the piece, reported that it was 'dismissed with a universal hiss' and went on to suggest that 'if Sheppard had been as wretched, and as silly a Rogue in the World, as the ingenious and witty Managers have made him Upon the Stage, the lower Gentry, who attended him to Tyburn, wou'd never have pittied him when he was hang'd.'

It was in the days of Grimaldi and the Dibdins that pantomime really found its satirical feet. As Charles Dibdin was to write: 'It was always my Custom to hold up to ridicule the monstrosities of the times.' Elsewhere in his *Memoirs* he adds: 'In these pantomimes I introduced a series of Caricature Scenes somewhat similar to the Print Shop Caricatures, and, like them, allusive to the reigning follies of the day ...' Dibdin's many targets included such fashionable manias as those for bare-knuckle prize fighting and for driving 'Four-in-Hand' in which the young bloods of the aristocracy attempted to ape the skills, the dress and even the language of the great stage and mail-coach drivers, who had become the heroes of their day. 'Prime' (meaning 'first-rate') and 'Bang-Up' (meaning 'right up to the fashionable mark') were the watch-words of this set, and Dibdin tilted at them in his 1810 *Bang Up! or, Harlequin Prime* and also in a number of songs, among them 'The Whip-Club' which he wrote for the Sadler's Wells pantomime *Fashion's Fools; or, Aquatic Harlequin* of 1809. The song was sung by Grimaldi in the role of a *real* coachman:

> Since fashion's all fiddle-de-dee,
> For playing the fool I was made,
> But what will become of poor me,
> 'Tis the fashion to take up my trade.
> In the Whip Club exhalted I stand,
> As the cut of my coat will imply,
> And while driving, d'ye mind, four in hand,
> four in hand,
> Can completely cut out a fly's eye.

In a delightful little song sung by Grimaldi in *The Astrologer; or, Harlequin and Moore's Almanack* at Sadler's Wells in 1810, Charles Dibdin tilted at the then current craze among women for reading novels. Of his thus-addicted wife, Grimaldi complained:

> While dressing the dinner one day she'd got,
> A novel she was concluding-O,
> Quite absent with soapsuds she filled the pot
> And in it boil'd the pudding-O;
> My shaving brush mislaid had I,
> When a novel all day she'd cried o'er one,
> And I found the brush in the beef-steak pie,
> O wasn't she a tidy one!

And things got even worse:

> O'er 'The Victim of Feeling' she snivelling sat,
> While the child in the fire chanc'd falling O;
> And she feelingly bawl'd out, 'O curse the brat!
> The Devil can't read for his squalling O!'

Elsewhere, in a song called 'The London Cheats or There Never Was Such Times' (this one by C. Westmacott and H. Nicholson), Grimaldi laid into the then common practice among shop-keepers of adulterating both food and drink – sugar sold with sand in it; 'coffee' made of horse beans; 'turtle' soup derived from ox's shin; and gin that wasn't gin. 'It's all nothing at all but spirits of wine, you Bog-trotting swindler!' And the milk? Well, in a snatch of patter between verses, Grimaldi played a three-way conversation to explain about that:

> 'There's more milk drank in London in a week than all the cows in England cou'd give in a fortnight'.
> Says Blunderskull: 'How can that be, you Pump?'
> 'Why', says a Plasterer, 'Because two-thirds of it, you Judy, is white-wash.'

It was these same practices that Tobias Smollett had written of in *Humphrey Clinker*: 'The bread I eat in London, is a deleterious paste, mixed up with chalk, alum, and bone-ashes; insipid to the taste, and destructive to the constitution.' As Grimaldi was to sing:

> In London where comical jokes go free,
> There are comical modes of cheating,
> Birch brooms are cut up for Souchong and Bohea,
> And plaster for bread you're eating.

> Spoken: How do ye do, Mrs Caphusalum? I hope you approve of the genuine Tea. Oh yes New Brooms sweep clean, and I have no occasion to buy Birch ones, while I deal at your shop for Tea. There's nothing like my cheap bread, says Doughy the Baker. Oh yes, says Needy, you forget, Plaster of Paris is very like it.

> CHORUS
> What are you at each knave may cry,
> Who feels my honest rhymes,
> What are you arter's my reply,
> There never was such times!

Concern about the state of bread is frequently to be found in pantomime scripts. In the London Palladium's 1968 *Jack and the Bean-stalk*, for example, when the Giant did his, 'Fee, fi, fo, fum, I smell the blood of an Englishman; Be he alive or be he dead, I'll grind his bones to make my bread', Crone (his manservant) quipped: 'That's a good idea. You never know what they put in the bread nowadays.'

For anyone in search of topicality, even the titles of the old pantomimes can be informative. *Harlequin and the Wild Fiend of California; or, the Demon of the Diggings and the Gnome Queen of the Golden Lake*, for example, which was staged at the Grecian in December 1849, reminds us that that was the year of the 'forty-niners' and the Californian Gold Rush. Not surprisingly, gold rushes, with their opportunities for all manner of scenic excesses, were seized upon with great relish by the pantomime writers.

They certainly made good use of the Californian one. In December 1851, Sadler's Wells took one of Madame d'Aulnoy's fairy tales, 'The Yellow Dwarf' and staged it as *Harlequin and the Yellow Dwarf; or, the Enchanted Orange Tree and the King of the Gold Mines*. Both the orange tree and the King of the Gold Mines figure in the original story, but at the Wells that year the King was called 'California' and the audience was 'carried in imagination' to the diggings. A year later at the Adelphi one of the best tricks in the Harlequinade is said to have been the changing of a betting office, the proprietor of which had 'gone to the diggings' to 'the placers, with a view of the gold regions with the miners at work'.

Some attempts to work topicality into pantomime titles served merely to make them sound singularly unentertaining. In the 1850s, for example, there was one called *Harlequin Genius; or, the Progress of Free Trade, the Spirit of Improvement, and the Great Exhibition of 1851*; and another, snappily titled *Barber, Barber, Shave the Cat; or, Harlequin Monopoly Humbug, Free Trade and the Magic Pins*. Equally dispiriting is the title of the Pavilion's 1852 Christmas piece, *Uncle Tom and Lucy Neal; or, Harlequin Liberty and Slavery*. Harriet Beecher Stowe's *Uncle Tom's Cabin* had been published in book form that year (it had previously been run as a serial in America) and within a few months of publication had achieved phenomenal sales both here and across the States. That Christmas, in addition to pantomime versions and tilts at Uncle Tom 'mania' in numerous Harlequinades, no fewer than four London theatres (Drury Lane, the Adelphi, the Victoria, and the Surrey) preceded their pantomimes with straight dramatisations of the book. Most of them appear to have been rather dull. At the Surrey, we are told, 'the audience were evidently little interested either in the horrors of slavery or the particular fate of Uncle Tom, and kept up a succession of noisy demonstrations from beginning to end.' It would appear that the managers had found a worthy successor to *Jane Shore* and *George Barnwell*.

Just as 'Uncle Tom' pervades the pantomime scripts and reviews of 1852, so 'The Wellington Statue' had pervaded those of 1846. Indeed, one journal completed its round-up of that year's Christmas entertainments by remarking: 'We may add as a rider (though it is scarcely necessary to do so) that the Wellington Statue forms a prominent feature in *all* the pantomimes.' This was James Wyatt's unfortunate colossal statue of the Iron Duke which had been erected that September in all its inappropriate massiveness atop the arch at Hyde Park Corner, opposite his London residence at Apsley House. It had caused an outcry. *Punch* in particular had heaped, and continued to heap, ridicule upon it in both word and drawing. The best pantomime 'hit' against it was, without doubt, that staged at Sadler's Wells where, 'at the touch of Harlequin's wand, the arch at Hyde Park corner crumbled into ruins beneath the weight of the Duke's statue; and a colossal representation of his Grace, some ten feet high, which tumbled about the stage as if in doubt where to find even a local habitation, drew down the vociferous approbation of the gods.' (The statue was eventually removed and, in 1912, Adrian Jones's bronze four-horse chariot and figure of Peace took its place on the arch.)

At that point in the 1840s the pantomime was also much preoccupied with the rapidly expanding railway network and railway 'mania', as is evidenced by titles like *Harlequin and the Steam King; or, Perroule's Wishes and the Fairy Frog*, and *The Birth of the Steam Engine; or, Harlequin Go-a-Head and Joe Miller and His Men*. (The cast of the latter included 'an individual called Watt, by trade a mechanic', who later became Harlequin.)

The devisers and writers of pantomime have always shown a keen interest in the pantomimic possibilities of scientific advances, especially developments in travel. As early as 1820, a Covent Garden pantomime was ridiculing the public's obsession with speed. It showed how a 'safety coach' that took five hours to get from London to Brighton was put out of business by 'a steam coach' that could do it in one. And, of course, the moral was suitably pointed. As one reviewer noted: 'The passengers, by a sudden explosion are strewed about the stage, to the infinite diversion of the galleries.'

Hand-in-hand with the interest in steam went an interest in hot air. After the first manned hot-air balloon had risen above Paris in the November of 1783 ballooning became an instant craze. From the end of the eighteenth century, and through the first quarter of the nineteenth, the balloon made regular appearances in pantomime, particularly at Covent Garden. In the 1814 *Harlequin Whittington* at the

Garden, a balloon with a child in the basket actually ascended from the stage and 'after losing itself in those mysterious regions sacred to the magazines of theatrical thunder and lightning, descended through an aperture in the middle of the roof of the house, and moving over the heads of the upstaring, and half-startled pit, rested once more on the place from which it rose.' In the Garden's 1823 *Harlequin and Poor Robin; or, The House that Jack Built*, Clown and Pantaloon took 'an Aeronautic Excursion' from Vauxhall Gardens to Paris. This, we are told, was 'a revolving scene – the balloon ascends – and the English landscape gradually recedes from view – the gradual approach of night – the rising of the moon – and passing of the balloon through heavy clouds – and the return of day' being 'beautifully represented', before the balloon finally descended into a scene representing the Tuileries Gardens. In 1826 the balloon turned up again, this time carrying a young lady, and 'traversed the whole circle of the theatre, by means of a rope from the ceiling, which passed round the chandelier'.

By the first years of the twentieth century public interest had long since turned from the balloon and man's dream of flying now, and very briefly, centred on the powered airship. Count Zeppelin had completed his prototype in 1900, and interest in these curious craft had been enormously heightened in the October of 1901 when Santos Dumont had navigated his ship round the Eiffel Tower. The following year the Brazilian Monsieur Severo and his engineer had been killed when their airship exploded above Paris. That Christmas the airship featured in several pantomimes. There was one at Drury Lane and another at the Prince of Wales Theatre, Birmingham. Here, it made a dramatic entrance over the Village of Tweedle Dee (the pantomime was *Jack and the Beanstalk*) when it 'dashed' across the stage, and with much 'noise, commotion, etc.' crashed into some houses. As Captain Gottem explained to 'the Village coquette' as he stepped from the wreckage: 'You see, missie, we're what they call aeronauts – Air or nothings, as one might say. As a rule we're killed on trips like this.' Later, his airship repaired, the good Captain offers to fly Dame Trot to Cloudland, in search of her son, Jack:

DAME: You're sure it's safe? Isn't there a lot of danger in balloons?
CAPTAIN: Not at all. Not at all. Besides, this yer ain't a balloon marm; she's a ship. Say the word and off we go!

And off they went!

Progress even caught up with *Cinderella* when, at Drury Lane on Boxing Day 1895 she set out to the Ball in an 'automotor carriage encrusted with incandescent jewels'. It was the first time the motor car had been seen on the London stage. Indeed, there were at that time no more than fourteen or fifteen of them on the roads of Britain, the first having been introduced the previous December. The Lane's car had, according to an article in *The Idler*, been 'especially constructed by Messrs Windover, the celebrated carriage builders, and ornamented by Messrs Jackson of Rathbone Place, the work being carried out in *carton pierre*, *papier mâché*, and gold leaf.' It was powered by an electric motor stored in the floor and was, hardly surprisingly, acclaimed 'one of the principal sights' of the pantomime.

Actually, Cinders has always been a bit of a pioneer in her way. In Drury Lane's 1883-4 version of the story, she was at first reluctant to wear the glass slippers:

> CINDERELLA: What beauteous slippers! – yet I cannot take them;
> For should I dance in them I'm sure to break them.

To which her Fairy Godmother replied:

> FAIRY: Fear not, sweet maid, whate'er may come to pass;
> These cannot break – they're made of toughened glass.

The pantomime has never been ashamed of introducing such incongruities in the cause of topicality. It has never been ashamed of 'advertising' either. Both traits are, of course, common in the pantomimes of today. We have recently had Ugly Sisters who have entered the Ball-Room Scene exclaiming 'Gateshead Revisited!' and a Buttons (at Weston-super-Mare) who confessed to the audience that he loved Cinders enough to give her his last Rolo, whereupon he propped a huge packet of them up against the proscenium arch. We are thoroughly familiar with characters who enter to proclaim that they've 'just been to the Sales', and name the local department store.

None of this is new. In the 1905-6 Drury Lane *Cinderella*, the Fairy Godmother announced:

> In crystal slippers you shall trip it lightly;
> I have them here – for I'm the Fairy Whiteley.

Whiteley's was, of course, London's very first department store, and the Fairy went on, in typical department store manner, to summon her elfin shoe-makers with the cry: 'Shoes forward! Quick! The best you have to show!'

In an 1883 *Jack the Giant Killer* at the Theatre Royal in Walsall, 'Queen Butterfly' suddenly stepped forward to announce:

With your permission, if you'll be so kind
To give us time to set the scene behind,
We now intend – you won't refuse, I'm certain –
To let us, for five minutes, drop the curtain.
The art of advertising I'm not skilled in,
But refreshments may be had within the building,
So if you're thirsty, you won't have far to walk;
We supply them here, by Beebee of 'The Stork'.

Mrs Beebee was proprietor of the local Stork Hotel which, the programme informs us, was 'Family and Commercial' and offered 'First-Class Wines and Spirits. An Ordinary Every Day at 1.30. Spacious Billiard Room' and 'Good Stabling'.

The pantomime's readiness to make capital out of its popularity has seldom been more blatant than it was at Sadler's Wells in the early 1800s under the management of Charles Dibdin, Jnr. In his 1808 Easter pantomime *Thirty Thousand; or, Harlequin's Lottery*, he went out of his way to 'plug' the then famous Mr Bish, who was one of the contractors for the National Lottery and for whom Dibdin wrote (and was 'very liberally' paid for writing) complimentary songs that were printed on the back of the Lottery Bills which were distributed to the public. Such bills would carry simple little verses like:

The lottery contract's fallen to Bish;
    Heighho says Fortune:
There isn't a man that is more to your wish,
And he'll carve you a slice of his Capital dish,
With his rowly, poly, luck and Lottery!
    Heighho! says Rowly.

Dibdin actually set one scene of *Harlequin's Lottery* in Bish's Lottery Office on Cornhill. He was subsequently approached by numerous tradesmen to exhibit their premises on his popular stage. The advantages were plain. As he wrote: 'The Proprietor of some Manufactory, a Scene of which I introduced, actually, on the first Night of the Piece, sent his Foreman, with from 150 to 200 of his Men, to the Wells, and paid 2/- each, for their Admission into the Pit. At the least, all those connected with any House etc. we so advertised, were sure to advertise Sadler's Wells in return; and it was a maxim with our Partner, Mr Hughes, that the most effective advertisement for a Theatre, was a "walking advertisement".'

The methods of working such advertisements into the pantomime have varied enormously down the years. In 1856 we find a character in *The Magic Mistletoe; or, Harlequin Humbug and the Shams of London*

at the Strand Theatre who was actually called 'Sir Rowland Macassar'. Rowland's Macassar Hair Oil (against the ravages of which on
chairbacks and sofas the antimacassar had been designed) frequently
advertised in pantomime programmes.

More original was London perfumier Eugene Rimmel, whose dis-
creet credit 'The Perfumes by Mr. Rimmel' sometimes blossomed
into more extravagant form as at the Theatre Royal, Liverpool, in
1862. The pantomime was *Harlequin and the Three Bears; or, Little
Goldenhair and the Fairies*, and its grand transformation scene ended in
the 'Fuchsia Bower of the Fairies in the Gardens of Never-Fading
Bloom'. The programme contains the announcement: 'During this
Scene the perfume of Flowers will be diffused throughout the Theatre
by means of Rimmel's Perfume Vaporizer patented by Mr E. Rimmel 96, Strand, London.' An advertisement in the programme explained that 'Mr Rimmel, the perfumer, has recently invented a small
apparatus termed the "perfume vaporizer" for diffusing a grateful
vapour in crowded assemblies or private dwellings, which effectually
destroys unpleasant vapours.' It went on to claim that 'it diffuses the
perfume of any flower in all its freshness and purity, emitting the
balmy fragrance of a blooming parterre on a fine spring morning.'

And so the 'commercials' roll on: 'Babes' in the wood in the 1920s
who were dressed as 'Bisto Kids'; a 1929 *Sleeping Beauty* with a scene
set in 'Meccanoland' where 'dainty little children, dressed in the
knickers and jerseys of the familiar Meccano boy, romp about
amongst full sized models made up of gigantic Meccano parts.' Even
the frequently-heard modern references to the 'Fairy Liquid' have
their ancient and venerable counterparts. In an 1892 *Little Bo-Peep*, for
example, Prince Poppetty challenges Squire Oofless (of Oofless Hall,
Pebbly Beach, Stoneybrokeshire) to a duel, with the cry: 'Draw, sir!
This can only be washed out by blood!' To which the Squire coolly
replies: 'I wouldn't use that. Try Sapolio!' 'Sapolio' was the brand
name of a household soap.

Future historians will find our own age just as sharply mirrored in
the scripts and reviews of pantomime. They will have little difficulty
in understanding the point being made by the 1973 Widow Twankey
who, in bemoaning the fact that she is getting fewer and fewer bras-
sieres at her laundry each week, blames it on 'this women's liberation';
nor will it be difficult to discover why a 1983 Dame sang a song
called 'I'm on the Dole'. But what, one wonders, will they make
of the Ugly Sister who, at the end of one scene, suddenly glances
heavenwards and commands: 'Beam us up, Scottie!'

ELEVEN
TRICKS·TRAPS·AND·TRANSFORMATIONS

n inventory that was taken of the scenery, properties and the like stored at the Theatre Royal, Covent Garden, midway through John Rich's period of management includes the following items:

> Medusa's cave and 3 pieces Grotto that change to Country house; inside of Merlin's Cave, outside of ditto; dairy; Inn Yard; Arch to Waterfall; the sea back cloth; 6 ground pieces to the trees in 'Orpheus'; the burning mountain, two pieces; 8 wings to great machine in 'Rape'; the great travelling machine made for 'Orpheus'; 6 handles and 12 brackets for the sea; a barrel, groove and weights to trees in 'Orpheus'; the statue in the 'Rape', the buck basket, the tubb, egg, wheelbarrow, dunghill, child's stool, gardener's basket, a raree show, 3 green banks, a lyon; cupid's chariot, two rain trunks and frames; a hook to draw off the cloudings; a flying chariot; three lightning sticks; 2 barrels, weights, wires and scaffoldings to dragon; 86 thunder balls; and 192 tinn candlesticks.

It was from this and similar stuff (the inventory runs over many pages) that Rich created the visual 'magic' and splendour that was an essential part of the first pantomimes. César de Saussure, whose letters written from London in the eighteenth century have been edited as *A Foreign View of England in the Reigns of George I and George II*, saw several of Rich's productions. Of his *Orpheus and Eurydice* he wrote:

> This piece is full of wonderfull springs and clock work machinery. When Orpheus learns that his beloved is dead, he retires into the depth of the stage and plays his lyre; presently out of the rock appear little bushes; they gradually grow up into trees, so that the stage resembles a forest. On these trees flowers blossom, then fall off, and are replaced by different fruits, which you see grow and ripen. Wild beasts, lions, bears, tigers creep out of the forest attracted by Orpheus and his lyre. It is altogether the most surprising and charming spectacle you can imagine.

The rising of the trees obviously involved the use of the 'barrel groove and weights to trees in "Orpheus"' referred to in the inventory; the 'trees', one assumes, rising from beneath through slots in the stage (forerunners of the 'sloats' or 'slotes' of the Victorian theatres) and utilising a counter-weight system.

This was the world of 'green paper trees' and 'gilt apples'; of 'new-burnished copper Dragons' and enormous birds 'formed of leather covered with raven's feathers' that flapped their wings by means of wires, and were frequently of 'such prodigious bigness' that they could be made to 'flap out the candles'. It was the world of 'oiled-paper moons', in which the sound of thunder was achieved by rolling cannon balls down wooden channels set in the roof (the 'thunder-run' they called it), and lightning by throwing powdered resin or the like into candles set high above the stage. 'One shower of snow in the whitest French paper', announced the *Tatler* in a mock-inventory of theatrical properties and effects published in 1709. It was just such a shower that Pope had in mind when he wrote of Rich sitting at ease 'Mid snows of paper, and fierce hail of pease.' The *Tatler's* list also included 'spirits of Brandy for Lambent Flames and Apparitions', a sea 'consisting of a dozen large waves; the tenth bigger than ordinary, and a little damaged', and 'a dozen and a Half of Clouds, trimm'd with Black, and well conditioned'.

It was a world created jointly by machinists, painters and carpenters. The importance of the pantomime carpenters (who in those days also 'worked' the show) is tilted at in Fielding's *Tumble-Down Dick*:

MACHINE: Pray, let the carpenters take care that all the scenes be drawn in exact time and tune, that I may have no bungling of the tricks; for a trick is no trick, if not performed with great dexterity. Mr Fustian, in tragedies and comedies, and such sort of things, the audiences will make great allowances; but they expect more from an entertainment; here, if the least thing be out of order, they never pass it by.

FUSTIAN: Very true, sir, tragedies do not depend so much upon the carpenter as you do.

A hundred years later, Tom Dibdin, as a writer, had to confess that 'the best pantomime ever constructed depends on strings, and flaps, and traps; and, if machinery does not work, the pantomime must fail.' By the 1850s it was being suggested that the stage carpenter only really worked once a year, at pantomime time, when 'the genius of stage carpentry' was properly appreciated and authors, actors, composers, musicians, and 'such mere idlers' sank into their 'proper insignificance'.

The pantomime's preoccupation with trick and spectacle has been deprecated and ridiculed by sobersides right down the years. When Rich, in *The Necromancer; or, Harlequin Dr Faustus*, introduced a working windmill and a fire-spitting dragon, the satirists had a field-day. In a piece called *The British Stage; or, the Exploits of Harlequin*, which was written in the form of a farce 'for the study' and printed in 1724, the anonymous author introduced an assortment of

148

devils, conjurors, harlequins, ghosts, a windmill and numerous animals, among them a dragon, an ass (representing 'The Town'), and
an owl (representing 'The Theatre'). He gave the last three these
speeches:

ASS: Adzooks I would not give a farthing for a play without a windmill
in't. Methinks there's so much wit in it, that the Author of it deserves
a statue of brass.

DRAGON: You're right. What is a play without a Windmill? Then there must be
a Dragon, or the drama will not be complete.

OWL: And an owl, too, to furnish proper music. Observe the harmony of
this voice. (*And he hollows.*)

ASS: Excellent! Surely this is the politest age of the world; it so suits my
elegant inclinations, that I bless and hug myself with the thought of
coming into life at a time so gallant.

The scenic style of the early pantomimes, with their heavy depend-
ence on stage machinery and spectacular trick-work, in fact harked
directly back to the work of the designers and technicians of Renaissance Italy as expounded by the likes of Sebastiano Serlio in his *Regole
generali di architettura*' (published in English translation in 1611), and
Nicola Sabbattini in his *Pratica di fabricar scene è machine ne' teatri* (*The
Practice of Making Scenes and Machines*). It was a visual style that had
been introduced into England for the great Court Masques of Inigo
Jones. However, very little of it had spilled out into the public theatres
by the time the Puritans closed them down in 1642, and when they
re-opened some twenty years later the style, though revived, was on
a much-reduced scale. By the eighteenth century spectacle had all but
vanished, except in the opera, and in the pantomime as devised by
Rich. Indeed, in the drama even new scenery was a rarity, old stock
stuff being constantly re-used. Tate Wilkinson recalled one scene that
had been in use at Covent Garden for over forty years. 'I never see
those wings slide on,' he wrote, 'but I feel as if seeing my very old
acquaintance unexpectedly.'

Rich's principal machinist for his staging of *Orpheus and Eurydice*
was a man called Sam Hoole, whose triumphant contribution to the
piece was a mechanical serpent described as being 'of enormous size'
and covered all over with gold and green scales, of which it was said,
'nothing ever crawled across the stage with more accomplished sin-
uosity'. It 'twirled and twisted and wriggled' about, its eyes shining,
its head upraised, 'making an awful but very natural hissing noise'. Its
task was, of course, to kill Eurydice, and that done, it shot off behind
the stage curtain 'with a velocity scarcely credible'. It is said to have
been so life-like 'as to frighten half the ladies who see it'. The whole

town, including the entire royal family, turned out to see Sam Hoole's serpent which, according to one estimate, had cost more than £200 to make. Unfortunately, its success went to Hoole's head. He became obsessed with making serpents. He would make nothing else. He made them in all sizes, and they 'crawled about his shop as if he had been chief snake-catcher to the Furies'. Alas, there was no sale for them and 'with nests of them yet unsold' Hoole was finally 'ruined, bankrupt and undone'.

Equally famous as a machinest was Drury Lane's Alexander Johnson, 'celebrated for his superior taste and skill in the construction of flying chariots, triumphal cars, palanquins, banners, wooden children to be toss'd over battlements, and straw heroes and heroines to be hurl'd down a precipice'. He was further famous for his wickerwork lions, his pasteboard swans, and 'all the sham birds and beasts appertaining to a theatrical menagerie'. On one occasion, having just managed to secure a sneak preview of a real live elephant that the rival Covent Garden Theatre intended to introduce into its pantomime *Harlequin and Padmanaba*, Johnson is said to have remarked contemptuously: 'I should be very sorry if I couldn't make a much better elephant than that at any time.' And he did. Indeed, it was afterwards written: 'The elephant in Blue Beard, stuffed by his hand, wound round his lithe proboscis as spruce as he who roared in Padmanaba.'

The early pantomimes were stuffed full of technical tricks. We find, for example:

> The Guardian and Clown enter. The former seats himself on a bench, which is converted into a railing and encloses him, while a block of wood, on which the Clown was seated, extends itself upwards to a pole of an amazing height, diversified with a variety of colours, and exhalts him in the air - while this is acting in the front of the stage, some sailing boats appear on the Thames, which have a most beautiful and picturesque appearance.

Especially popular were 'trick' changes - 'a box into a table, splendidly furnished; a Baggage Waggon into a Stage Coach; a Windmill into a ship; and a Colonnade into a Triumphal Car.' Such changes were accomplished by means of hinged flaps. The '3 pieces Grotto that change to Country house' which is listed on the Covent Garden inventory would seem to have been just such a piece of trick scenery. It probably stood as a three-fold screen representing a grotto and, at a given cue, was 'changed' into a Country House by the tripping and falling of the hinged flaps. Such flaps might also sometimes be 'sprung' so that they could flap upwards.

A typical trick of Grimaldi's day was to 'change' a post-chaise into a wheel-barrow. Of this operation we are told:

> The chaise is to be merely a profile but when the door opens a piece of hanging canvas is to give the appearance of substantiality. On entering, Pantaloon is to stand in a wheel-barrow. When he undoes a brace, the upper part of the chaise will be hauled up while the lower sinks through a cut in the stage and into the cellar leaving the wheel-barrow exposed.

These stage 'cuts' were essential to the achievement of pantomime 'magic'. Writing in the 1880s, Leopold Wagner described them in some detail:

> They appear as a series of planks, or pairs of planks, let into the surface and running straight across from wing to wing, at intervals of every few feet in the stage-depth. When required these 'cuts' are opened by sliding the 'planks' apart from the centre, and in the narrow space presented, sufficient room is afforded for the passage of the scenes to be sent up slowly or shot up for quick-change purposes.
>
> When a group of figures have to ascend, say, mermaids in the transformation, it will be necessary to make a larger and much wider opening in the stage which is easily affected, since between each of the cuts, the entire flooring can be taken up in separate square portions, thus allowing an opening of any dimensions to be made at the very point required. The ascension of the group, however, is more difficult, being wholly dependent upon the raising machinery in the cellar.

A good deal of pantomimic fun was derived from the use of the numerous and varied stage 'traps' through which performers could be 'shot' onto the stage or permitted, apparently, to vanish through it. Thus did the Demon King 'shoot' into view; Harlequin dive through the wall or the clock-face; and Clown get 'hammered into the ground'. Basically, a 'down-trap' enabled a performer to take a header through the stage or merely to vanish feet first through it. All he had to do was stand on a flapped India-rubber mat which would allow him to pass through it and immediately closed over him; he would then be caught in a hammock or blanket suspended beneath the stage.

The most famous of all the traps was the 'star trap', with its circular opening and series of triangular-shaped segments of wood hinged around the circumference their points meeting in the middle. Through this, with the aid of perhaps six men and a weight of 4 hundredweight, a performer could 'materialise' and be catapulted 14 feet or more above the stage floor. To quote Leopold Wagner again:

> During the 'fight scene' in the pantomime at some of our theatres, upwards of a dozen traps of various kinds are often 'open' from which it may be inferred that the position of the actor having to pick his way between them, as he combats the sprites springing up or diving below on all sides, must be more than ordinarily dangerous.

No matter how elaborate the 'tricks' and mechanical devices of the pantomime, however, it was ultimately a remarkable succession of brilliantly talented painters, artists in their own right, many of them Royal Academicians, who bestowed upon these shows their crowning scenic glory. One of the earliest of these, John Rich's scenic artist, George Lambert, who has been mentioned already, was himself a powerful landscape painter in the manner of Gaspar Poussin. It has even been suggested that a number of his pictures have since been sold as Poussin's. From 1771 onwards at Drury Lane, David Garrick had the services of perhaps the most famous of them all, the great Alsatian painter Phillipe Jacques de Loutherbourg. This was the same De Loutherbourg whose 'miraculous powers' were acknowledged by Mr Puff in Sheridan's *The Critic* (he continued as scenic artist to the Lane when it came under the playwright's management). De Loutherbourg brought a new form of illusionist 'realism' to stage design, his many innovations including the introduction of set scenes and raking pieces which broke up and gave new depth to the old wing-and-border stage. This had hitherto been an arid box-like affair, framed by vertical 'wing' pieces that stood on either side of the stage and 'borders' that hung horizontally above it. De Loutherbourg also introduced startling new effects in lighting and sound. He introduced new elements of colour into stage lighting by placing squares of vari-coloured silk in front of the lamps; and by using pivoting silk screens created the effect of clouds fleeting across his painted landscapes that were in themselves marvels of perspective painting. He may be said to have brought a vivid touch of 'nature' to theatrical design.

> What to spectators such new pleasure brings,
> From wonders done by cloudings, flats and wings;
> The Painter custom marks, he notes the clime,
> And then adapts his scenes to place and time;
> Observes what seasons, morning, noon or night,
> Sun-rise, sun-set, and Stage devoid of light.

Thus, in his *Recollections*, published in 1826, the Irish actor and dramatist John O'Keefe paid a special verse tribute to some of the scene painters he had worked with – among them, once again, de Loutherbourg who, for the 1785 pantomime 'OMAI; or, a Trip Round the World' with its theme of Captain Cook and the South Sea Islands, had based both scenery and costumes on sketches made by John Webber during Cook's last voyage. Omai, incidentally, was the name of a South Sea islander who had been brought to England previously and who returned home, much Europeanised, on the fatal final expedition. Of Loutherbourg's work for this piece, O'Keefe wrote:

> A Loutherbourg's bold genius took full range,
> Through Cook's South Islands, savage, wild and strange;
> In pieces cut, broad scene that seem'd so nigh,
> Thus spreading miles of distance to the eye;
> Opaque he made transparent on occasion,
> Volcano, sun-set, or a conflagration;
> And my Omai furnish'd him with scope,
> To give a full effect to ardent hope.

One of the major scenic innovations of the early nineteenth century was the introduction into the theatre of the moving diorama. This was, in effect, a vastly long canvas back-cloth (perhaps 270 feet or more in length) which, when wound from a vertical roller on one side of the stage onto a similar one on the other, gave the impression of 'moving' scenery. Especially effective in the representation of 'journeys', it was first seen in Covent Garden's 1820 pantomime *Harlequin and Friar Bacon; or, The Brazen Head*, of which *The Times* wrote:

> The transformations of the pantomime are not numerous: one of the best is the change of the lighthouse at Holyhead into a ship, in which the lovers embark, and cross the Channel. It is accompanied with a mechanical contrivance, both new and ingenious, by which the back scene is put in motion, showing a succession of sea views till the vessel anchors in the Bay of Dublin.

No scenic artist ever made better use of the diorama than Clarkson Stanfield, for whose brush it might have been specifically intended. Stanfield was born in Sunderland in 1793 and at an early age joined the Navy. He was at one time a ship-mate of Douglas Jerrold's aboard H.M.S. *Namur*, when Jerrold (later to become famous as the author of the nautical melodrama, *Black-Eyed Susan*), was a middy and Stanfield a foremast man. In 1815, disabled by an accident, he left the service, and having already painted scenes for ship's theatricals, turned to scene-painting for a living. He went on to become not only one of the greatest theatrical painters but, subsequently, one of the greatest of seascape artists. With his 'jolly red sailor face', he was known to his friend Charles Dickens as 'my tarry friend' or 'dear old Stanny', and we can see him arriving at Tavistock House to paint the scenes for one of Dickens' private theatrical performances with 'seventy pots of paint, a ball of string, and an umbrella for measuring boards, backcloth and curtain'. Stanfield was one of several artists commissioned to execute frescoes for the pavilion in the gardens of Buckingham Palace, and Macready, having viewed the work of them all, pronounced: 'Stanfield's looks best!'

Some of the dioramas painted by Stanfield for the Theatre Royal, Drury Lane, have been described by E. L. Blanchard. For the 1825 *Harlequin Jack of All Trades*, he executed a 'panoramic display' showing 'the adventures of a man-of-war, from the launch at Dover, its encounter with a gale, the wreck, and the towing into a foreign port'. For *The Queen Bee; or, Harlequin and the Fairy Hive* of 1828 it was a 'moving diorama' representing 'Spithead at Sunrise, the entrance to Portsmouth Harbour, the Dockyard, Gosport, the Isle of Wight with the Royal Yacht Club, Cowes Regatta, the Needles by Moonlight, the Ocean, and the Rock of Gibraltar.' As Blanchard commented: 'He created, and afterwards painted out with his own brush, more scenic masterpieces than any other man, and in his time Clown and Pantaloon tumbled over and belaboured one another in front of the most beautiful and dazzling pictures which were ever presented to the eye of the playgoer.'

Stanfield's 1829 diorama, incidentally, concluded with 'the striking effect of the Falls of Virginia Water' in which thirty-nine tons of real water were used. Not that 'real water' was anything new to pantomime. Sadler's Wells, under Charles Dibdin's management, had huge water tanks set both in and above the stage for the display of aquatic spectacles, and Garrick had 'happily introduced a cascade of real water' into Drury Lane's pantomime in 1753. (To this day, one sees on Christmas bills the alluring line: 'Speciality – Spectacular Waterfall'.)

Next to Stanfield, the most distinguished scene painter of the nineteenth century was William Beverley, who began his career as a scenic artist at the Theatre Royal, Manchester, and went on to work at the Lyceum and, for thirty years, at Drury Lane. Of his work for Planché's fairy extravaganzas George Henry Lewes (writer, critic, and famous for his long-standing liaison with George Eliot) wrote: 'One had dreamed of fairy-land like this.' Beverley may be said to have invented what became known as 'the transformation scene', when the principal purpose of it was no longer the simple 'transformation' of characters, but rather the exhibition of an ever-more splendid display of scenic virtuosity, when the gauzes lifted slowly, one by one, to reveal what Arthur Quiller Couch has described as a 'new and unimagined world, stretching deeper and still deeper as the scenes were lifted; a world in which solid walls crumbled and forests melted, and loveliness broke through the ruins, unfolding like a rose.'

It was a moment in the pantomime described more cynically by W. S. Gilbert as:

... the foolish culmination in a weary 'transformation',
Whose complete elaboration takes a twenty-minutes' space!

Sir Augustus Harris, the ebullient manager of the Theatre Royal, Drury Lane, and producer in the 1880s and 1890s of its extravagantly spectacular Christmas shows, once referred to Wagner's *Das Rheingold* as 'a damned pantomime'. It was a description which Bernard Shaw considered 'thoroughly sound'. Shaw went on to suggest that had it not been for the pantomime, the British would, in all probability, never have been able to stage the piece, because the stage machinist, the costumier, and the illusionist scene painter, so long neglected by the legitimate stage, would have been extinct. Thus, 'nobody would have known how to work the changes, to suspend the Rhine maidens, to transform Alberich into a dragon, to assemble the black clouds that are riven by Donner's thunderbolts, or to light up Froh's rainbow bridge.' Shaw concluded that 'we owe the present enormously effective form of the Nibelung tetralogy, a work which towers among the masterpieces of the world's art, to the persistence of just such entertainments as Aladdin.'

TWELVE
YOU·ARE·ALWAYS·SURE·TO·FETCH·THEM

I.

How d'ye do? wst, wst!

How are you? wst, wst!

You are always sure to fetch them with a wst, wst, wst!

Come along, wst, wst!

Nothing wrong, wst, wst!

Oh! wont you come and take a walk and wst, wst, wst!

When 'The Great' Macdermott's song 'You Are Always Sure to Fetch Them with a Wst, Wst, Wst!' was sung in pantomime at the beginning of the 1880s, it was seen by many people as symptomatic of what the pantomime, 'as performed in most provincial and several London theatres', had in their view become by then – 'a mere mass of coarse vulgarity and worse'.

As one irate correspondent wrote to *The Theatre* in October 1881: 'To see Cinderella represented as a fast young person, a singer of "Wst! Wst! Wst!" and its kindred, a beef-ankled hammerer of imbecile breakdowns – ugh!' Earlier in his piece he had remarked ominously: 'Small wonder many of the boys develop a taste for music-halls, and surprise their exemplary parents by going utterly to the bad.'

The following February, W. Davenport Adams, in an article headed 'The Decline of Pantomime', contributed to the same journal, similarly attacked 'the music-hall element'. He pointed out that such songs as 'Wst, wst, wst!' would never be tolerated 'by pater-familias in his drawing-room, and yet, when he takes his children to the pantomime, they are the most prominent portion of the entertainment'. Of the music-hall performers generally, he wrote: 'They have the effect of familiarising audiences, and children especially, with a style and kind of singing, dancing, and "business" which, however it may be relished by a certain class of the population, ought steadily to be confined to its original habitat.'

In fact, artists from the 'halls' had started to infiltrate the pantomime towards the end of the 1860s. In 1866, E. L. Blanchard, then at the height of his forty-year reign at the Lane, had tilted at 'the easy airs of Music Hall society' and the introduction of their 'Costermonger Joe' type of song. And in reviewing the 1869–70 pantomime at the New East London Theatre, *The Illustrated London News* had noted: 'Several music-hall celebrities are specially engaged in its representation.' But the crowning success of the 'invasion', as it was called, was proclaimed in the December of 1880 when music-hall artists, for the first time, headed the pantomime company at the Theatre Royal, Drury Lane. They had been brought in by the Lane's new manager, Augustus Harris, who had taken over just the previous year.

Harris, the son of a celebrated theatrical manager and producer, was, at twenty-seven years old, the youngest manager the Lane had ever had. By the time he died, some seventeen years later, he'd won the nickname 'Druriolanus' (in addition to the less imposing one of 'Gusarris'). Outside the Theatre Royal, on the corner of Catherine Street, there stands to this day a drinking fountain that carries a bust of him and is dedicated to his memory.

When Harris arrived at the Lane in 1879, the pantomime there had long since been settled in a cosy rut. Blanchard (whom Harris referred to as 'The Old Man of the Sea') was onto his twenty-eighth 'Annual'; and the Vokes family, 'a remarkable, if undisciplined and aggressive troupe' of five who had regularly dominated the Lane's pantomimes under the previous management, were preparing yet again to monopolise all the principal parts, as they had done for the past decade.

The Vokes, the children of a theatrical costumier, were talented all-rounders – dancers, singers, acrobats and actors. Led by Fred Vokes ('the man with elastic legs'), the troupe included his three sisters, Jessie, Rosina and Victoria, and an adopted 'brother', Walter Fawdon. (Rosina, once described as 'the life and soul of that merry family', was later replaced by Fred's wife, Bella.) Since their first pantomime appearance together at the Lyceum back in the 1860s they had been enormously successful and hugely popular, but by the time Harris arrived at the Lane the press was beginning to complain that 'they dance exactly as they have danced for years past', and that 'through attempting to do too much', they 'eventually succeeded in provoking a feeling of depression'. As an indication of their domination of pantomime, the Lane's 1874 *Aladdin* can be cited: Fred Vokes appeared as Abanazar; Fawdon as his dumb slave Kazrac; Victoria as Aladdin; Rosina as the Princess Badroulbadour; and Jessie as the Genius of the Lamp.

The Vokes survived one year under Harris's management, but by 1880 had departed to Covent Garden. At Drury Lane that year the company was headed by Kate Santley, who had graduated from the 'halls' to opera *bouffe*; Arthur Roberts, once described as 'the comedian *in excelsis* for the man about town'; and James Fawn, sometime singer of that famous morning-after-the-night-before lament, 'It Must Have Been the Lobster, It Couldn't Have Been the Booze'. The 'music-hall element' had arrived, 'wrecking the expected cue with the wanton wit of gagging'.

By the December of the following year, Blanchard was writing in his diary: 'Look over the ghastly proofs of my Drury Lane Annual, in which I find my smooth and pointed lines are turned into ragged prose and arrant nonsense. Consider the payment to me as an equivalent for the harm done to my literary reputation.' A sympathetic reviewer that year acknowledged: 'Mr E. L. Blanchard's text is cut down to the very narrowest limit. I don't think I ever followed a book of a pantomime of which so few lines were spoken. The author's text has been literally wiped out.'

The Illustrated London News, however, considered it 'a capital pantomime' (it was, indeed, a triumphant success), but took Blanchard to task for, of all things, the brevity of the title. It was called simply *Robinson Crusoe* and the reviewer, dismayed, asked: 'Where is Harlequin?' There was, in fact, a Harlequinade, but that wasn't good enough. He found the 'terrible brevity' of the title most unseasonal. 'To be properly redolent of Christmas', he insisted, 'it should have been called "Harlequin Robinson Crusoe; or, the Spirit of Youth and the Demon Vice, the Storm-Lashed Lugger, the Enchanted Silver Fish, the Bold Buccaneer, and the King of the Cannibal Islands."' This same reviewer – it was George Augustus Sala – reviewing the pantomime at the Surrey Theatre in which 'The Great' Macdermott sang the lines 'Whenever I sees a copper/I always tells a whopper', felt it necessary to explain to his readers: 'A "copper" is a police-constable.' The artists from the halls were, through pantomime, reaching a whole new audience, and one that would never have dreamed of attending a music-hall.

Over the next few years Harris increasingly packed his shows with stars from the music-halls, none more so than his 1892 *Little Bo-Peep, Little Red Riding-Hood and Hop o' My Thumb*, in which Dan Leno appeared as Daddy Thumb, Herbert Campbell as his wife Goody Thumb, Little Titch as Hop o' My Thumb, Ada Blanche as Little Boy Blue, Arthur Williams as Dame Mary Quite Contrary, Marie Loftus as Little Bo-Peep, and Marie Lloyd as Little Red Riding-Hood. The essential music-hall tone of the piece, so different from the rhymed elegance and studied prettiness of Blanchard's work, may be judged from this typical scene:

DAME: Now, where is my daughter Red Riding-Hood?

POLLY PERKINS: Oh, where's Red Riding-Hood? What do *you* think?

SALLY WATERS: Where's Red Riding-Hood indeed! Ask where is Boy Blue and then put two and two together!

MISS MUFFET: No – put one and one together.

ALL: Here she is!

Red Riding-Hood runs on.

RED RIDING-HOOD: What cher, good old ma?

DAME: Child! I have to correct you of a bad habit. 'What yer good old ma' is distinctly low. Your sister – your foster sister Bo-Peep – would never use language *a la Romano*.

RED RIDING-HOOD: Well then, what are you going to back for the Derby, old woman?

DAME (*with dignity*): I am not an old woman, and I am not going to back anything for the Derby. I want to keep on the right side of the ledger. Now Red Riding-Hood, look here, here's your grandmother ill again. I'll get you to take her something in a basket, but *nothing* in a bottle. I'll give her something that will settle her for good; something that will make her squirm.

(*Exits into cottage*).

RED RIDING-HOOD: A visit to Grandma! Ugh! How lively! She's generally taken a little too much – well, you know – tea, and if she hasn't she wants to. Still, it's an excuse to stroll through the wood . . .

Shortly after this, a Chorus 'behind the stage' pipes up with:

Little Bo-Peep, she tends her sheep,
With her you always will find them,
She leaves 'em to roam, but they always come home
While she stays flirting behind 'em!

The script is pervaded by a fondness for sex and alcohol. Even the wolf (a self-proclaimed socialist) is a drunk. He makes his first entrance in Scene 3, which is set outside 'The Spotted Sun', the stage direction reading: 'Mr Wolf very drunk, fired out of door by Barman.' Outside the pub Mrs Wolf catches up with him as he is now vociferously demanding 'a bottle of sorra warrer', and a 'matrimonial fight' breaks out. The script at this point contains the note: 'Any special business of the Bros Griffiths could come in here,' it being suggested that this famous speciality act might like to insert their 'Burlesque Kangaroo Boxing Match'.

The music-hall tone also dominated the music. The Dame sang 'I Haven't Been Kissed for Weeks'; Daddy and Goody Thumb rendered 'I'll Give Him Ta-ra-ra-boom-de-ay'; Marie Lloyd's Red Riding-

Hood had 'Give Me Some Almond Rock' and a version of 'Oh Mr Porter' that included the lines 'Oh Mr Boy Blue – what shall we do/ We've captured both the wolves and now we'll take them to the Zoo'; and the Grand Finale was sung to the tune of 'The Man Who Broke the Bank at Monte Carlo':

> As you go along
> In joyful song,
> Now mind you all declare,
> With most contented air,
> That you've had good Christmas fare,
> Here at our jolly Pantomime,
> You've enjoyed a better time
> Than the man who broke the bank at Monte Carlo.

Some people looked nostalgically back to a time when 'White-chapel songsters' and other music-hall novelties were 'not considered indispensable for success', and especially objected to the introduction of 'clog dancers, gymnasts, contortionists' and the like. In fact, such speciality acts had been with the pantomime from the beginning. John Rich himself had employed 'Schwartz's Dancing Dogs', and frequently used rope-dancers and tumblers. In the 1780s and 1790s the renowned pugilist Daniel Mendoza had appeared in a number of pantomimes, among them one at Birmingham called *Robinson Crusoe; or, Friday Turned Boxer*, in which his 'speciality' spot was a sparring match with Man Friday. Drury Lane's 1826 pantomime included an appearance by Ramo Samee, the Indian juggler; and the following year its *Harlequin and Cock Robin; or, the Babes in the Wood* concluded with 'various dances on the tight and slack rope, which excited great astonishment'. Reviewing the Surrey Theatre's 1844 pantomime, *The Illustrated London News* tells us that 'Herr Von Joel considerably added to the evening's amusement, by giving his extraordinary imitations of Beasts, Birds, etc.' Down the years we also find 'feats of strength by the Italian brothers'; and appearances by Professor Anderson, 'The Wizard of the North'; Master Hiram, 'The Juvenile Leotard'; Cinquevalli, the great juggler (it was said that he could play billiards better on his own back than most people could on a table); and Dezano, the contortionist 'who gives some clever illustrations which have nothing whatever to do with the play'.

The method of launching into such specialities has changed very little between Queen Victoria's day and our own. Almost a century ago, for example, we find a couple of comedy aerialists standing outside Old Mother Hubbard's home in a Bristol pantomime won-

dering how best they can contrive to pass the time until the Dame
wakes up:

STOUT: Let's practise our gymnastics, what d'ye say?
GREEN: Oh, anything for fun, so fire away!

Visually, the late Victorian pantomimes, reflecting late Victorian
taste, tended towards the massive and the opulent. They were frequently studded with grand processions and lavishly extravagant ballet
sequences in which literally hundreds of supers, dancers, and
specially-recruited children might take part. None, however, was
more lavish and extravagant than those staged at Drury Lane under
Augustus Harris. Harris thought and worked in superlatives. His company was always 'the largest and most expensive' ever gathered together for a pantomime; his costumes always 'the most costly that
have ever been produced'; his spectacles the 'most brilliant and glittering' ever seen on a stage. It was 'nothing but the best' in a 'Gusarris'
show. On one occasion Harris announced: 'The ballet and chorus
have been most carefully selected, and will consist of a hundred pretty
girls, without a single ugly face amongst them.' In his 1881-2 *Robinson
Crusoe* he even had a *double* panorama, so that in a scene in which a
ship sailed up the Thames, *both* river banks could be seen. In the same
pantomime he staged a procession through the streets of London in
which every single trade of the town was 'either comically or prettily'
represented. We are told that 'M. Labhart, the celebrated property-
master' worked almost night and day for six months on this one
scene, 'a fact which speaks for itself.'

One of Harris's most celebrated processions was in the 1882-3
Sinbad the Sailor, in which every single king and queen of England
from William the Conqueror to Queen Victoria, all costumed with
immaculate historical accuracy, processed from the Tower of London
and 'welcomed the conquering heroes from Egypt'. (In September
that year a British army under Sir Garnet Wolseley had defeated the
revolt of Arabi Pasha at the battle of Tel-el-Kebir.) The 'conquering
heroes' in this scene were represented by 'an army of boys and girls,
fitted out and accoutred in the most wonderful little uniforms ever
devised. They represent the Army of Egypt under Sir Garnet Wolseley, in fighting trim, complete and accurate to every haversack and
button.'

But thirty-odd kings and queens and 'the Army of Egypt' was not
enough for Harris. He feared that 'the Kings and Queens by themselves, would not present such an imposing array', so, when they

161

finally marched forth from the Tower of London they were 'severally followed by so many knights, pages, and men-at-arms' that there were upwards of five hundred people on stage at once. The Drury Lane stage was described as looking 'like a town'. As Jimmy Glover once put it: 'Harris had a penchant for over-doing it.'

But Harris wasn't the only one. 'There is enough beauty, taste and richness at Covent Garden for at least two pantomimes,' wrote one critic in the 1880s. 'The mind wearies over so much elaborate spectacle. Ballet succeeds ballet until the attention becomes dazed and the wonder is how these young ladies can find time to change their dresses so many times.' A few years later, William Archer was to refer to 'these monster extravaganza-spectacles which flare forth each Boxing Night all over England, like the beacon-fires that heralded the Armada'.

2.

A glance at the pantomimes staged at the major provincial theatres during the 1885-6 season shows just how general the tendency toward spectacular ballet and processions had become. At the Grand Theatre, Leeds, we find a *Dick Whittington* that included a Ballet of Elves, 'an interesting procession of the trades typical of the various Yorkshire Towns', and 'a review of representatives of the troops of all nations'. In Edinburgh, the 'big show scene' of the Theatre Royal's *Babes in the Wood* was the 'Hall of Dazzling Light' in which 'dancers and bicyclists precede a wonderfully well-arranged procession of all nations'. The Lyceum in Edinburgh offered an *Ali Baba* that boasted 'a beautiful fan ballet and an equally good Oriental ballet', plus a troupe of 'wonderfully clever bicyclists'. And at the Grand Theatre, Glasgow, another *Ali Baba* was described as 'one of the most extensive and artistic spectacular displays to be seen out of London'.

Of this production, the roving critic wrote: 'Nothing could be better than the Eastern bazaar, with its pretty slave dance; and the robbers' prismatic cave, with its evolutions of the famous forty in their sparkling, golden-jewelled, electric armour is a particularly brilliant sight.' There was, too, an 'exceedingly brilliant' scene in Ali Baba's Palace which boasted a procession of 'splendidly attired guests' and an 'impressive Oriental Ballet'. All too frequently, as this critic pointed out, the actors in these pantomimes were completely overshadowed by the brilliancy of their surroundings. At the Princess's Theatre, Glasgow, however, Ramsey Danvers' Mrs Crusoe (the 'old woman' *par excellence* of the Scottish stage) managed to dominate the proceedings, despite competition from a 'Sailors' Ballet' and a 'Ballet of the Months adapted from "Excelsior"'.

At the Alexandra Theatre, Liverpool, that year, the production of *Cinderella* was described as 'mainly a great scenic display'. It included 'an historic procession by children', a fox hunt with an old English hunting chorus, and a 'really beautiful' Swan Ballet. In Manchester, we are told, the Theatre Royal and the Prince's Theatre vied with each other in the matter of scenery, the Royal's *Dick Whittington* winning by a short head on account of its Highgate Hill By Night scene complete with Ballet of Elves. The Prince's, however, laid claim to 'the best acting in the country pantomimes', Edith Brandon proving 'the ideal Cinderella', and Edward Righton and Walter Wardroper 'the funniest of sisters even seen'.

But it was the *Robinson Crusoe* at the Theatre Royal, Birmingham, that finally carried off the scenic palm in that spectacular season one hundred years ago:

> To particularise all the scenery would occupy more space than is at my disposal, but I cannot refrain from alluding to the effective nature of the ship scene, the beauty of the Fairy Queen's bower, and the brilliancy of the tropical island, with its ballet of squaws, its procession of tribes, and the final arrival of a British war ship. A ballet of fire fiends is wonderfully well done, and by way of contrast to this nothing could be better than the school scene with its seventy scholars decked out in Kate Greenaway costumes.

The star of the show was Vesta Tilley, for whom this critic (it was Austin Brereton) had nothing but praise, and of whom he wrote with obvious relief, 'There is no sign of the music-hall about her.' Mind, he was not so happy with some of the popular songs that cropped up in the provincial pantomimes that year, complaining that 'What Cheer, Ria?' and 'What a Happy Land is England' pursued him nearly everywhere.

So pleased was Brereton with Birmingham's *Robinson Crusoe* that he advised his readers to waste no time in 'finding their way to Euston, and travelling thence by the well-ordered, fast, and punctual trains of the London and North-Western Railway'. A few years previously 'pantomime trip trains' had started running from London to Leeds to afford people an opportunity of seeing the spectacularly lavish pantomimes being staged by Wilson Barrett at the Grand. Indeed, such a draw did Barrett's 'Annual' become that frequent excursion trains were laid on to ferry people from Manchester and other large towns.

Many provincial pantomimes were acknowledged as having been 'reconstructed and localised' from the work of London writers. 'Lyrics and locals by ...' is a recurring additional programme credit. Then, as now, local references were an essential ingredient that added fun and immediacy and also provided a 'burlesque' contrast between the lavish fantasy of the on-stage story and the work-a-day world outside. In many pantomimes such references would be limited, as they tend to be nowadays, to the odd line or two. There was a Dick Whittington who was told in the 1880s:

> If Princes ever come to Leeds, young man,
> They leave the Town as quickly as they can.

And there was the Whittington in Bristol in 1900 who, on hearing Bow Bells, exclaimed:

> What sweet sounds!
> Not like the bells of a Clifton Church
>   jangling out of tune!

But, on occasion, 'localisation' went a good deal further. A splendid example of a 'local' pantomime is one performed at the 'Theatre Royal, Agricultural Hall' in Walsall in 1883. It was called *Jack the Giant Killer; or, Harlequin Old Dame Trot and the Fairies of the Enchanted Glade*, and it was written by 'Mr F. Bousfield', the theatre's resident acting manager, who also played Dame Trot. The opening is set in 'Mischief's Forge and Workshop' where are discovered Discord ('a very bad spirit'), Vulcanite ('a ditto, ditto'), Dynamite ('a double distilled ditto, ditto, ditto'), other bad spirits too numerous to mention, and Mischief himself, described as the 'Presiding Genius and Managing Director of the above Unlimited Company – naughty and not very nice'.

DISCORD: Well, now to business; what brings you here?
But tell us the events of the closing year.

MISCHIEF: Well, first I must your kind attention call
To improvements at the Agricultural Hall;
The road outside, so long well-known to fame,
And designated charming, sweet Mud Lane,
Is now repaired, pedestrians inviting.
Though, I must say, it wants much better lighting.

DISCORD: Is that all?

MISCHIEF: No, the Railway Station, I don't doubt it,
Will be finished sometime, but they are
        very slow about it.

DISCORD: Slow and sure; can do no harm.

MISCHIEF: The same applies to the Sewage Farm!
'Twill purify the town, make us as sweet
        as honey;
But eighty thousand pounds is a tremendous
        lot of money.

DISCORD: There's one thing, though, we haven't yet.
Although it's wanted quite as much, I bet;
'Twould be a boon to great and small,
And that is a Public Market Hall!

MISCHIEF: That's true; on rainy days the public
have a treat
By going to purchase in the open street.

DISCORD: A Covered Market it should be; egad it
Has long been wanted, and its time we had it.

MISCHIEF: A truce to joking, and to business come:
Our friend the Giant, Fi fe fo fum . . .

. . . and we are suddenly whisked off into an exposition of the plot. But that is by no means the end of the local references. When, for example, some time later, Jack is told that he is destined to become the king's son-in-law, he very soon manages to turn the conversation from kings and man-eating giants back to locally more pressing issues:

JACK: Son-in-law! How will it come to pass?
Please illuminate – turn on the gas;
No stop! That phrase ain't right,
I mean turn on the electric light!

MISCHIEF: And what is that, my bold commissioner?

JACK: The electric light is a gas extinguisher.

MISCHIEF: And where can we see this wondrous light?

JACK: Almost in every town, and every night,
Many streets are lighted, and they say
that all shall:
But I haven't seen it yet in Walsall.
Though that's not strange, and ten to one
I'd bet it
When anything's invented, we're the last
to get it!
The tram-way, too, is also on a par,
They've laid some rails – but I haven't
seen a car!

Walsall itself pervades this *Jack the Giant Killer* from start to finish. Not that it lacked spectacle. One scene included 'Characteristic Dances of Holiday Juvenile Festivities' performed by 'highly-trained children too numerous to mention', and the Grand Transformation Scene, which preceded the three scenes of the Harlequinade, transported the audience to 'The Arcadian Bowers of Golden Palms', amid the exotic splendours of which, one imagines, the uncompleted tramway beyond the doors might momentarily be forgotten.

3.

A little over seven months before Mr Bousfield's *Jack the Giant Killer* opened in Walsall, and some seventy-odd miles to the north, at the People's Music Hall in Oldham, the twenty-two-year-old Dan Leno had been proclaimed 'Champion Clog Dancer of the World' at the end of a contest that had lasted for six whole days. Within half-a-dozen years of this he was to be acknowledged as the greatest pantomime artist since Grimaldi.

Leno was born George Galvin at Eve Court, Somers Town, in a part of London that was demolished to make way for St Pancras Station. His parents were small-time music-hall artists, and Dan made his first appearance, aged four, as 'Little George, the Infant Wonder, Contortionist and Posturer'. While he was still a child, his father died and his mother married again, her second husband working the halls under the name of 'Leno'. The family subsequently travelled the length and breadth of Britain with little Dan dancing on pub table-tops for coppers, and eventually branching out into comedy patter songs as 'The Great Little Leno, the Quintessence of Irish Comedians' (his father had, indeed, been Irish).

It was this mixture of song and monologue that was to make his name when he began to play the London halls in the mid-1880s, a diminutive figure with a mobile face and strange, tragic, enquiring eyes which 'seemed to look out far beyond the world that held its sides with laughter'. 'I have suffered, although I look so gay and kittenish. My word I have put up with something.' It was said of him that no matter what he did to his face, its air of wistfulness 'always conquered the pigments'. Yet no one could express happiness with more joyous intensity than Leno did, for example, in the song 'The Grass Widower', written for him by J. H. Woodhouse.

VERSE

I feel so over-joy'd, I do, for Mrs Tumkins, she
Was order'd by the doctors to take a trip to sea;
I don't mean for to go upon the ocean, oh! dear no;
But just to take a sniff, you know, where briny breezes blow.

Spoken: And she's gone away for a week - fancy being a grass widower for a week. This is the first week's holiday I've had since we've been married, and we've been married four years and six weeks come half past 11 tomorrow morning. When she told me the doctor had ordered her to go away for a week I said, 'Go away for two years'. I packed her up some currant cake - well, there were no currants in it, but the holes were there where the currants had been. And we took a cab. Well, when we got on the platform, I felt so overjoyed I could have cuddled the engine. I asked the guard what time the train went, he said 'In five minutes'. I said, 'Send it off in three, and there's a pot of four-half* for you'. He said, 'Shall I lock the lady in?' I said, 'Nail her in! Hammer her in!' And when the train left the station, I turned round and kissed all the porters; and I had two cabs home and ran between them. You know, she never would let me have a latch-key; but I've got three in my pocket now, and I've ordered another gross of 'em. I shall keep going in and out our house till I wear the lock out.

CHORUS

> Oh! what a day I'm going to have tomorrow!
> My liberty I will regain, no more to be put down;
> Oh! what a spree! I'll pawn, beg or borrow,
> For my old woman, for a week, has just gone out of town.

As the essayist E. V. Lucas wrote of him: 'Part of Leno's amazing success was his gift of taking you into his confidence. The soul of sympathy himself, he made you sympathetic too. He told you his farcical troubles as earnestly as an unquiet soul tells its spiritual ones. You had to share them. His perplexities became yours.'

> Where is there an article that compels you to tell more lies than an egg? There's something artful about an egg. There's mystery in it. Of course, there are three kinds of egg: there is the new-laid (which is nearly extinct); there's the fresh egg, which is almost the same as the new-laid, but with an additional *something* that makes all the difference. Then comes The Egg: that's the egg that causes all the trouble. It's only a little round white thing; but you can't tell what it's thinking about. You daren't kick it, and you daren't drop it. It's got no face. You can't get it to laugh. You simply look at it and say, 'Egg'!

Thus, Leno in the role of a grocer's assistant:

> On New Year's Day I made a resolution: I made up my mind that, whatever happened, I would always speak the truth – *whatever* happened, I would never tell another lie as long as I lived – and I was feeling *so* happy and comfortable and angelic about it as I was taking down the shutters in the morning when – what do you think? What *do* you think? The very first customer who came into the shop asked me – straight out – 'Are those eggs fresh?'

Two steps back, hands flung out in a mute despairing appeal, and the story was told. As Marie Lloyd once said: 'If we didn't laugh at him, we'd cry our eyes out.'

It was George Conquest who first took Leno into pantomime, engaging him to play Dame Durden in his 1886-7 *Jack and the Beanstalk* at the Surrey Theatre. 'A more amusing Dame Durden than Dan Leno it would not be easy to discover,' wrote one critic. The following year, Augustus Harris paid a visit to the Surrey to see Leno play Tinpany the Tinker in *Sinbad and the Little Old Man of the Sea*, and booked him at once for Drury Lane. Between 1888 and 1903 Leno was to appear in sixteen consecutive pantomimes at the Lane. Harris's

---

* An alcoholic drink, half-ale, half-stout that sold for fourpence a quart.

master-stroke was to team him with another famous music-hall comedian, Herbert Campbell, who had been playing pantomime there since 1882. Campbell was over six feet tall, weighed more than twenty stone, and with his huge voice and jolly red face, made the perfect foil for the small, wan, wiry Leno. But it was under Harris's successor, Arthur Collins, that Leno reached his peak as a pantomime performer. As James Glover, Musical Director at the Lane under both Harris and Collins, wrote: 'Leno's successes with Harris were as nothing compared to his triumphs with Collins. Harris let him come on and simply "be Dan Leno". Collins thought out the Leno style, and gave him the Leno material for the Leno triumph. Every funny situation or scene was built for him, first by the producer, and then written round by the librettist.'

The most successful of these producer/librettist collaborations was that of Collins and J. Hickory Wood, a Mancunian and one-time insurance clerk, who was to become Leno's first biographer. Take, for example, their 1900 *The Sleeping Beauty and the Beast*, in which Dan Leno appeared as Queen Ravia and Herbert Campbell as King Screwdolph, the Sleeping Beauty's royal parents, who awake from their long sleep to find that the country has become a republic and that they are powerless and penniless. In Scene 11 they are discovered walking in the Grove of the neighbouring Prince (who has been changed by the Wicked Fairy into 'The Beast!'). The Queen stops to pick a rose, but the moment she plucks it there is a fearful crash of thunder, and the scene is changed in a flash to 'The Enchanted Crystal Garden'. The pair of them, visibly shaken, stand there trembling, the Queen still holding the rose in her hand:

KING: Good gracious! What have you done?
QUEEN: I don't know! I think I must have pulled up the world by the roots.

There is music, and the Prince (in the guise of 'The Beast') enters, followed by his Guards.

PRINCE: Rash mortals, who have dared to pluck my flowers,
          You well may tremble. Numbered are your hours.
KING: I do believe he's going to kill us.
QUEEN: Well, let's talk to him nicely, and perhaps he won't.
KING: Yes, but he talks in rhyme.
QUEEN: Well, *we'll* talk in rhyme.
KING: Can we?
QUEEN: We'll try. You begin.
KING:
(to Prince): Although you've caught us in the act of sneaking –
QUEEN: He *should* say prigging – that's his way of speaking.

168

KING: We only took the flower as a joke.

QUEEN: We are a pair of monarchs – stony broke. (*To King*) Here, it isn't fair! I'm finding all the rhymes.

KING: Never mind! You're doing very nicely.
(*To Prince*) As you may know, we have a lovely daughter.

QUEEN: A very clever girl, and *I* have taught her.

KING: Who simply dotes upon the scent of roses –

QUEEN: As ev'rybody does – if they have noses.

KING: And since, from many causes, she does suffer –

QUEEN: We thought we'd give her this, because – we luff her.

KING: We couldn't help it, for we love her dearly.

QUEEN: And we remain, sir, yours most sincerely.

An especially popular feature of the Leno-Campbell pantomime partnership was the 'Topical Duet' they sang each year – of political satire and backstairs gossip about the famous, 'carefully culled', as the carping correspondent of *The Theatre* put it, 'from the fetid columns of so-called "society papers", which seem to be extensively read amongst music-hall people'. Alas, little of the real 'tittle-tattle' found its way into the printed versions of these songs, but the style of them may be gauged from this verse and chorus of 'Shout Hurrah! Shout Hooray', written by Arthur Sturgess and composed by Jimmy Glover for *The Forty Thieves* of 1898-9:

LENO: I hear the Lib'ral party is without a leader now,
For Rosebery and Harcourt are – Ta-ra-ra-ra-ra *row!*

CAMPBELL: The temper of the party will, I fancy, shortly fail,
And all because – Ta-ra-ra, ta-ra-ra-ra-*Daily Mail!*

LENO: I've sent my competition in, perhaps I may be wrong,
I've named the leader – Ta-ra, ta-ra, ta-ra-ra-Rougemong.

CAMPBELL: And all the same I wonder why the party's gone to pot.
The reason is –

LENO: The reason is, of course – ta-ra-ra – what?

CHORUS

BOTH: Then, shout hurrah; Shout hooray!
It is difficult our meaning to convey;
But when Radicals are dumb, it's ta-ra-ra-ra-ra-rum.
Shout hurray! Shout hurrah! Shout hooray!

The events referred to in this verse indicate that it was added to the song early in 1899. At that time the Liberal Party was out of office and in some disarray. For a couple of years after Gladstone's retirement in 1894 the party had been led by Lord Rosebery, but in 1896 he had resigned. Sir William Harcourt had acted as its interim leader in the House of Commons, but in December 1898 he, too, resigned. There followed 'exasperated revelations' of conflict among the leadership. The party was unable to agree on a leader, and in 1899 *The Daily Mail* proposed a plebiscite. Dan Leno's irreverently suggested candidate for the post, 'Rougemong', was in fact one Louis de Rougemont who had arrived in London from Australia in 1899 with amazing tales of having been lost for thirty years among the aborigines. In a series of articles contributed to *Wide World Magazine* he told of life among a 'lost' tribe of cannibals; of having been made their chief; of the performing of strange black magic arts; and of priceless treasure for the gathering. He became a sensation and was 'lionised' in London, until exposed as a Swiss-born adventurer (real name Louis Grine), most of whose tale was hearsay. All grist to the mill of the topical songwriter.

For the Christmas of 1899, Drury Lane's pantomime was *Jack and the Beanstalk* with Dan Leno as Dame Trot and Herbert Campbell as the King. By the time it opened the Boer War was eleven weeks old, so the Giant's name was changed from the customary 'Blunder*bore*' to the more up-to-the-minute 'Blunder*boer*', and at the end of the show Collins staged one of his most famous scenes. Jack, Dame Trot, Bobbie (Jack's younger brother), the Princess, the King *et al.* escaped down the beanstalk with the Giant in menacingly noisy pursuit and Jack, using the magic sword given him by the Good Fairy, set energetically about hacking the beanstalk down. In the nick of time he managed to sever it. There followed 'a noise of twenty avalanches', and everything was plunged into darkness as the Giant tumbled, tumbled, blotting out the sun. When the lights went up again, the Giant's body was discovered lying at full length on the ground, taking up almost the entire area of Drury Lane's vast stage. Cheering townspeople swarmed around and over it; one brave soul actually opened one of the dead Giant's pockets – and out marched 'the entire British Army', horse, foot, artillery, even nurses, the troops clad not in the familiar scarlet but in the new khaki uniforms that had been introduced just that year and were still a novel sight. The audience went wild with delight. They were all familiar with the Boer leader Kruger's boast that he could put the little British army in his pocket.

The 'Army' for this scene, like Gus Harris's 'Army of Egypt' thirteen years earlier, was composed entirely of children. Children have long found employment in pantomime, being used from the beginning to play its imps, its fairies, its sprites and most of its animals (wasn't Grimaldi's mother, when a child, rented to David Garrick as an 'occasional fairy'?). There were even a number of professional

companies composed entirely of children. Peg Woffington began her
career in one such in Dublin in the 1730s.

In 1826 in Covent Garden's *Harlequin and Mother Shipton*, we find
'a little regiment of children dressed as turn-spit dogs'. These were
dogs kept specially in inns and large houses for turning the roasting-
spits which they did by running inside a tread-wheel device that drove
them. And as early as 1842 a spectacular pantomime battle was staged
between an army of malevolent imps on the one hand, and a ship-
load of British sailors on the other, the British party including a
complete marine band and all of them, imps, sailors and bandsmen,
played by children.

Children were also extensively used in the processions and ballet
sequences when they might be called upon to play anything from a
trump-card or a chess-man to a carrot, a pumpkin, or a mangel-
wurzel. 'Sometimes', wrote George Augustus Sala of a small boy in
the 1870s, 'he is Tom Thumb's aide-de-camp, or Cinderella's train-
bearer; but occasionally he sinks so low as to enact the role of an
animated stick of celery.' There is a sad story of a child found sobbing
his eyes out back-stage who, when asked what was the matter, replied:
'Please, sir, I'm a whelk, and somebody has taken my shell.' And
there is the tale, too, of the small boy cast as a domino who was
furious when he found himself dressed as a 'double-blank' instead of
the 'double-six' he had been promised.

In the nineteenth century it became the custom to hold mass open
auditions for children, mainly those of 'poor working people or petty
shop-keepers', and it was said that 'pantomimes afford bread to those
who are often in want of it at other seasons.' Among the children
thus chosen to play 'the British Army' in Drury Lane's Boer War
Jack and the Beanstalk was a one-time newspaper seller called Jimmy
Harrington, an 'urchin' who 'becomes a performing diminutive
guardsman'. He had already made an earlier appearance in another
role, and by a quirk of fate was destined, thus, to enter the history
books. It was toward the end of the pantomime season on 28th
February 1900. The house was in; the pantomime was about to commence; when the news arrived that Ladysmith had been relieved.
Jimmy Glover, who was as usual conducting the Drury Lane orchestra
that night, takes up the story:

> Two great comedians – one Herbert Campbell, the other Dan Leno – consult in
> their dressing-rooms as to the scene in which they should break the news to the
> audience. They arrange Scene VII, Part II, but in Scene I, Part I, three hours
> earlier, a boy brings on a pie to Dame Trot (Dan Leno), who according to the

plot is running a bakery. On this particular night the boy comes on gaily – more joyous than usual. Dances round Dame Trot, but speaks not his accustomed lines. Stage waits – Leno annoyed. But the boy budges not. At last the great comedian, somewhat chagrined at this interruption of his scene, says, 'Boy, why so gay this evening?' A pause – a huge giggle by the boy, and then this reply: 'Oh, 'aven't you 'eard, I've just relieved Ladysmith?' – sensation.

Leno and Campbell are said to have been furious.

On the last night of Drury Lane's 1903-4 pantomime *Humpty Dumpty*, the famous partnership, who once again had been playing Queen and King, clasped hands and sang:

> In the panto of old Drury Lane
> We have both come together again,
> And we hope to appear
> For many a year,
> In the panto of old Drury Lane.

On 19th July that year Herbert Campbell died, at the age of fifty-seven. Three months later, Leno, too, was dead. He was forty-three. In its obituary *The Times* wrote: 'To find anything like a close parallel to his style we should probably have to go back to the Italian *commedia dell'arte*.'

4.

Although Dan Leno played a wide range of pantomime roles, among them many male ones such as Idle Jack in *Dick Whittington*; Daddy Thumb in *Little Bo-Peep*; Mr Lombard Streete in *Beauty and the Beast*; Reggie, one of the babes, in *The Babes in the Wood*; and Abdallah in *The Forty Thieves*, he has come, above all, to stand as the archetypal pantomime Dame.

We see him as Jack's mother in *Jack and the Beanstalk*, the very picture of an embarrassed widow, running constantly between two wedding breakfasts set out in different rooms of the same house, because she's promised to marry two different men on the same day. Or we see him as Widow Twankey entertaining the Slave of the Lamp (juggler Paul Cinquevalli) in her humble kitchen and held utterly spellbound by the feats of 'magic' he performs with an ordinary saveloy sausage. She simply can't believe her eyes, and to make sure she's not being 'spoofed' she picks up the sausage between tricks, examines it, and tells herself reassuringly: 'Yes, it *is* so! That's a saveloy right enough!'

But above all, perhaps, we see Leno in the bun-wig, shawl, button-boots and voluminously-aproned skirts of 'Mother Goose', of which role, as we know it, he was the creator. It is said that his first entrance in the role 'aroused his audience to a degree of mirthful enthusiasm such as even he had never seen surpassed'. Hickory Wood has described that entrance:

> Picture Dan Leno, attired as a humble rustic widow, seated in a little cart, alongside a crate containing live geese, and peacefully driving a pair of donkeys along a Surrey lane. As the cavalcade reaches the cross-roads a motor horn is heard, and a car, driven by a huge gentleman, enveloped in the orthodox furs, dashes broadside into the little country cart. Over goes the cart, and there ensues a scene of the wildest confusion, amid which one has visions of Dan Leno in all parts of the stage at once; Dan Leno raising the struggling donkeys to their feet; Dan Leno rescuing geese that have escaped from the crate, and are wandering down the stage to investigate Jimmy Glover, and, finally, of Dan Leno firmly grasping by its neck an excited and struggling goose in either hand, and alternately 'slanging' the chauffeur in English, French, German and Italian.

The role of 'Dame' has a genealogy that stretches back to the earliest days of theatre, when girls and young women were played by youths and old women by men, usually comically. The earliest English ancestors of the pantomime Dame are no doubt Mrs Noah and Mac the Sheepstealer's Wife in the miracle plays of the Middle Ages. There's broad comedy a-plenty in both roles, as when Mrs Noah flatly refuses to board the newly-built Ark because she doesn't want to leave the 'gossips' who are her friends, or when Mac's wife, Gill, hiding the stolen sheep in her cradle, pretends to the suspicious and searching shepherds who call that it's her newly-born child – despite its 'long snout', 'horns', and 'four feet':

> A pretty child is he,
> As sits upon a woman's knee;
> A dylly-downe perdie!
> To make a man laugh.

Even after actresses entered the theatre at the Restoration, the convention of a man playing a comic old woman continued in the drama. Samuel Foote, for example, played Mrs Cole, the bibulous and disreputable old procuress (and convert to Methodism) in his own play *The Minor*, written in 1760.

> MRS COLE: The time has been, when I could have earned thirty shillings a day by my own drinking; and the next morning was neither sick nor sorry: but now, O laud! a thimble-full turns me topsy-turvy!

Nevertheless, when offered a drink during a visit to the home of a friend she takes the bottle: 'I won't trouble you for the glass; my hands do so tremble and shake. I shall but spill the good creature.' And, on departing in her sedan-chair, she instructs the servant:

'Richard, you may as well give me the bottle into the chair, for fear I should be taken ill on the road.'

In the earliest pantomimes, as we have seen, such parts as witches, the original Mother Goose, and Mother Shipton (both 'Dames' in the true, rather than the theatrical meaning of the word) were played by men. Grimaldi played several female roles in various pantomime 'openings' before being 'transformed' into Clown. Among these were Queen Rondabellyana in *Harlequin and the Red Dwarf; or, The Adamant Rock* (1812); Dame Cecily Suet in *Harlequin Whittington, Lord Mayor of London* (1814); and the Baroness in *Harlequin and Cinderella; or, The Little Glass Slipper* (1820), a role played later, and in another *Cinderella*, by Dan Leno. Since the Ugly Sisters became the property of the comedians, the Baroness's role has much diminished and in many cases vanished altogether.

As with so much else in pantomime, the Dame roles remained variable until the end of the last century. In Covent Garden's 1826 and 1836 versions of Aladdin, for example, the Widow Ching Mustapha was played by women. In 1856, at the Princess's Theatre, the Clown Redigé Paulo took the part. The original Widow Twankey of the Byron burlesque was played by James Rogers; and in E. L. Blanchard's 1865 version of the story, the Widow Ching Ching was Charles Steyne. But when Blanchard tackled the story again in 1874, Harriet Coveney took the part. And one of the greatest of Dames was Nellie Wallace. However, as V. C. Clinton Baddeley has pointed out, for a woman to play Dame is to attempt to make sense out of nonsense. 'And the queer fact is that no woman is ever as convincing as a man in a Dame part.'

It was on a night after Christmas that Hugh Walpole's 'Jeremy', then a small boy, sat in the gallery of a provincial theatre and experienced for the first time the wonder of this curious business:

In the middle of the scene was a funny old woman, her hat tumbling off her head, her shabby skirt dragging, large boots and a red nose. It was from this strange creature that the deep ugly voice proceeded. She had, this old woman, a number of bales of cloth under her arms, and she tried to carry them all, but one slipped, and then another, and then another; she bent to pick them up and her hat fell off; she turned for her hat and all the bales tumbled together. Jeremy began to laugh – everyone laughed; the strange voice came again and again, lamenting, bewailing, she had secured one bale, a smile of cautious triumph began to spread over her ugly face, then the bales all fell again, and once more she was on her knees. It was then that her voice or some movement brought to Jeremy's eyes so vividly the figure of their old gardener, Jordan, that he turned to Uncle Samuel and exclaimed convulsively: 'Why, she's a man!'

THIRTEEN
ADVENTURES·IN·THE·'SKIN'·PARTS

AUTHOR: Now, sir, I want to introduce my Hero at this part of the pantomime.

MANAGER: You have introduced him; isn't Harlequin the hero?

AUTHOR: Bless your unpractised head! Harlequin! Who thinks of Harlequin
while there's a chimpanzee, a bear, a reindeer, a cat, or a goose to be
had? I must have something that will strike. Something that will
make a noise in the world. I'll have a grand necromantic lover,
disguised like – like a lion!

Thus, in 1814, did Tom Dibdin in his *Harlequin Hoax* poke
fun at the pantomime's delight in the use of people disguised as animals. Dibdin's 'author' claimed a family 'bred
to the boards' and announced proudly: 'My mother was a
mute, and my Daddy a dumby; I was the original Goose in the
Golden Egg and work'd the whiskers of the White Cat.' Even as early
as 1752, a writer in *The Adventurer*, satirically projecting a pantomime
to be called *Harlequin Hercules* devoted to the performing of the
twelve labours, gleefully describes the number of 'animals' such a plot
affords him. Some of them he envisages as mechanical; others as 'skin'
parts. For the Nemean Lion, for example, he announces that he has
'a tawny coloured hide made of coarse serge with the ears, mane and
tip of the tail properly bushed out, with brown worsted'. And for the
fourth labour he has 'a beautiful canvas wild boar of Erymanthus'.
This, as Hercules has to carry it off the stage on his shoulders, 'has
nothing in its belly but a wadding of tow', and 'a little boy who is
to manage its motions, to let down the wire jaw, or grind the wooden
tusks.' The writer does confess to one slight problem with the little
boy: 'Though I could rather wish he were able to grunt and growl,
yet as that is impossible, I have taught the urchin to squeak prodigiously like a pig.'

Such animal roles go back to the very earliest days of the theatre,
and the pantomime has used them from the start. After all, Hogarth,
in his picture of 'Rich's Triumphal Entry', portrayed pantomime's
founding father 'invested with the skin of the famous dog in 'Perseus

and Andromeda'. Many theatrical children began their careers in 'skin' parts. It is said that Grimaldi, aged three, was very nearly killed whilst playing a monkey at Sadler's Wells. His father had him on a chain and was swinging him round and round above his head when the chain broke, sending young Joey flying out into the pit – but, happily, into the arms of a spectator. There was many a 'serious' actor, too, in the old stock companies who found himself donning a 'skin' come Christmas. In the 1850s, for example, we find the nineteen-year-old Henry Irving 'curdling the blood of ecstatic children' as Scruncher, Captain of the Wolves, in a *Little Bo-Peep* at the Theatre Royal, Edinburgh.

It was common practice at one time to mix the live 'animal' performer with mechanical animals. In Covent Garden's *Harlequin and Mother Shipton; or, Riquet with the Tuft* (1826), Mother Shipton's 'owl' and 'magpie' were played 'by machinery', and her cat by Mr E. G. Parsloe, who, according to the *Sunday News*, impersonated the animal 'with much ingenuity, effect, and feline peculiarities'. We are told that he 'squatted and "purred" about, set his "cat's eyes" at strangers, stretched out his paws, "washed his face", be-sunned himself on the cottage roof, and pursued other equally appropriate gambols to the wonderous merriment of the juvenile portions of the audience in particular.' Nevertheless, the *Sunday News* reviewer was not totally happy with Mr Parsloe's cat. 'We have only one fault to find with him', he went on, 'and that fault is his skin; we never heard of any witch having a cat that was not all black – a white hair was, in olden time, fatal to the charmed powers of a witch's cat – but this mimic cat was black and white, somewhat like the hide of the Newfoundland dog that afterwards ran away with Pantaloon's head.'

In the second half of the nineteenth century there came a number of specialist performers who raised 'skin' parts to a level all their own and branched out well beyond the cat, goose, cow and donkey of the ordinary pantomime. A *Dick Whittington* played at the Grand Theatre, Leeds, in 1886 actually boasted 'an individual who impersonates a frog with surprising success'.

The most famous and spectacularly creative of them all was George Conquest whose succession of brilliantly conceived and played 'animals' and 'grotesques' became one of the special attractions of the pantomimes at the Grecian and later at the Surrey Theatre. Conquest was the son of actor-manager Benjamin Conquest, and one of a large and many-talented theatre family. *The Times* described him as 'one of the most remarkable artists of the day', who combined the qualities of actor and acrobat 'to a degree which could not easily be found elsewhere' and who could 'tumble, jump, execute feats on the trapeze and walk on stilts to perfection, at the same time allowing histrionic feeling to shine through all his athletic exploits.' He could execute 'the most astounding leaps, dives and flights' and, using sometimes as many as twenty-nine stage traps, would be seen 'flying through the air or projected through the floor'.

Another amazing aspect of Conquest's work was the variety of roles which he would exhibit in each pantomime. He might appear first as 'a giant of most portentous size', then change, 'by a wonderful compression', into a 'little dwarf', and then – hey presto! – and 'a vivid green version of the Brighton Octopus is dancing about the stage'. In an interview with *Chums* in December 1897, Conquest confessed that playing the octopus (it had been 'taken from life' at the Brighton Aquarium) had been extremely hard work. With the tentacles fully extended, the costume measured twenty-eight feet across! 'I was appearing in two different pantomimes at the time, and I can tell you the effort well nigh killed me,' he told his interviewer. 'As it was, it killed the horse which used to take me to and fro.'

Another famous creation of Conquest's was a giant porcupine which consisted of over 2500 pieces, each with an individual movement, and all actuated by Conquest as he raised and lowered his quills. But the most famous of all was, arguably, the title role of *Spitz-Spitz, the Spider Crab* in the Grecian's 1875 pantomime. 'All its joints were perfect, and it took eleven months to construct. I made every bit of it myself.'

Every animal role Conquest played was taken from life:

> I watch the originals of the various things I am about to portray for weeks. For the spider crab I used to go to the Zoological Gardens in the early hours of the morning before the public were admitted and study a crab. When I made up my mind to play a parrot in the pantomime I spent a great deal of time in the parrot-house at the Zoo. I studied the parrots' ways of talking, and practised their manner of walking by tramping backwards and forwards with my toes turned in. Then I started screeching like the birds themselves, and in a very short space of time they began to answer me.

Ranking second only to Conquest as an 'animal pantomimist' was Charles Lauri, the son of a famous Clown, who made his debut, aged six, as a cat in a Birmingham pantomime. He went on to appear as a bear, a wolf, an ostrich, a kangaroo (he found the jumping 'very fatiguing'), and in 1891 appeared with wings for the first time, 'flying about the stage as an ibis'. He also appeared as a frog, but found that

role somewhat limiting as he could 'go through all the known antics
of a frog in five minutes'. The roles Lauri most enjoyed were those
of the ordinary domestic animals. 'The public really prefers domestic
animals', he once said. 'People like to watch the things with which
they are already familiar.' It was Charles Lauri's 'cat', which used to
run round the front of the dress circle, that ousted the 'Buttons' role
from the Lyceum's 1893–4 *Cinderella* by appearing as a 'stray' in the
kitchen scene.

Lauri had no greater admirer among the critics than William
Archer of the *World*, who wrote of the Lyceum's 1894–5 *Santa Claus*
(it was a version of the 'Babes in the Wood' story):

> There is only one thing against which I must enter a vehement protest, and that
> is the death of the Babes' faithful collie, Tatters. As embodied by Mr Charles
> Lauri, Tatters is the most popular and sympathetic character in the pantomime,
> and his untimely end is too harrowing to be borne. Pray believe that I make this
> protest quite seriously. Children ought not to have their feelings wrung and their
> pleasure saddened in this way.

A footnote to Archer's collected criticisms adds: 'Tatters was eventually brought to life again, in deference to many protests.'

For many years one of the most successful of animal acts was the
Brothers Griffiths, who specialised in comic animals such as a wrest-
ling lion which 'gave its trainer no end of trouble', and the Blondin
Donkey (created in the 1880s) which, emulating its namesake, the
French aerialist, 'exhibited on the tight-rope'. (In fact, a plank of
wood the edge of which was painted to resemble a rope.) This donkey, according to one who saw it, was 'at one moment life-like' and
at the next was 'twisted into shapes which would have been impossible
had not the forelegs and the hindlegs been experienced acrobats'.

Of the more traditional 'skin' parts, 'Goose' is generally considered
the hardest to play. As one famous animal impersonator, Gerry Lee,
explained in a BBC radio interview in January 1963:

> The frame of the goose is made of iron.... And you're strapped in it.... Your
> arm-pits are strapped in for the wings ... you can't sit down ... you can't stand
> up.... If you're waiting to go on, somebody has to push a stool gently under you
> to give your legs a rest.... You'd have to have at least twenty minutes to half an
> hour to get out of the goose skin, so you're in it for the length of the show.

More recently, Barbara Newman (she's been playing 'Goose' since
1946) described the awkwardness of the posture within the frame:
'You've got to bend your knees, and bend your back, and put your
head up straight, otherwise you'd be looking on the floor all the time.
You've got to get the outline of the Goose inside the Goose's skin.'

Her 'skin' is built on a wicker frame and she, like most animal impersonators, made her own. To buy a goose skin these days can cost £1400. Every feather, perhaps two thousand or more, has to be sewn or glued separately. Kay Lyell, another famous 'Goose' (she claims her greatest asset is that she stands only four feet eleven inches tall) has confessed that the role has two great drawbacks. One is that children will try to stuff ice-cream down your beak; the other is that the fat ones – 'it's always the fat ones' – invariably want to sit on your back!

One of the most shameless scene-stealers in the whole pantomimic repertoire has long been 'Daisy' the cow in *Jack and the Beanstalk*. Desmond and Marks, a famous 'skin' duo (one of the most peculiar things they ever played was a fire-and-smoke-belching alligator!) have explained that the front does all the work of moving the tongue, the eyes, and the ears; the rear being what they call a 'sleeping' part. 'All he has to do is work the tail, if, indeed, the tail be workable.' He has also to 'lift the front if they're doing a "rear-up" onto the hind-legs'.

One 'Daisy the Cow' became a national celebrity when the mother-and-son team of June and Paul Kidd, currently one of the most distinguished animal acts in the business, took their creation into the children's television programme *Five O'Clock Club*. Son Paul plays the 'most expressive' front in this act, and mother June takes the rear. In fact, they do nine different 'skins', plus a 'Giant', a stilt-walking act, and a very spectacular 'skeleton' routine using ultra-violet light. June, who was trained as a ballet dancer and spent twelve years at Sadler's Wells, was married to a member of the famous Pender Troupe which specialised in 'skins', acrobatic dancing and stilt-walking. A one-time member of the team (he 'used to be the third stilt-walker in the line') was young Archie Leach from Bristol, who went on to make a name in the movies as Cary Grant.

The Kidds play *Jack and the Beanstalk* every year now, providing both the cow and the Giant, and if they cannot do the Giant they do not do either. 'The children go to see "Beanstalk" to see a Giant,' says Paul. 'And how do you slay an off-stage voice?' They, too, make their own skins, June doing most of the sewing ('We take a lot of care in choosing the right fabric, hard wearing, very good quality'), and Paul handling the heads and the mechanisms, 'which take a great deal of time to perfect'. (All these animal impersonators are pretty secretive about their 'mechanisms'.) And the cost? In January 1984, June said: 'The Daisy we're using now, with all the mechanisms, and the fabric, and two pairs of trousers, and hoofs and that, cost us just on £500.'

Sadly, the number of 'animal specialists' is dwindling year by year and the 'skin' parts are increasingly being handed back to the dancers, children, and straight actors who played them in the earliest days of pantomime. There simply isn't sufficient year-round work to support more than a handful of 'traditional' skins. But, then, even Desmond and Marks had never played a 'skin' (though they had played just about everything else) until Emile Littler suggested one year that they might like to try it. For many 'skin' duos these days, though, there's only one solution. Like Peter Dayson and David Brody of the newer generation (they played Frankie Howerd's camel 'Mustaphabun' in Eastbourne's 1984 *Aladdin*) they have to work separately for the rest of the year.

FOURTEEN

ALL·TOGETHER·NOW

All too frequently people point to the dearth of pantomime in the West End of London (only one production, for example, in 1984–5) as an indication that pantomime is dying. Yet even in the 1900–1 season, in the pre-war heyday of pantomime, the West End could boast only two, one at Drury Lane, the other at the newly-built London Hippodrome. The Theatre Royal, Covent Garden, stopped producing a regular pantomime in the 1880s; Drury Lane in 1919, though three were produced there during the 1930s.

Nationwide, however, pantomime is booming. Recent years have been especially good. In the 1984–5 season some thirty-odd pantomimes were staged in the environs of London; seventy in the provinces; and twenty-two in Scotland, Wales and Ireland. Many of them claimed record attendances and profits, and some ran well into March, even though they had opened not on Boxing Day but perhaps as early as the middle of December. Producer Paul Elliott has claimed that his own production company derives half of its total annual profit from pantomime, and for many theatres the pantomime is the one copper-bottomed, financially successful certainty of the entire production calendar.

Essentially, the basic form of the modern pantomime is still as it had evolved in the late 1890s and early 1900s, and owes a good deal to the work of Arthur Collins and Hickory Wood at Drury Lane. The Harlequinade, reduced to an irrelevant appendage, was finally dropped. A natural prose dialogue was introduced, and the use of rhymed couplets restricted to the 'immortals'. This was common practice by the first years of the new century. Furthermore, a scheme of things was established which ensured that the story-line was properly forwarded while still permitting the stars sufficient artistic freedom to display their own personalities and talents, and affording ample opportunity for the introduction of specialities and scenic display. The balance is a fine one and it shifts a good deal from generation to generation, production to production. All too frequently it lurches in the direction of the star or stars, but on occasion it lurches equally fatally in the direction of the story, to provide a singularly dull evening devoted entirely to what is pretty, whimsical and fantastical. As Peter Hepple of *The Stage* has written, pantomime is essentially 'raucous, occasionally vulgar, and with an almost electric charge between audience and stage'. The formula that emerged in those turn-of-the-century years was ideally suited to the music-hall artists who then dominated the pantomime. But it has turned out to be equally suited to the stars of musical comedy, variety, radio, record and television who successively followed them.

It was Collins himself who introduced musical comedy stars into the Drury Lane pantomimes and also, in 1912, handed the role of Principal Boy back to a man, baritone Wilfred Douthitt who played Prince Auriol in *The Sleeping Beauty* opposite the Princess Marcella of Florence Smithson (from *The Arcadians*). *The Times* made special mention of the 'keen pleasure' of listening to accomplished singers like Miss Smithson and Mr Douthitt, 'singers whose like have never been heard before in any Drury Lane pantomime known to us'. So successful was this *Sleeping Beauty*, that it was repeated in a revised form with new scenes in 1913 and again in 1914 as *The Sleeping Beauty Re-Awakened* and *The Sleeping Beauty Beautified*. Douthitt again headed the cast in 1913, but was replaced in the 1914 production by Bertram Wallis, a gold medallist of the Royal Academy of Music, and star of operettas like *The Count of Luxembourg* and *The King of Cadonia*. In 1915, too, Collins used a male Principal Boy, this time Eric Marshall, who, according to *The Times*, was employed 'to warble sentimental ballads' as Florian in *Puss in Boots*. But the male Principal Boy was not limited to Drury Lane. In 1916, Randolph Sutton played Jack Goose in *Mother Goose* at the Empire Theatre, Wakefield (he had been very successful there in variety), and went on to play 'Boy' regularly for seventeen years. And in 1920-1 Fred Barnes appeared as Robin Hood in a *Babes in the Wood* at the Glasgow Coliseum.

The male Principal Boy was to have a new vogue in the late 1950s and through the 60s with, as *The Stage* put it, 'a host of rock'n'rollers and recording artists making their pantomime debuts throughout the country'. This was seen by many not only as a great (and deplorable) innovation but also as signalling the end of the female 'Boy'. Indeed, such famous 'Boys' as Marie Burke, Evelyn Laye, Clarice Mayne and Dorothy Ward were brought together by the BBC for a radio programme in which they paid tribute to vanishing femininity – and also defended the old 'tradition' against the new 'invaders'.

The vogue had started in 1956-7 when Norman Wisdom played Aladdin at the London Palladium, then still a variety theatre and one of the citadels to have been captured by the new wave of popular singers. (The Palladium's bill-toppers in 1957 included the Frankie Lymon Teenagers, Johnnie Ray, Eve Boswell, Howard Keel, the Platters, Frankie Lane, Max Bygraves and Joan Regan.) The Palladium was also the West End's only pantomime stronghold, so it was completely natural that in the cause of continuity the popular singer should move into this area, too: the only suitable role for the male balladeer or pop singer being that of Principal Boy.

Norman Wisdom was followed by Edmund Hockridge as Prince Michael in *The Sleeping Beauty*; Frankie Vaughan as Francesco in *Puss in Boots*; Cliff Richard as Aladdin (with The Shadows as Wishee, Washee, Noshee and Poshee); Frank Ifield as Robin Hood in *The Babes in the Wood*; Peter Gilmore as the Prince in *Cinderella*; Engelbert Humperdinck as Robinson Crusoe; plus comic Jimmy Tarbuck as Jack in *Jack and the Beanstalk*, and Edward Woodward as Robin Hood.

However, after more than a decade of incursion by male Principal Boys, the pantomime once again (with the occasional exception) reverted to girls. It was Cilla Black incidentally in 1971 who restored the female Boy to the London Palladium. In the radio programme referred to above, Evelyn Laye gave it as her opinion that men could never make really good Principal Boys 'because of their knees', a statement which prompted singer David Hughes to ask: 'Who worries about Robin Hood's knees?' A rather surprised Miss Laye replied with admirable seriousness: 'I hope Maid Marian!'

Principal Boys have changed enormously down the years, always reflecting the current fashion in the female form and appearance. The 'Boys' of the Victorian pantomimes, so graphically described by James Agate as 'the big-bosomed, broad-buttocked, butcher-thighed race of Principal Boys', and as 'walking definitions of what the scientist means by "mass" and the Victorians by the "statuesque"', gave way in the years before the First World War to a new, more severely masculine race, which mirrored the style and aspirations of the 'New Woman'. In the post-war years, a softer femininity returned, a change in which one of pantomime's most famous Principal Boys, Dorothy Ward, played no small part. She still remembers the revolution she caused when she asked for her costumes to be made by a dressmaker rather than a tailor! It was Dorothy Ward who pointed out 'the great heresy' of supposing that Principal Boys are concerned with male impersonation. As she has said: 'When a Principal Boy swings one shapely leg forward and thumps a well-kept fist into the opposite palm, she is imitating some lost vision of man; when she adopts a resolute – and deliberately unladylike – stance, feet firmly planted apart, or hooks her thumbs nonchalantly in her belt, she is assuming postures which are meant to be recognised as manly, but she is not trying to create an illusion of manhood.' In essence, she is presenting us 'with an attractive woman's version of how a man behaves in romantic circumstances'.

And today's 'Boys'? Well, when Aimi Macdonald played Prince Charming at Eastbourne a few years back, she announced that she was playing him 'fun-loving and democratic'. She also said, 'I never think about my legs.'

Curiously perhaps, one of the dressiest parts on the pantomime stage these days is the Dame. No longer is the bonnet and shawl sufficient for an entire evening. Indeed, many Dames these days change for every appearance, making the increasingly outrageous dressiness part of the fun. One of the first 'dressing-up' Dames was George Lacy, generally held to be the greatest Dame since Leno. (He began playing the part in 1924, the youngest man ever to do so, and now reckons he must be the oldest.)

Lacy claims to have introduced the idea of never appearing in the same costume twice, 'regardless of whether it made sense'. As he says: 'People accept that in a pantomime. And my excuse was that it was "magic". With that you can get away with murder, really.' One of Lacy's most outrageous costumes was a little green-baize affair, complete with carefully positioned pockets, and a full-sized snooker set sewn onto the front, in which he contrived to look just like a snooker table. Such outrageous costumes have long been part and parcel of the Dame role. That other great Dame, Douglas Byng, mocking the 1930s fashion for short fox-fur capes made out of single skins, got himself something similar run up entirely out of loofahs. When the Second World War broke out, these bathtime accessories soon became unobtainable and much sought after, so much so that Byng was forced to keep his cape locked up in a safe so that people couldn't steal the loofahs. Of the Dame role, Byng says: 'You can be more saucy as a woman than as a man. "What he did to me" is very different from "What I did to her". She's on the *defensive*. A man's on the *offensive*.'

These days the Dame enters not with a large wicker market-basket but, almost invariably, pushing a supermarket trolley from the bottom of which she's almost bound to produce a dead chicken – unfrozen, plucked and complete with head and feet (what *do* the

Children of Paradise

children make of it?), and a long string of plastic carrots which she places round her neck, so that she can ask: 'What do you think of it? It's eighteen carat!'

The jokes don't change much.

'Why don't you grow up, stupid?'
'I have grown up stupid!'

'I've got the skin of a baby.'
'Seal or elephant?'

'What was Gandhi's first name?'
'Goosey, Goosey!'

'Mother and father are in the iron and steel business. She irons. He steals.'

'I feel so effervescent'.
'I never knew you when you effer wasnt'.

'Right-o ... Right-o ... Right-o.'
'Why do you keep saying "right-o"?'
'Because you're standing on my right toe!'

Comedians to this day sit under 'the Tree of Truth', just as Dan Leno and Herbert Campbell did, though the acorns that grew on their tree and dropped onto the head of he who told the lies seem to have turned into oranges or grapefruit, or even coconuts, certainly something a good deal larger and more hurtful.

John Morley, currently Britain's most prolific pantomime writer (he can claim an entry in the *Guinness Book of Records*), even researched and dusted up a Grimaldi sketch for one of his pantomimes. Morley, incidentally, tailors his scripts very carefully to suit the stars who are cast to play in them. 'Each succeeding pantomime', he says, 'is written around its star.' If the star is playing Widow Twankey, the plot revolves round Twankey. 'Another year, the star might be playing the Emperor of China and I would write it round him.' But plot, he insists, is the public's first and foremost demand. They want the story told clearly and straight. Comedy comes next in importance. Current pop songs, splendid scenery and costumes, complete the list.

It is, perhaps, significant that the most popular characters these days are the 'baddies' – especially Abanazar and The Demon King. But possibly the greatest change in pantomime in our time is the amount of audience participation involved. It is, after all, the only form of entertainment which still permits its audience the pleasure of joining in, and in many pantomimes the company keep up an almost constant running dialogue with the 'customers', more redolent of a music-hall than any legitimate theatre. It has also acquired an attractive willing-ness to confide its little secrets and to confess its limitations. Richard Murdoch as Alderman Fitzwarren in *Dick Whittington* greeting an audience at Windsor with: 'How nice of you to come, when you could all have been at home enjoying yourselves.' Francis Matthews, playing Widow Twankey in a Bath *Aladdin* admitting joyously: 'That's what I like about panto. You can bring the whole plot up to date with just one line. It saves all that boring talk.' But Bill Maynard, playing the Squire of Sweet Content in a Birmingham *Mother Goose*, summed it all up when he suddenly turned on his audience and bellowed: 'That's the level! You'd better get used to it!'

It all adds up to something refreshingly honest and utterly disarm-ing. We all know the man's a woman; we all know the woman's a man; and anyone can see that the cow has got people in it. But isn't that the whole point?

As *The Times* wrote over a century ago:

> ... it were a queer world and a sad if two and two were four inevitably and at all periods of the year; and if the impossible and the fantastic were not at certain epochs allowed to strut about in the guise of the possible and real.

THE END

BOOK LIST

Adams, W. Davenport, *A Book of Burlesque*, 1891

Anon, *The Playhouse Scuffle*, 1710 (pamphlet)

Archer, William, *The Theatrical 'World'*

Arnold, Walter, *The Life and Death of the Sublime Society of Beef Steaks*, 1871

Arundell, Denis, *The Story of Sadler's Wells*, 1978

Avery, Emmett L., *The London Stage 1660–1800*, 1960

Beaumont, Cyril W., *The History of Harlequin*, 1926

Blanchard, E. L., *The Life and Reminiscences of E. L. Blanchard* (ed. Clement Scott & Cecil Howard), 1891

Broadbent, R. J., *A History of Pantomime*, 1901

Burnand, Sir Francis, *Records and Reminiscences*, 1904

Cibber, Colley, *An Apology for the Life of Mr Cibber*, 1756

Clinton-Baddeley, V. C., *The Burlesque Tradition*, 1952

Colman, George, the Younger, *Random Records*, 1830

Cook, Dutton, *A Book of the Play*, 1876

Cumberland, Richard, *Memoirs*, 1806

Dibdin, Charles, *Memoirs of Charles Dibdin*, ed. George Speight, 1956

Dibdin, Tom, *Reminiscences*, 1837

Dickens, Charles (Boz), *Memoirs of Grimaldi*, 1838

Disher, M. Willson, *Clowns and Pantomimes*, 1925

Dunbar, Janet, *Peg Woffington and Her World*, 1968

Elliston, Robert, *Memoirs*, 1844

Fielding, Henry, *Tumble-Down Dick; or, Phaeton in the Suds*, 1736

Findlater, Richard, *Grimaldi; King of Clowns*, 1955

Fitzgerald, Percy, *The World Behind the Scenes*, 1881

Fleetwood, Frances, *Conquest: The Story of a Theatre Family*, 1953

Fothergill, Brian, *Mrs Jordan: Portrait of an Actress*, 1965

Gascgoigne, Bamber, *World Theatre*, 1968

Gibbs, Lewis, *Sheridan*, 1947

Glover, James M., *Jimmy Glover His Book*, 1912

Johnson, James, *An Account of Pantomimes*, 1882

Lawrence, William John, *Old Theatre Days and Ways*, 1935
Macready, Charles, *Diaries of Charles William Macready* (ed. William Toynbee), 1912
McKechnie, Samuel, *Popular Entertainments Through the Ages*
Mander, Raymond & Mitchenson, Joe, *Pantomime, A Story in Pictures*, 1973
Mayer III, David, *Harlequin in His Element*, 1969
Morley, Henry, *Journal of a London Playgoer*, 1854/5
Nagler, A. M. (ed), *A Source Book in Theatrical History*, 1952
Nicoll, Allardyce, *A History of Late 18th Century Drama; The World of Harlequin*, 1963
Niklaus, Thelma, *Harlequin Phoenix; or, The Rise and Fall of a Bergamask Rogue*, 1956
O'Keefe, John, *Recollections*, 1826
Pope, W. Macqueen, *Theatre Royal, Drury Lane*, 1945
Planché, J. R., *The Recollections and Reflections of J. R. Planché*, 1872
Rennel, Gabriel, *Tragi-Comic Reflections*, 1725
Roberts, Arthur, *Fifty Years of Spoof*, 1927
Sherson, Erroll, *London's Lost Theatres of the 19th Century*, 1925
Short, Ernest, *Fifty Years of Vaudeville*, 1946
Schneider, Ben Ross, Jnr, *Index to London Stage*, 1979
Southern, Richard, *Changeable Scenery*, 1952
Timbs, John, *Clubs & Club Life in London*, 1872
Wagner, Leopold, *The Pantomimes and All About Them*, 1881
Weaver, John, *A History of Mimes and Pantomimes*, 1728
Wilkinson, Tate, *Memoirs*, 1790
Williams, Clifford John, *Madame Vestris*, 1973
Wilson, A. E., *Christmas Pantomime*, 1934; *Pantomime Pageant*, 1946
Wood, J. Hickory, *Dan Leno*, 1905

INDEX